SUPPORT
NETWORKS FOR
INCLUSIVE SCHOOLING

W9-AHK-872

SUPPORT NETWORKS FOR INCLUSIVE SCHOOLING

INTERDEPENDENT INTEGRATED EDUCATION

Edited by

William Stainback, Ed.D.
and **Susan Stainback, Ed.D.**
College of Education
University of Northern Iowa
Cedar Falls, Iowa

·P·A·U·L·H·
BROOKES
PUBLISHING Cọ

Baltimore • London • Toronto • Sydney

Paul H. Brookes Publishing Co.
P.O. Box 10624
Baltimore, Maryland 21285-0624

Typeset by The Composing Room of Michigan, Inc., Grand Rapids, Michigan.
Manufactured in the United States of America by
The Maple Press Company, York, Pennsylvania.

Library of Congress Cataloging-in-Publication Data

Support networks for inclusive schooling : interdependent integrated
    education / edited by William Stainback, Susan Stainback.
        p.   cm.
    Includes bibliographical references.
    ISBN 1–55766–041–7
    1. Handicapped children—Education—United States.
    2. Mainstreaming in education—United States.   I. Stainback,
William C.   II. Stainback, Susan Bray.
LC4031.S88   1990
371.9'046'0973—dc20   89–48390
                                                              CIP

Contents

Contributors

Kathryn D. Bishop, M.A.
Assistant Professor
College of Education
University of San Diego
San Diego, CA 92110

Barbara E. Buswell, B.A.
Co-Director PEAK Parent Center
6055 Lehman Drive
Suite 101
Colorado Springs, CO 80918

Jennifer J. Coots, M.A.
Doctoral Student
School of Education/Division of
  Special Education
California State University,
  Los Angeles
5151 State University Drive
Los Angeles, CA 90032

Dale L. Dutton, B.S.
California Supported Employment
  Training Project
University of San Francisco/
  Rehabilitation Administration
346 19th Street
Santa Monica, CA 90402

Donna H. Dutton, M.A., M.S.
Executive Director
Computer Access Center
2425 16th Street
Santa Monica, CA 90405

Mary A. Falvey, Ph.D.
Professor
School of Education/Division of
  Special Education
California State University,
  Los Angeles
5151 State University Drive
Los Angeles, CA 90032

Marsha Forest, Ed.D.
Center for Integrated Education
Frontier College
35 Jackes Avenue
Toronto, Ontario, M4T 1E2
CANADA

Alan Gartner, Ph.D.
Professor and Director
Office of Sponsored Research
The Graduate School and University
  Center
City University of New York
33 West 42nd Street
New York, NY 10036

Kathleen C. Harris, Ph.D.
Associate Professor
School of Education
California State University,
  Los Angeles
5151 State University Drive
Los Angeles, CA 90032

Lawrence J. Johnson, Ph.D.
Area of Special Education
University of Alabama
P.O. Box 870231
Tuscaloosa, AL 35487

Dorothy Kerzner Lipsky, Ph.D.
Senior Research Scientist
The Graduate School and University
   Center
City University of New York
33 West 42nd Street
New York, NY 10036
and
Assistant Superintendent for
   Curriculum and Instruction
Oceanside Union Free School District
Oceanside, NY 11572

Jack Pearpoint, B.S.
President
Frontier College
35 Jackes Avenue
Toronto, Ontario M4T 1E2
CANADA

Marleen C. Pugach, Ph.D.
Department of Curriculum and
   Instruction
School of Education
University of Wisconsin, Milwaukee
P.O. Box 413
Milwaukee, WI 53201

Mara Sapon-Shevin, Ed.D.
Associate Professor
Elementary and Special Education
Center for Teaching and Learning
University of North Dakota
Grand Forks, ND 58202

C. Beth Schaffner, B.A.
Teacher/Integration Facilitator
6565 Ashcroft Drive
Colorado Springs, CO 80918

Susan Stainback, Ed.D.
Professor
College of Education
University of Northern Iowa
Cedar Falls, IA 50614

William Stainback, Ed.D.
Professor
College of Education
University of Northern Iowa
Cedar Falls, IA 50614

Jacqueline S. Thousand, Ph.D.
Assistant Professor
University of Vermont
Center for Developmental Disabilities
499C Waterman Building
Burlington, VT 05405

Terri Vandercook, Ph.D.
Associate Director
Institute on Community Integration
University of Minnesota
13 Pattee Hall
150 Pillsbury Drive, S.E.
Minneapolis, MN 55455

Richard A. Villa, Ed.D.
Director of Instructional Services and
   Staff Development
Winooski School District
80 Normand Street
Winooski, Vermont 05404

Jennifer York, Ph.D.
Associate Director
Institute on Community Integration
University of Minnesota
104 Pattee Hall
150 Pillsbury Drive, S.E.
Minneapolis, MN 55455

Foreword

When we ask: "Why should all children learn together in regular education classrooms?" we are asking the *wrong* question. And when we ask: "Can the child who is not toilet trained benefit from learning with his or her same-age peers?" or, "Why should the child who cannot sit in his or her chair for more than a short time be allowed into a regular education classroom?" we continue to ask the wrong questions. The *only* question that we should be asking is: "What would it take to have this child in a regular classroom with his or her same-age peers?" This question allows us to focus our attention and efforts on what is most important—how to support *all* students in a fully inclusive classroom.

This book focuses on inclusive schooling where all students learn together in integrated regular classrooms. It is our hope and desire that as we approach the year 2000 all classrooms will have an array of diverse students. We hope that all schools will truly be inclusive; a place where diversity is highly regarded; a place where all parents will want their children to have friendships with the other members of the classroom, regardless of others' backgrounds, learning styles, talents, and gifts.

To realize the dream of inclusive education in our schools, we need to consider how best to provide supports to students and teachers in the mainstream of education. To best support all people in regular classrooms an individualized approach is needed, rather than using a cookie cutter approach where everyone receives the same support and instruction whether or not they need or want it. We also need to consider when to use natural supports, when to use paid supports, and how to move from one to the other in order to meet the unique needs of the person receiving those supports.

Integrated schools and classrooms should provide all students with opportunities to receive supports when and if they need them. In such schools and classrooms not only will the student who has been previously segregated in a self-contained classroom be given support, all students in the regular classroom will be supported within the course of a typical school day.

Providing support in the classroom to enable each student to feel that he or she is an important part of the whole group is critical. Classrooms need to pull together and form a *community.* Such a community will teach children at a young age to share, to really communicate with one another, and to join together to overcome the prejudices of those who do not believe that everyone belongs. *A sense of community can and does break down barriers.*

Providing support to students in an inclusive classroom requires sensitivity, individualization, and balance to ensure that we provide *only* the support that is needed with the intensity, duration, and frequency that is needed. This approach will help us to empower those students who have too often been disempowered in the past. Whenever support is provided, it should be provided in a way that empowers students, that is, helps them learn to help themselves and others.

When we provide support with respect we demonstrate on a small scale how communities and society should act. The classrooms of the future should be a microcosm of our neighborhoods and communities.

In order for us to provide supports that are truly individualized and useful, we need to listen to the people requesting the supports. For some students this will be easy; they will just tell us. Others may not be able to communicate as clearly what they need; thus, we need to be more attentive to what these people are saying (both with words and actions) so that we can respond appropriately.

Initial support should always be provided to enable all students in the classroom to learn and develop. These initial supports may be providing team teaching situations, cooperative learning centers, student assistants, sign language instruction for a student who is deaf and his or her friends, peer tutors, adaptation of the curriculum, or other supports designed to specifically meet the needs of all concerned.

The supports noted here are just some of the methods that can be used. However, it must be noted that providing supports must be done for all students and be seen as something that schools do in order to be inclusive, rather than doing it just for one student or a subgroup of students. The potential for perverting any of these supports to make people stand out and be separate is always present. Safeguards must be in place to prevent this from happening.

The major safeguard that must occur for all individuals is the need for all people to have a circle of friends—people to stand with one another. A network of concerned people is brought together for the express purpose of being a protection not only for the person who is obviously vulnerable, but for each other. This circle is an absolute key to ensuring that people's lives are filled with a richness of life's experiences. In addition, in the final analysis, the only true protection and advocacy that any individual has is caring peers, friends, family, and community members.

Since the mid-1980s there has been a movement toward inclusive education for all people. This movement does not discriminate based upon labels, levels of need, and so forth. The concept of full inclusion is no longer a "dream" of a few visionaries, but it has become a reality for many students and teachers.

Growing numbers of families are realizing that creating a desirable future for their child means that they must include their child in the mainstream of their neighborhood school. They also are realizing that their child must receive a quality education and have friends in the neighborhood school. Thus, as educators, we need to focus our attention on the question of how to make this a rich and rewarding experience for all students, rather than on whether we should do this or this cannot be done because . . .

It is time to recognize that all students perform an important and critical role in our society—that of social change agent. It is our strong belief that students such as our daughter, Shawntell, a student who in the early 1970s would have been denied inclusion in any school program much less a regular classroom, as well as many others, have brought about a revolution in the way our schools are configured and in the philosophy underlying education. They have demonstrated time and time again that inclusive education is possible and even more importantly it is critical if we are going to be a just and humane society. Through the vigilance of these young activists, they have "shown us the path" toward inclusive education.

This book provides practical strategies for providing supports to all students. *It is right and it is time* to make inclusive education a reality.

Jeffrey L. Strully, Ed.D.
Executive Director
Association for Retarded Citizens
Denver, Colorado
and
Cindy Strully, M.A.
Director of Case Management
Centennial Developmental Services
Evans, Colorado

Preface

Growing numbers of parents and educators are advocating for full inclusion of all students in the mainstream of school and community life. But there are still many parents and educators who disagree. For example, Ginger Greaves, a parent of a child who is deaf, disagrees. Ms. Greaves's son was mainstreamed for years, but as a result had no friends he could communicate with, had minimal access to teachers and peers who knew sign language, and made virtually no progress in his language competence and schoolwork (Siegel, 1989).

Few, if any, people, including the editors of this book, would blame Ms. Greaves for being less than enthusiastic about her son being in the mainstream of school and community life. Unfortunately, Ms. Greaves's son's experiences with the mainstream are true for far too many students. The mainstream is too often a place where the communication methods, tools, techniques, and support some children need to develop friends and to be successful educationally are *not* provided. In addition, teachers, because of lack of resources and support, are frequently required to teach to the so-called average student. As a result, the curriculum and instructional program is too difficult and frustrating for some children, while at the same time, it is not challenging enough for others.

This is a sad commentary on how accepting, adaptive, and flexible the mainstream of school and community life is for some students. Thus, it is essential to work to make the mainstream a place where *all* children's educational and related needs are met, where they can communicate with peers and teachers, and where they have friends and are made to feel welcome and secure. To do otherwise is to chance losing the participation and contributions of many people, including those classified as having disabilities, to the mainstream of society.

Developing an educational mainstream that meets all student's needs is not easy, but a growing number of people are joining the struggle (Strully, 1989). The process begins when students, parents, and teachers develop a vision of the classroom as an inclusive community; a community where everyone belongs, where the needs of all members are met, and where people care about and support each other.

As this book describes, the focus is on recognizing and enhancing the talents and gifts of *all* class members to learn and empowering everyone to help others. As noted by Wilkinson (1980) ". . . people are interdependent; everyone has a function and everyone has a role to play, and that's what keeps people together and forms a community" (p. 452).

While specialists and professionals usually play a key role, the emphasis in inclusive classrooms, and throughout this book, is on joining people together by facilitating them to help each other rather than relying too much on "outside" support. An overreliance on specialists and professionals can destroy the sense of community in a classroom since it reduces the need for people to develop relationships and learn to support each other. Practical strategies are suggested in this book for achieving full inclusion of all students in a mainstream that is challenging to each student but is also adaptive and sensitive to each student's needs.

The book is divided into three major sections. In Section I, inclusive schooling and support networking are addressed in three chapters. Chapter 1 defines and discusses what is meant by inclusive schooling or full-time regular class integration for all students. In Chapter 2, the importance of interweaving a network of varying supports into a comprehensive and coordinated support system for classroom teachers and all students in the mainstream is discussed. Chapter 3 focuses on how present-day "special" educators can join regular education and facilitate a network of supports for teachers and students.

There are nine chapters in Section II, (Chapters 4 through 12), all of which focus on specific supports that can be employed to help classroom teachers and students. Supports such as the following are discussed in detail: peer friendships, cooperative learning, peer tutoring, teacher and student assistance teams, professional peer collaboration, collaborative consultation, team teaching, technological supports, and supports for dealing with severe maladaptive behaviors.

In the four chapters in Section III, the emphasis is on how administrators, parents, and general community members can work together to achieve supportive and caring schools. School administrative supports are discussed in Chapter 13, parental supports in Chapter 14, general community supports in Chapter 15, and some initial, concrete steps that can be taken for developing supportive and caring schools are outlined in Chapter 16.

In this edited book, a number of people need to be thanked. We are grateful to the contributors who provided excellent and progressive information in a timely fashion. They deserve special thanks for their willingness to adjust their busy professional and personal agendas for the production schedule of this book. In addition, we wish to acknowledge Vince Ercolano, the acquisitions editor, and Sarah Cheney, the production editor, at Paul H. Brookes Publishing Co. for their professional assistance and friendly and cheerful attitude throughout the development and completion of this book.

REFERENCES

Siegel, L. (1989). Educational isolation of deaf children. *IMPACT-HI Newsletter,* 1st quarter, 1, 4.
Strully, J. (1989, December). *The future is now.* Paper presented at the 16th Annual TASH Conference, San Francisco.
Wilkinson, J. (1980). On assisting Indian people. *Social Casework, 61,* 451–454.

To Samantha Stainback,
our significant, supportive other.

SUPPORT NETWORKS FOR INCLUSIVE SCHOOLING

SUPPORT
NETWORKING FOR
INCLUSIVE SCHOOLING

Susan Stainback
William Stainback

1

Inclusive Schooling

This chapter introduces the concept of inclusive schooling. The purpose is to provide background information and considerations requiring attention when all students are included in the mainstream of their regular neighborhood schools.

The chapter is organized around a series of questions frequently asked about inclusive schools and the integration of all students in the mainstream. The answers provided are based on information the authors have gathered from a variety of sources, including parents, students, and educators who have been involved in the development of inclusive schools.

WHAT IS AN INCLUSIVE SCHOOL?

An inclusive school is one that educates all students in the mainstream. Educating all students in the mainstream means that every student is in regular education and regular classes (Lusthaus & Forest, 1989). It also means providing all students within the mainstream appropriate educational programs that are challenging yet geared to their capabilities and needs as well as any support and assistance they and/or their teachers may need to be successful in the mainstream (Stainback & Stainback, 1988). But an inclusive school also goes beyond this. An inclusive school is a place where everyone belongs, is accepted, supports, and is supported by his or her peers and other members of the school community in the course of having his or her educational needs met.

Portions of what is presented in this chapter are based on material in Stainback, Stainback, and Forest (1989).

3

Inclusive schooling is the process of carrying out the operation of supportive schools. That is, it is the process of operating a classroom or school as a supportive community where the needs of all members are met and people support and accept responsibility for each other. Inclusive schooling is related to, but different from, the movement to integrate or mainstream students with disabilities into their regular neighborhood schools. Integration and/or mainstreaming is the process of having students with disabilities (who have been excluded) become an integral part of the mainstream of their schools. Inclusive schools do not focus on how to assist any particular category of students, such as those classified as disabled, fit into the mainstream. Instead, the focus is on how to operate supportive classrooms and schools that include and meet the needs of everyone. Thus, the focus of this chapter, and the book in general, is *not* on how to mainstream or fit students into regular education classes. Rather, the focus is on how to develop regular school and classroom communities that fit, nurture, and support the educational and social needs of every student in attendance.

An inclusive school and the process of inclusive schooling is the ultimate goal of the integration and mainstreaming process. Once inclusive schooling and inclusive schools are achieved, integration and mainstreaming will no longer be necessary since there will no longer be anyone left out to be integrated or mainstreamed into regular educational settings.

It should be stressed that inclusive schooling means that all students should be included in the mainstream with appropriate programs and support to meet their individual needs. Success occurs when all students are provided appropriate educational opportunities and support. These can and should be provided in the educational mainstream.

HOW CAN INCLUSIVE SCHOOLS BE ACHIEVED?

To achieve inclusive schools, special and regular educators must come together to work to achieve the goal of effective and appropriate education for every student in the mainstream. Full inclusion does *not* mean that special educators are no longer necessary; rather, it means that special educators are needed even more to work with regular educators in teaching and facilitating challenging, supportive, and appropriate educational programs for all students. However, special educators do need to be integrated into, and in effect, become "regular or general" educators in the mainstream who have expertise in specific instructional, curricular, and assessment areas. (This is discussed in more detail at a later point in this chapter.)

The resources, knowledge base, and personnel of regular education cannot serve the needs of all students. Special education resources and personnel cannot serve all needs either. However, if special education resources are teamed with regular education resources to become an integral part of the regular education mainstream, then all students' needs are better met. In other words, students cannot be successfully integrated without integrating personnel and resources. The reason is that both research and experience have shown that the *key* to success is that the students be provided appropriate programs and educational opportunities in integrated settings (Certo, Haring, & York, 1984; Madden & Slavin, 1983; Stainback & Stainback, 1985).

Thus, it is no longer sufficient to simply advocate for access to the mainstream of school life. It is also essential to facilitate appropriate educational programs and supports for every student in the mainstream.

WHY SHOULD ALL STUDENTS BE EDUCATED IN THE MAINSTREAM?

The basic underlying purpose of educating all students in the mainstream is to provide each student the opportunity to learn to live and work with his or her peers in natural, integrated educational and community settings. Vandercook, Fleetham, Sinclair, and Tetlie (1988) noted:

> In integrated classrooms all children are enriched by having the opportunity to learn from one another, grow to care for one another, and gain the attitudes, skills, and values necessary for our communities to support the inclusion of all citizens. (p. 19)

Since the mid-1980s, the movement to include all students in regular neighborhood schools and classrooms has gained increased momentum for a number of reasons. One reason involves the benefits to the students. When provided appropriate educational programs and support in integrated settings, students tend to learn more than they do in segregated settings (Brinker & Thorpe, 1983, 1984; Madden & Slavin, 1983). Additionally, when given guidance from adults in integrated settings, students can learn to understand, respect, be sensitive to, and grow comfortable with individual differences and similarities among their peers (Voeltz, 1980, 1982). Students can also learn to interact, communicate, develop friendships, work together, and assist one another based on their individual strengths and needs (Forest, 1987; Stainback & Stainback, 1988; Strully, 1986, 1987; Vandercook et al., 1988). Finally, the 1982 report of the *Disability Rights, Education, and Defense Fund* found "that regardless of race, class, gender, type of disability, or its onset, the more time spent in integrated public school classes as children, the more people achieved educationally and occupationally as adults" (Ferguson & Asch, 1989, p. 124). Some parents intuitively know this. One parent stated:

> When she's finished with school, she'll be able to be in some sort of integrated situation. She'll have social skills she wouldn't have had and an ability to function in more complex situations than she would've been able to do if she'd stayed segregated. (Hanline & Halvorsen, 1989, p. 490)

A second reason to include all students in the mainstream is to avoid the effects of segregation inherent when students are placed in separate, special schools and/or classes. Lack of self-confidence, lack of motivation, and lack of positive expectations for achievement are all products of segregated learning environments. As Chief Justice Earl Warren noted in *Brown v. The Board of Education* (1954):

> [Separateness in education can] generate a feeling of inferiority as to [children's] status in the community that may affect their hearts and minds in a way unlikely ever to be undone. This sense of inferiority . . . affects the motivation of a child to learn . . . [and] has a tendency to retard . . . educational and mental development. (p. 493)

This concern voiced by Warren was confirmed by a statement from a student who attended separate, special classes throughout his school years. He stated:

> The only contact we had with the "normal" children was visual. We stared at each other. On those occasions, I can report my own feelings: embarrassment. . . . I can also report their feelings: YECH! We, the children in the "handicapped" class, were internalizing the "yech" message—plus a couple of others. We were in school because children go to school, but we were outcasts with no future and no expectation of one. (Massachusetts Advocacy Center, 1987, pp. 4–5)

Another student who moved from an integrated elementary class to a homogeneous, segregated class in junior high school also confirmed Warren's statement when she stated:

> I felt good when I was with my [elementary] class, but when they went and separated us that changed us. That changed our ideas, the way we thought about each other, and turned us to enemies toward each other because they said I was dumb and they were smart. (Schafer & Oleta, 1971, p. 96)

The third and perhaps most important reason to include all students in the mainstream is that it is the fair, ethical, and equitable thing to do. It deals with the value of *equality*. As was decided in *Brown v. The Board of Education* (1954), "separate is not equal." All children should be a part of the educational and community mainstream. It is discriminatory that some students, such as those "labeled" disabled, must earn the right to be in the regular education mainstream or have to wait for educational researchers to prove that they can profit from the mainstream, while other students are allowed unrestricted access simply because they have no label. No one should have to pass anyone's test or prove anything in a research study to live and learn in the mainstream of school and community life. This is a basic right, not something one has to earn.

Since students classified as having disabilities have constituted a major focus for exclusion from the mainstream of schools and communities, many disability rights advocates have been actively supporting the inclusive schooling movement. As one disability rights advocate has said, "From a minority group perspective, the principal change to be sought in education policy is the . . . integration of disabled students into regular classrooms" (Hahn, 1989, p. 233).

The basic premise of equality inherent in inclusive schooling was stated on the floor of the United States Senate by the former Republican senator from Connecticut, Lowell Weicker:

> Authorities on disabilities have often said, and I have quoted them on this floor before, that the history of society's formal methods of dealing with people with disabilities can be summed up in two words: SEGREGATION and INEQUALITY. Psychologist Kenneth Clark, whose testimony about the damaging effects of segregation provided pivotal evidence in the landmark case of *Brown versus the Board of Education,* stated that "segregation is the way in which a society tells a group of human beings that they are inferior to other groups of human beings in the society." As a society, we have treated people with disabilities as inferiors and made them unwelcome in many activities and opportunities generally available to other Americans. (Weicker, 1988, p. 1)

It is not comforting to think that in the past it was actually decided that some children or adults should be excluded from regular lives, classrooms, and communities. This exclusion has been justified on the basis that "it's for their own good," "they need special treatment or interventions," or "the research has not yet been completed." However, for a truly fair, egalitarian society in which all people are considered to have equal worth and equal rights, the school systems need to be reevaluated. If integration and equality for all people in society is desired, then segregation in the schools cannot be justified. Appropriate educational programs and interventions can be provided in the mainstream. Forest (1988) noted: "If we really want someone to be part of our lives, we will do what it takes to welcome that person and accommodate his or her needs" (p. 3). When a single person, who has not broken any laws, is excluded from the mainstream of school and community life, all of society becomes vulnerable.

WHAT ARE SOME PRACTICAL
STRATEGIES FOR PROMOTING INCLUSIVE SCHOOLING?

There are a number of strategies that can be used to make full inclusion a reality.

Establish a School Philosophy

The first and perhaps the most important strategy is to establish a school philosophy, based on egalitarian and democratic principles, where integration is valued. Ferguson and Asch (1989) noted, "Integration is not an experiment to be tested, but a value to be followed" (p. 137). The school board and the administration, particularly the school principal, can be instrumental in establishing a philosophy that all children can learn and belong in the mainstream of school and community life. Often, however, they need the encouragement, support, and assistance of parents and educators to enable them to do so.

Follow the Principle of Natural Proportions

A second strategy is to follow the principle of natural proportions. That is, inclusive schools generally accept those students who are a natural part of their neighborhood, zone, or district from which the school draws its students. As a consequence, students who have often been excluded from their neighborhood school, such as those with severe disabilities, for example, should attend the age-appropriate, regular neighborhood school they normally would attend if they were not classified as having a disability (Brown et al., 1989).

It is difficult for those schools that serve large numbers of students with disabilities to become inclusive schools. The reason is that due to the high density of students with disabilities within the total student population, natural or normal regular class integration is almost impossible to achieve.

Include Individuals Who Are Directly Involved

The third strategy is to include in any discussions and planning for integration the people who will be directly involved, such as the students traditionally classified as having disabilities, parents, students classified as nondisabled, and teachers. Those people most directly influenced have been excluded far too long from the planning and decision-making process.

Some schools, in the process of moving toward full inclusion, have found it helpful to *establish an inclusive schooling task force* made up of teachers, parents, students, counselors, administrators, and specialists. In addition to serving as a general advocacy group for integration, the purpose of the task force is to help all individuals involved with the school gain a better understanding of the whys and hows of developing and maintaining an integrated, caring, and inclusive school community. To do this the task force is often charged with several duties. One is to gather background information in the form of books, articles, and videotapes on the subject. These can be recommended to and shared with school personnel, students, parents, and school board members. A special section of the school library might be designated to maintain all the materials gathered. Also, when gathering background information, key task force or other school personnel may want to visit inclusive schools in one's own or nearby school district.

A second purpose of the task force is to organize and conduct information sessions for parents and school personnel where people knowledgeable and experienced in full integration can discuss reasons and provide suggestions as to how it might be accomplished. It is important that the key people invited to share information have direct experience in full-time regular class integration. Usually a combination of parents, students, teachers, and administrators from a school system that has successfully integrated their classrooms can be more "believable" and effective than hearing only from "experts." Some schools have the same information sessions for parents, educators, students, and administrators, which involves everyone "sitting down together" rather than each group communicating only among themselves.

A third purpose of the task force is to establish an integration plan that includes specific objectives for achieving full inclusion. This plan usually includes how the resources and professional and nonprofessional personnel in "special" education can be utilized to provide reduced teacher/pupil ratios, team teachers, consultants, teacher aides, and support facilitators in the mainstream of regular education. By establishing such a task force to help achieve inclusive schooling, community members, students, and a variety of personnel within a school can become involved and take ownership and pride in achieving a fully integrated school.

Develop Networks of Support

A fourth practical strategy for achieving mainstream education is to develop networks of support. Many school personnel are finding that successful inclusion of all students necessitates more than providing one or two types of support (e.g., having a specialist and/or teacher's aide in the regular class). Instead, it often requires an array of both nonprofessional and professional supports such as buddies, friendships, and peer tutors for students; and, for teachers, professional peer collaboration, team teachers, teacher and student assistance teams, collaborative consultation, and perhaps most important, time for planning and working with others. In addition, one or more technological supports may be needed. The array of supports needed and how they can be provided are discussed in Chapter 2 and throughout this book.

Integrate Students, Personnel, and Resources

A fifth strategy is to integrate not only students, but personnel and resources as well. Including all the students from the special education class in regular education allows the special education teacher and the teacher's aide(s) in the special class to be freed and integrated into the mainstream to serve as team teachers, support facilitators, and the like. When only one or two students from a special class are included, this usually means that the special education teacher must remain in the special class to teach the students who still remain, or try to serve the dual roles of a team teacher or support facilitator in regular education and a special class teacher. This dual role can be an almost impossible task. Furthermore, when all students are included, all the resources and energy of school personnel can be spent on assessing instructional needs, adapting curriculum, and providing support to students who need it in the mainstream rather than spending valuable resources and energy on classifying, labeling, and making "placement" decisions.

While it is being suggested here that *all* the students from a special class be included in the mainstream, it is essential *not* to include large numbers of the newly assigned students into any one regular education classroom. These students should be included across several classrooms. As noted earlier in regard to having "natural proportions" of students within schools and classrooms, one or a small number of new students can be more easily absorbed into a classroom than a large group. In addition, it is important to avoid clusters of "former special education" students being perceived as a "special" group within regular education.

Adapt the Curriculum

The sixth strategy is to adapt the curriculum when needed. In inclusive schools, the focus is not exclusively on how to help students fit into the existing, standard curriculum of the school. Rather, the curriculum in the regular education class is adapted, when necessary, to meet the needs of any student for whom the standard curriculum is inappropriate. For example, while most students in a science unit on temperature may focus on learning to understand Fahrenheit and Celsius temperature scales, one student might learn to recognize and point to items that are hot and cold. That is, while all students can pursue the same basic educational goal (what is temperature) and learn together in the same regular education class activities, it may be necessary for them to sometimes focus on and be evaluated according to specific curriculum objectives that are different. How the curriculum can be adapted is discussed in detail in Stainback and Stainback (in press).

Maintain Flexibility

The seventh and final strategy to promote inclusive schooling is to maintain flexibility. According to Vandercook, York, and Forest (1989):

> Flexibility . . . is necessary as even the most thoughtfully designed strategies and plans sometimes are not successful and need revision. False starts should be anticipated and a commitment made to ongoing problem-solving and change as needed. Initial objectives for student involvement in regular classes and the support necessary to achieve individualized objectives may need to be modified after the students actually participate in regular classes. (p. 2)

Vandercook et al. (1989) essentially recommended that educators adopt a problem-solving approach. That is, when problems occur, as they inevitably will, the best strategy is to go back to the drawing board and come up with another plan or a different way to proceed, rather than to retreat into segregated, special education classes. While in some cases retreat may be the easiest route, it is not in the long-term best interest of the students classified as having disabilities or the ultimate achievement of integrated, inclusive communities.

CAN ALL STUDENTS PARTICIPATE IN MEANINGFUL WAYS IN REGULAR EDUCATION?

A number of educators have demonstrated that students with diverse educational needs can participate and learn in meaningful ways in regular education classes (See Biklen, 1988; Discover the Possibilities, 1988; Forest, 1987; Porter, 1988; Vandercook et al., 1988). For instance, during a map reading activity, one student may be called upon to discuss the economic system of a country, another may be requested to identify a color, while another student may simply be requested to grasp and hold a corner of the map. In reading class, during oral reading activities, one student may be requested to read out loud, another listen to a story and answer questions, while another student may be asked to pick out pictures that describe the story. In inclusive, heterogeneous classrooms, what any student is requested to do to participate in a group or individualized class activity is based on what the student needs to learn and is capable of doing. Within a single math class, for example, objectives may range from grasping an object or following a one step direction to computing or analyzing a highly complex problem. Thus, when appropriately organized, regular education classes can provide a variety of appropriate learning activities and challenges for students with a range of learning needs, interests, and capabilities.

In addition, many school personnel are finding that all types of skills can be taught within regular neighborhood schools and classrooms. For example, daily life functional skills, such as cooking, can be learned in home economics classes, and alternative communication skills using pictures or other methods can be learned in reading or language arts classes. Also, lunch and snack times in regular education can be used to develop eating and dining skills, bus riding skills can be taught when students need to travel back and forth to school or in the community, braille can be taught and practiced during reading classes, and mobility skills can be taught to students who need them when they are called upon to maneuver around the regular education classroom, school building, and playground.

Finally, it should be stressed that adapting instruction to individual differences does not mean that educational standards need to or should be lowered for any student, whether traditionally classified as retarded, normal, or gifted. Every student should be challenged to be the best he or she can be. That is, while the goals and methods of educational programs should be individualized to meet the unique needs of each student, high expectations and challenges for each student, based on his or her unique capabilities and needs, are essential to providing all students a quality education.

DO STUDENTS ALWAYS HAVE TO BE
HETEROGENEOUSLY GROUPED WITHIN REGULAR EDUCATION?

Educating all students in the mainstream essentially means the heterogeneous grouping of students of similar ages in the same regular neighborhood schools, classes, programs, and activities. Experience and research have shown that there are advantages to heterogeneously grouping students (Dawson, 1987; Slavin, 1987). For instance, heterogeneous grouping can allow for shared responsibility among students and skill guidance and modeling in which peers learn from and help each other. In addition, heterogeneous grouping can offset the potential stereotyping and/or stigmatization that often results when students are frequently associated with a particular ability, disability, or achievement group, and can promote better understanding of individual differences and similarities among all students. Thus, heterogeneous grouping should occur whenever possible.

However, some students may need to be homogeneously grouped occasionally for instruction within a class or across classes according to their interests, needs, and capabilities (Slavin, 1987; Stainback, Stainback, & Forest, 1989). For example, some students may desire or need instruction in computers, advanced physics, calculus, a foreign language, a musical instrument, gymnastics, braille, sign language, mobility orientation, or community-referenced instruction that other students either do not need or choose not to take. When such groupings occur, they should be based on the instructional needs of the students as they relate to the instructional focus of the class or grouping, rather than according to a categorical label such as retarded, normal, or gifted. Care also must be exercised to minimize such groupings to the greatest extent possible; but when they are used, they should be flexible, fluid, and short term to avoid the development of a tracking system and to allow students to move in, out, and across the groupings according to their individual needs and interests.

Robert Slavin, a well-known researcher on grouping, recommended that homogeneous grouping plans be used _only_ when the following conditions can be met:

1. The grouping plan measurably reduces student heterogeneity _in the specific skill being taught;_
2. The plan is flexible enough to allow teachers to respond to misassignments and changes in student performance level after initial placement; and
3. Teachers actually vary their pace and level of instruction to correspond to students' levels of readiness and learning rates. (Villa & Thousand, 1988, p. 149)

Slavin (1987) stressed that, if limited grouping is necessary, students should be grouped according to their specific instructional needs and for no more than a couple of subject areas. Thus, they are allowed to spend the majority of their school day in heterogeneous groupings.

Grouping of students for instructional purposes occurs at the high school level more often than it does at the preschool or elementary school levels. In fact, many parents and professionals believe that it occurs much too frequently (Forest, 1987; Goodlad, 1984; Oakes, 1986). Even if a student cannot read, multiply, or write, it does not necessarily preclude the functionality and importance of him or her taking core regular education high school courses such as basic science, history, and literature. By allowing all students to enroll in basic core high school classes and participate, if in only small ways, they all profit from high school educational experiences designed to help them reason, think, and learn about how society and the world around them operates. Similarly, by having students with diverse characteristics in such basic information, idea developing, and sharing classes, students can share common experiences, learn to better understand what people with different perceptions think, and also have an opportunity to learn from and interact with their peers. These are all functional and necessary skills.

Although a student may not be as intellectually astute or physically adept as many of his or her classmates, he or she will still be expected to and have the right to vote, live, and recreate in, adapt and contribute to, and understand the surrounding world (Guess & Helmstetter, 1986). Thus, it is important to evaluate what learning opportunities some students miss in order to make time for teaching such things as fluency in a job or daily activities, under the guise of providing a functional curriculum, that may virtually become obsolete in the future (e.g., pumping gas, washing dishes). Some educators believe that it is essential to guard against preparing a subgroup of students for the future who share few common experiences and understandings with people they are expected to live with in the community (Goodlad, 1984; Oakes, 1986). In addition, any student's education would be incomplete without at least providing him or her an *opportunity* to be introduced to materials and discussions in history, literature, music, art, and science that promote an understanding of the world, sensitivity to the human condition, and reasoning and thinking skills during the school years. It is difficult, at best, to predict what the future might be for any student; thus, a growing number of people believe that it is a mistake to limit any student's education to learning *only* "daily life, functional" skills (Forest, 1987; Goodlad, 1984; Oakes, 1986; Stainback et al., 1989).

It should be noted that if a class is reading the novel *Red Badge of Courage,* for example, a student, who cannot read and comprehend the novel, can still participate (Baumgart et al., 1982). He or she can listen to a brief tape recorded simplified version based on the story or be told the basic or rudimentary elements and ideas through picture cards or by some other means and answer a few basic questions. Even a small understanding of the story and participation with peers can be a helpful and worthwhile learning experience.

Formerly excluded students often gained more than was anticipated when included in basic regular education classes. For instance, a student, classified as having a severe disability, surprised everyone when he was included in an eighth grade science class:

> Initially, science class was selected because the teacher was an enthusiastic individual who was very interested in involving all learners in his class. The team struggled with how science related to a functional, life space domain curriculum but went ahead with the plans to include the learner in the science class anyway. After several weeks in the class, it became apparent that the student enjoyed the science subject area. His spoken vocabulary increased dramatically to include science jargon including e.g., "rocks," "rivers," "stars." (York & Vandercook, 1989, p. 16)

Increasing one's vocabulary is certainly functional. Thus, it is important not to assume that formerly excluded students will fail to benefit from regular education classes.

In short, while teaching floor sweeping, dish washing, grocery shopping, bus riding, vocational, and other skills is important, it is essential not to overlook the other side of any person, that is, the more intellectual and human side. All students—including those traditionally classified as having severe, profound, and multiple disabilities—need to be provided *opportunities* to think, reason, and make moral and ethical decisions; become sensitive to the needs of others; appreciate art, music, and poetry; and understand the world in which they live. In addition, all students need to share common experiences together so that they can gain a better understanding of one another and learn to live and function together in an integrated society. When subgroups of students are provided an almost totally different curriculum throughout their school years, there is a real danger they will have little in common and little understanding of each other later in life.

IS THERE EVER A NEED FOR SPECIAL EDUCATION?

The personnel, curriculum, and methods in special education are definitely needed to provide all students educational and related services that meet their individual needs. However, in truly integrated schools they, too, need to be integrated into regular education and become "regular" education personnel, curriculum, and methods.

The reason for changing from the special to the regular label is that the terminology used to describe personnel and programs as well as students is important to achieving truly integrated schools. Will (1986) stated, "The terminology we use in describing our educational system is full of the language of separation, of fragmentation, of removal" (p. 412). For example, at present, students, educators, and programs are separated and fragmented by labeling some "special" and others "regular." Even when everyone is physically placed in the mainstream, separation still occurs on a psychological level in the minds of students, teachers, and parents.

This psychological separation can be avoided. All students can be viewed simply as students, each with his or her own unique characteristics, rather than viewing some with "special needs" and others with "regular needs." All classrooms and programs can be referred to by their function or instructional focus. For example, Ford and Davern (1989) changed a high school special education classroom into an apprenticeship center or classroom. All students, whether classified disabled or nondisabled, who were engaged in community-based, work-study, supported employment, or cooperative education type programs, used the classroom as a place to receive instructions, gather belongings, and prepare for community outings. Finally, all educators can be referred to as regular educators or just simply educators rather than some being "special" educators. To accomplish this, special educators can become educators with expertise in, for example, community-referenced instruction, supported employment, school administration, behavior management, braille, learning strategies, and/or support facilitation.

There is more to integration than just physical proximity. Integration on a psychological level in the minds of everyone is also important to achieve a sense of oneness or community, where everyone belongs and is a natural and integral part of the mainstream.

IS IT REALLY POSSIBLE TO
EDUCATE ALL STUDENTS IN THE MAINSTREAM?

Students display a range of physical, intellectual, and psychological characteristics. No one denies this. Yet, the school's response to individual differences need not be to classify, label, and/or segregate. If educators want to, it is possible to organize the mainstream of schools to appreciate and celebrate differences.

If a child fails to be successful in the mainstream, whose fault is it? Walter Lippmann said more than a half century ago:

> If a child fails in school and then fails in life, the schools cannot sit back and say: you see how accurately I predicted this. Unless we are to admit that education is essentially impotent, we have to throw back the child's failure at the school, and describe it as a failure not by the child but by the schools. (quoted in Block & Dworkin, 1976, p. 17)

After extensive research on effective schools, Edmonds (1979) stated:

> We can, whenever and wherever we choose, successfully teach all children whose schooling is of interest to us. We already know more than we need in order to do this. Whether we do it must finally depend on how we feel about the fact that we haven't done it so far. (p. 29)

This, of course, will require the identification of appropriate but challenging goals for each child in the mainstream rather than requiring them all to learn the exact same thing or always be at the same level of proficiency. It also will require that support and assistance be provided, when necessary. This can be done if the will to do so exists.

Some parents and educators have said that they thought it may be possible. Growing numbers of people are now convinced that it can be done, *given that the mainstream is sensitive to individual differences and teachers and students are provided adequate support and assistance.* The reason is that it is beginning to be done successfully in some schools in the U.S., Canada, Italy, and a number of other countries (Berrigan, 1988; Biklen, 1988; Blackman & Peterson, 1989; Forest, 1988; Porter, 1988; Schattman, 1988; Villa & Thousand, 1988; York & Vandercook, 1989).

However, it will be difficult to achieve widespread success if society is unwilling to: 1) provide each student the support necessary for him or her to be in the mainstream, and 2) adapt and adjust, when necessary, the mainstream to accommodate all students. Thus, the key is the *willingness* to visualize, work for, and achieve a mainstream that is adaptive and supportive of everyone.

It should be emphasized that saying it can be done is not the same as saying it will be easy. Segregation has been practiced for centuries, and there are entrenched attitudes, laws, policies, and educational structures that work against achieving full inclusion of all students on a widespread basis. In addition, because a second system of education (i.e., "special" education) has operated for so long, many schools unfortunately do not know at the present time how to adapt and modify the curriculum and instructional programs to meet diverse student needs, deal with behavioral difficulties, and/or provide the tools, techniques, and supports some students need to be successful in the mainstream. Thus, achieving full inclusion of all students is likely to be a challenging undertaking. However, the goal of having inclusive schools where everyone belongs, has friends, and is provided appropriate educational programs and supports is far too important not to accept the challenge.

Finally, the best way to learn how to make full inclusion a reality is to establish integrated schools and classrooms and work every day within these "real" world integrated settings to find solutions to problems. People in school systems that are doing this are sometimes experiencing frustration and roadblocks; however, most are not giving up. Instead, they are finding that by going back to the drawing board and gradually coming up with ways to overcome barriers, they are creating educational structures and opportunities that benefit everyone.

CAN FULL INTEGRATION BE ACHIEVED WITHOUT SACRIFICING PEOPLE'S DEVELOPMENT OF A SELF-IDENTITY?

Many people identify with others with whom they share a common characteristic, concern, or interest (e.g., physical characteristic, religion, cultural background). This self-identity or sense of self influences a student's confidence and feelings of worth, which, in turn, impacts the way he or she interacts with the environment. As with many other groups, developing a positive self-identity that includes one's disability is a particularly important consideration for individuals with disabilities (Hahn, 1989) and needs to be incorporated into the integration movement. Ferguson and Asch (1989) described the issue as follows:

> How do disabled people come to think of themselves in ways that incorporate their disability as an important part of their personal and social identity? It is a theme that complicates the call for educational integration. In both the literature and our personal reflections we find an undeniable recognition that a well-developed sense of identity as a disabled adult needs some significant involvement as a child with other people (children and adults) who have similar disabilities. (p. 131)

While this is an important factor to consider, most people also believe it is essential to work for and foster an integrated society and integrated schools where everyone can learn to live and work together and care about each other. The authors believe that this can be done without trampling on the rights of any person or group to identify with or freely form friendships and bonds with whomever they choose. The key here is free choice. For example, if people who share a common characteristic (e.g., deafness) want to bond together, that is their personal choice. However, one should never impose the arbitrary homogeneous clustering together of people perceived as having a common characteristic(s) in segregated settings, such as group homes for individuals with mental retardation; schools or classes for students who are black, non-English speaking, gifted, or deaf; or scout troops for those with handicaps and for those without handicaps.

In educational organizational structures, the prearranged homogeneous grouping or clustering of individuals based on a common characteristic is inappropriate for moral reasons involving equality. Such grouping is also less than optimal for learning to live, work, and care about one another in integrated communities. However, when integrated classrooms are organized in the schools, often individuals with certain characteristics that have relatively low incidence in the general population, such as blindness, deafness, or spina bifida, often do not have the *opportunity* to get to know and interact with other children and adults who have similar characteristics, interests, or backgrounds. Thus, *purposeful access* (i.e., planned opportunities) for people who share common characteristics with one another to gather through the availability of *support or interest groups* can be a worthwhile and desirable practice. For instance, Adrienne Asch, a colleague who is blind, clearly pointed out that while it was important for her educational and social development that she attend regular neighborhood public school classes, being able to have some opportunity to "compare notes" and share experiences with peers who were also blind was helpful to her. She stated:

We talked about how our parents, teachers, and the kids in our schools treated us because we were blind. Sometimes someone who solved a problem told the rest of us what she or he figured out. Sometimes we complained together about those problems none of us had managed to solve. It was important to compare notes, have solid friendships where sight or lack of it did not affect the terms of the interaction, and just in general not feel alone. (Ferguson & Asch, 1989, pp. 132–133)

Similarly, there has been much emphasis since the mid-1980s on the importance of students who are deaf getting to know others who are deaf and being introduced to the culture of the deaf (Padden & Humphries, 1988). In addition, benefits of formal and informal support or common interest groups have been cited for other areas, such as students of divorced parents, victims of abuse or rape, future farmers of America, religious youth groups, wheelchair sports, teenage girls, and so on. Although such experiences may be needed, they can be gained while maintaining integrated schools and classrooms through after-school, weekend, and summer social clubs and groups. In rural or sparsely populated areas it may be necessary to form regional advocacy groups, social clubs, or other activities. An important element of such access groups is that their membership and participation should not be imposed (individuals can choose or not choose to participate).

Care must be exercised to ensure that any organized grouping of people does not violate their interests, needs, and basic rights. There is a hazard that people in authority, including educators and parents, might focus on any one of a child's characteristics (e.g., disability, race, religion) and organize his or her life around that characteristic. Parents encouraging their children with disabilities to have only friends who have disabilities and to participate in social events for people with disabilities just perpetuates the well-intentioned segregation of years past (Strully & Strully, 1985).

As previously noted, homogeneous group activities should be voluntary, but also, encouragement should be based on an individual's unique needs and interests, not what others consider to be an individual's identifying characteristic (e.g., blindness, deafness). In an investigation of a work situation in which adults who were classified as mentally retarded were learning job skills, a number of the staff expressed concern about the interactions of one young woman. The woman chose to socially interact with the staff rather than her peers who were also classified as mentally retarded. When asked, the woman explained, "I am normal inside and I can't seem to get that out" (Kauffman, 1984, p. 89). The point is that everyone is "normal inside," and each person chooses different talents, characteristics, and interests to develop his or her sense of personal identity and friendships. Each person should have the right and be encouraged to define and nurture his or her identity in any positive way that he or she chooses, whether it be by sex, physical or mental characteristics, abilities, race, religion, cultural heritage, interests, and/or any combination thereof, while maintaining an awareness of his or her membership in and responsibility for a larger group of human beings. That is, if a group of individuals who share the common characteristic of being deaf or black or female or Catholic want to get together, share experiences, or form an advocacy group, that is their personal choice, but it should never be mandatory.

In addition to sharing or identifying with common characteristics through support or interest groups, purposeful access should occur in terms of *representation and role models* available in schools. Having people with varying characteristics as administrators, teachers, and other school personnel is an important factor to consider for quality inclusive education. For instance, having a school principal who is nonambulatory can not only set a positive role model for both ambulatory and nonambulatory students but will also assure representation of the access needs for wheelchairs in the school's decision making. Thus, including students with all types of characteristics in integrated schools will likewise require having educators and other personnel with various characteristics, including those who are deaf, black, female, blind, and so on, operating the schools. This is important not only to help all students to develop a positive self-image but also for more inclusive representation of the diverse needs among individuals and positive role models within the schools.

CONCLUSION

An inclusive school is one that educates all students in the mainstream. However, educating all students in the mainstream does *not* mean merely "dumping" students into regular education classes. It also does *not* mean that all students will necessarily have to achieve the same educational objectives and/or utilize the same methods to learn. It does mean including all students in a mainstream that is sensitive, flexible, and adaptive to unique needs where all students can receive whatever support and assistance they may need to fulfill their potential and develop friendships with their peers.

Few people—whether classified as disabled, nondisabled, or with any other label—want to be in a mainstream that does not meet their needs or does not make them feel welcome or secure. In fact, when students in segregated, special classes are asked about mainstreaming some of them will say that they are hesitant and unsure because they see the mainstream as a place where their needs may not be met and where they may feel unwelcome and uncomfortable. Some parents agree with their children. Thus, if an integrated society is desired, it is essential that the mainstream be adaptive and sensitive to the unique needs of all students and that positive peer relationships and friendships be fostered for all students so they will feel welcome and secure.

Experience has shown that it is possible to have a mainstream that meets everyone's needs *if* ample support and assistance is provided to both teachers and students in regular education classes. Throughout this book, parents who have been involved with the inclusive schooling movement and educators experienced in educating a diversity of students in the mainstream outline and discuss some of the major supports needed and how such supports can be provided.

REFERENCES

Baumgart, D., Brown, L., Pumpian, I., Nisbet, J., Ford, A., Sweet, M., Messina, R., & Schroeder, J. (1982). Principle of partial participation and individualized adaptations in educational programs for severely handicapped students. *Journal of The Association for Persons with Severe Handicaps, 7,* 17–27.

Berrigan, C. (1988, February). Integration in Italy: A dynamic movement. *TASH Newsletter,* pp. 6–7.

Biklen, D. (Producer). (1988). *Regular lives* [Video tape]. Washington, DC: State of the Art.

Blackman, H., & Peterson, D. (Eds.). (1989). *Totally integrated neighborhood schools.* LaGrange, IL: LaGrange Department of Special Education.

Block, N., & Dworkin, G. (Eds.). (1976). *The I.Q. controversy.* New York: Random House.

Brinker, R., & Thorpe, M. (1983). *Evaluation of integration of severely handicapped students in regular classrooms and community settings.* Princeton, NJ: Educational Testing Service.

Brinker, R., & Thorpe, M. (1984). Integration of severely handicapped students and the proportion of IEP objectives achieved. *Exceptional Children, 51,* 168–175.

Brown, v. The Board of Education of Topeka. 347 U.S. 483, 493 (1954).

Brown, L., Long, E., Udvari-Solner, A., Davis, L., VanDeventer, P., Ahlgren, C., Johnson, F., Grenewald, L., & Jorgenson, J. (1989). The home school. *Journal of The Association for Persons with Severe Handicaps, 14,* 1–7.

Certo, N., Haring, N., & York, R. (Eds.). (1984). *Public school integration of severely handicapped students.* Baltimore: Paul H. Brookes Publishing Co.

Dawson, M. (1987). Beyond ability grouping. *School Psychology Review, 16,* 348–369.

Discover the Possibilities. (1988). Colorado Springs, CO: PEAK Parent Center.

Edmonds, R. (1979). Some schools work and more can. *Social Policy, 9*(5), 25–29.

Ferguson, P., & Asch, A. (1989). Lessons from life: Personal and parental perspectives on school, childhood, and disability. In D. Biklen, A. Ford, &

D. Ferguson (Eds.), *Disability and society* (pp. 108–140). Chicago: National Society for the Study of Education.

Ford, A., & Davern, L. (1989). Moving forward with school integration. In R. Gaylord-Ross (Ed.), *Integration strategies for students with handicaps* (pp. 11–13). Baltimore: Paul H. Brookes Publishing Co.

Forest, M. (1987). *More education integration.* Downsview, Ontario: G. Allan Roeher Institute.

Forest, M. (1988). Full inclusion is possible. *IMPACT, 1,* 3–4.

Goodlad, J. (1984). *A place called school.* New York: McGraw-Hill.

Guess, D., & Helmstetter, E. (1986). Skill cluster instruction and the individualized curriculum sequencing model. In R. Horner, L. Meyer, & H. Fredricks (Eds.), *Education of learners with severe handicaps* (pp. 221–248). Baltimore: Paul H. Brookes Publishing Co.

Hahn, H. (1989). The politics of special education. In D. Lipsky & A. Gartner (Eds.), *Beyond special education* (pp. 225–241). Baltimore: Paul H. Brookes Publishing Co.

Hanline, M., & Halvorsen, A. (1989). Parent perceptions of the integration transition process: Overcoming artificial barriers. *Exceptional Children, 55,* 487–493.

Kauffman, S. (1984). Friendship, coping systems and community adjustment of mildly retarded adults. In R. Edgerton (Ed.), *Lines in process* (pp. 73–92). Washington, DC: American Association for Mental Deficiency.

Lusthaus, E., & Forest, M. (1989). Promoting educational equality for all students. In S. Stainback, W. Stainback, & M. Forest (Eds.), *Educating all students in the mainstream of regular education* (pp. 43–57). Baltimore: Paul H. Brookes Publishing Co.

Madden, N., & Slavin, R. (1983). Mainstreaming students with mild academic handicaps: Academic and social outcomes. *Review of Educational Research, 53,* 519–569.

Massachusetts Advocacy Center. (1987). *Out of the mainstream.* Boston: Author.

Oakes, J. (1986). *Keeping tracking: How schools structure inequality.* New Haven, CT: County Office of Education.

Padden, C., & Humphries, T. (1988). *Deaf in American: Voices from a culture.* Cambridge, MA: Harvard University Press.

Porter, G. (Producer). (1988). *A chance to belong* [Video tape]. Downsview, Ontario: Canadian Association for Community Living.

Schafer, W., & Olexa, C. (1971). *Tracking and opportunity.* Scranton, PA: Chandler.

Schattman, R. (1988). Integrated education and organizational change. *IMPACT, 1,* 8–9.

Slavin, R. (1987). Ability grouping and student achievement in elementary school: A best-evidence synthesis. *Review of Educational Research, 57,* 293–336.

Stainback, S., & Stainback, W. (1985). *Integration of students with severe handicaps into regular schools.* Reston, VA: Council for Exceptional Children.

Stainback, S., & Stainback, W. (1988). Educating all students with severe disabilities in regular classes. *Teaching Exceptional Children, 21,* 16–19.

Stainback, S., Stainback, W., & Forest, M. (Eds.). (1989). *Educating all students in the mainstream of regular education.* Baltimore: Paul H. Brookes Publishing Co.

Stainback, W., & Stainback, S. (in press). Meeting the curriculum needs of mainstreamed students with severe intellectual disabilities. *Teaching Exceptional Children.*

Strully, J. (1986, November). *Our children and the regular education classroom: Or why settle for anything less than the best?* Paper presented at the 13*th* annual conference of The Association for Persons with Severe Handicaps, San Francisco.

Strully, J. (1987, October). *What's really important in life anyway? Parents sharing the vision.* Paper presented at the 14th annual conference of The Association for Persons with Severe Handicaps, Chicago.

Strully, J., & Strully, C. (1985). Friendship and our children. *Journal of The Association for Persons with Severe Handicaps, 10,* 224–227.

Vandercook, T., Fleetham, D., Sinclair, S., & Tetlie, R. (1988). Cath, Jess, Jules, and Ames . . . A story of friendship. *IMPACT, 2,* 18–19.

Vandercook, T., York, J., & Forest, M. (1989). *MAPS: A strategy for building a vision.* Minneapolis: Institute on Community Integration.

Villa, R., & Thousand, J. (1988). Enhancing success in heterogeneous classrooms and schools: The power of partnership. *Teacher Education and Special Education, 11,* 144–153.

Voeltz, L. (1980). Children's attitudes toward handicapped peers. *American Journal of Mental Deficiency, 84,* 455–464.

Voeltz, L. (1982). Effects of structured interactions with severely handicapped peers on children's attitudes. *American Journal of Mental Deficiency, 86,* 380–390.

Weicker, L. (1988, July). On the Americans with Disability Act. *D.C. Update,* p. 1.

Will, M. (1986). *Educating students with learning problems: A shared responsibility.* Washington, DC: U.S. Department of Education, Office of Special Education and Rehabilitation Services.

York, J., & Vandercook, T. (1989). *Strategies for achieving an integrated education for middle school aged learners with severe disabilities.* Minneapolis: Institution on Community Integration.

Susan Stainback
William Stainback

2

Facilitating Support Networks

In general, most professionals, parents, and advocates agree with the social justice and philosophical tenets underlying the movement to educate all students in the mainstream of regular education; however, there have been some major implementation problems encountered. Regular education teachers are being faced with the job of providing students, who have increasingly diverse educational needs, an appropriate education. Unfortunately, too often teachers do not have the time, assistance, resources, or expertise to deal with this added responsibility. Likewise, students are being included in regular classrooms with existing peer social groups and friendship patterns that are unfamiliar to them, and as a result, they sometimes feel unsure and unwelcomed. While "special" education teachers, resource room teachers, and consultants often try to help these teachers and students, they also are generally responsible for a full work load in what is known as special education and cannot devote the time to provide the degree of support needed. Thus, because of the way schools are organized, the potential benefits of all students being in the mainstream are not being realized in some cases.

Since the basic goal of inclusive schooling is desirable for a number of reasons, a major task facing educators is to determine ways to make it work. The purpose of this chapter is to examine ways to make inclusive

Appreciation is extended to Kathleen Harris, California State University, Los Angeles, for her critical reading and contributions to this chapter.

schooling successful by building a support network for teachers and students in regular schools and classrooms.

OVERCOMING THE BARRIERS

A range of supports are needed for teachers and students to reach several goals. These goals include:

1. Meeting the unique educational objectives and curriculum and instructional needs of *all* students within inclusive general education classes

2. Helping all students feel welcome and secure in the educational mainstream through the development of friendships and/or peer supports

3. Challenging every student to go as fast and far as possible in fulfilling his or her unique potential

4. Developing and maintaining a positive classroom atmosphere that is conducive to learning for all students

5. Arranging the physical and organizational characteristics of the classroom to accommodate the unique needs of each student

6. Providing every student any ancillary services he or she might need, such as physical, occupational, or speech therapy, or instruction in braille, sign language (and peers and teachers who know sign language), English as a second language, mobility and orientation, voice synthesizers, and so forth

In order to address these goals a number of changes need to take place in the schools. A smaller pupil/teacher ratio through such methods as team teaching will be required to make a teacher's task of meeting the needs of all students possible. Furthermore, considerable resources and expertise in a range of curricular areas and classroom management need to be available within regular education to provide assistance and support. Finally, time for teachers to meet to problem solve and to assist and support one another in daily classroom activities is required to promote the confidence and information sharing necessary to develop successful inclusive classrooms. While these goals are difficult to realize in some regular neighborhood schools, with the development and maintenance of a strong *support network,* these goals can be achieved.

SUPPORT NETWORKING

What is Support Networking?

There is growing recognition that no single type of support can provide the range of assistance needed by both teachers and students in inclusive classrooms. Generally, there is a need to interweave a network of varying supports into a comprehensive and coordinated system of supports (Stainback, Stainback, & Forest, 1989; Stainback, Stainback, & Harris, 1989).

In support networking, the types of supports being recognized as helpful to teachers and students in inclusive classrooms have expanded considerably since the mid-1980s. For instance, support is being provided by involving a variety of educators, specialists, students, parents, administrators, and community members on a volunteer or paid basis to give assistance and/or suggestions through informal and formal consultation, collaboration, and various integration task forces or teams (Forest, 1987; Fuchs & Fuchs, 1988; Haydek, 1987; Idol, Paolucci-Whitcomb, & Nevin, 1986). There is also a growing interest in providing support through cooperative learning activities, peer tutoring, volunteers from the community, buddy systems, and/or friendship development (Falvey, 1989; Grenot-Scheyer, Coots, & Falvey, 1989; Sapon-Shevin, 1987). In fact, attention has focused on encouraging informal, nonprofessional support in the form of friendships and the like as well as professional support from specialists and teachers (Perske & Perske, 1988; Stainback et al., 1989; Vandercook & York, 1988). All of these supports, when used in a coordinated fashion with physical and technological supports such as ramps, wide aisles, auditory direction and safety signs, computers, voice synthesizers, and/or braille typewriters, can provide a comprehensive *support network* for teachers and students in regular classrooms to make the goals of the inclusive schooling movement a reality.

Purpose of Support Networking

The primary purpose of support networking is to promote inclusive schooling. As noted in Chapter 1 of this volume, inclusive schooling involves the development of a classroom and school in a supportive community, a community where the needs of all members are met and people care about and support each other. Wilkinson (1980) described a supportive community as follows: ". . . people are interdependent; everyone has a function and everyone has a role to play, and that's what keeps people together and forms a [supportive] community" (p. 452). Thus, the purpose of support networking is to develop neighborhood schools and classrooms into places where everyone belongs, is accepted, supports, and is supported by his or her peers and other members of the school community in the course of having his or her educational needs met.

Assumptions of Support Networking

1. Support networking is based on the premise that everyone has capabilities, strengths, gifts, and talents, including students classified as having disabilities, that they can use to provide support and assistance to their fellow community members.
2. In support networking, all people are involved in helping and supporting one another in both formal and informal support arrangements. Relationships are reciprocal, rather than some people always serving as helpers and others always being helped.
3. Natural supportive relationships in which individuals support one another as peers, friends, or colleagues are as important as providing professional support. A focus on natural supports helps connect people together in classrooms and schools and thus fosters supportive communities.
4. Individuals are unique and differ in what they require, and their needs often change over time. Thus, any supports inherent in support networking should *not* be based on a predefined, ironclad list of support options that cannot be modified.
5. Support networking works best in integrated, heterogeneous classrooms and schools. The diversity inherent among the members increases the likelihood that all class and school members, including students, teachers, parents, specialists, administrators, and other school personnel, will have the assets and resources necessary to support the needs of and become interdependent with each other.

Operational Considerations of Support Networking

1. Supports should be consumer driven. That is, the focus should be on what the consumer (the person receiving support) wants and needs as stated by the consumer (or if the person is very young or unable to communicate, his or her advocate should state what the consumer wants and needs).
2. Supports used should focus on empowering a person to assist him- or herself and others. This includes empowering a person to seek assistance when required and provide assistance to others.
3. School personnel in administrative or decision-making situations need to not only provide opportunities for informal support development among all members of the school community but also,

when possible, empower and encourage people to provide support to each other.

4. Support networking should be a natural and ongoing part of the school and classroom community. It should not be episodic or reserved only in times of difficulty or crisis.

5. Support networking should be run by insiders (i.e., those individuals directly involved in the school and classroom community). This may include students, teachers, secretaries, administrators, parents, specialists, and other school personnel and community volunteers.

6. Support networking is for everybody. Plans that focus on and operate for a single student or teacher generally are inefficient in promoting and maintaining the development and operation of an inclusive supportive community.

7. Support networking starts with an examination of the social interactions and supportive characteristics that naturally operate in regular classrooms and school settings and builds upon these.

8. An inherent danger in providing some types of support is that, if done incorrectly, it can make the person unnecessarily dependent upon the support. For example, if someone helps a particular student find his or her way to the school cafeteria, without at the same time helping the student learn the route and the skills necessary to do it alone, then that student may never learn to travel to the cafeteria independently. Thus, it is critical in supportive classroom communities that everyone understand that the goal is to provide support to others whenever it is needed but in the process of doing so always work to empower people to assist and support themselves and others.

Interweaving Informal and Formal Supports

The fundamental purpose behind support networking is to develop classrooms and schools into supportive communities where people support each other in natural ways. This does not mean that only informal supports available within a classroom are necessary. Formal professional resources and supports available from the school and community are also essential. Formal professional supports are often required to provide the expertise to ensure that the educational needs of each student are being met. For instance, there are some types of assistance and help that teachers and students may need that can best be provided in the mainstream by a professional or specialist (e.g., braille instruction). Thus, it will take a well coordinated network of informal and formal supports to make inclusive schooling a reality.

HOW CAN SUPPORT NETWORKING BE FACILITATED?

The informal and formal supports needed to operate inclusive class-rooms that are responsive to the needs of all students can be facilitated by phasing out special schools and classrooms. Special educators can become regular classroom teachers, team teachers, resource and con-sulting specialists, and facilitators of support networks within regular education. In addition, the wealth of materials, procedures, supports, equipment, and resources in special education can be integrated into regular education.

There are literally billions of dollars being spent and hundreds of thousands of personnel working in segregated special education pro-grams. All of these dollars and personnel can and should be integrated into the educational mainstream to facilitate support networking and whatever else is needed to achieve inclusive schools. Schenkat (1988) estimated that $20–$25 billion is being spent annually in special educa-tion. This money could provide considerable support and assistance for the establishment of inclusive schools and support networking for teachers and students in the mainstream. Reynolds (1989) estimated that:

> One teacher out of eight in the United States is employed in special educa-tion. If we add the school psychologists, school social workers, occupa-tional therapists, and other professional personnel who work main-ly . . . [in special education] . . . we come to a total of about 400,000 professional employees in U.S. schools—about one-sixth of the total number of professional school employees. (p. x)

In the remainder of this chapter, the emerging role of support facili-tators (that is, facilitators of comprehensive and coordinated support networks) is discussed. The authors' provide a rationale for support facilitators, outline the emerging support facilitator role, delineate some skills needed to carry out the role, and discuss possible pitfalls of using support facilitators.

RATIONALE FOR SUPPORT FACILITATORS

While there are many individuals within a school who can provide support to each other (e.g., teachers, specialists, aides, students), there is no individual responsible for facilitating supportive relationships and/or other supports that may be needed. As the supportive roles are recog-nized and developed, there is a need for personnel knowledgeable in the facilitation of supportive relationships to work with regular classroom teachers and students to organize, coordinate, and promote the variety of supports needed. This role could be assumed by former special educators, consultants, supervisors, or other educators interested in assisting classroom teachers to coordinate support networking.

THE SUPPORT FACILITATOR ROLE

The support facilitator's role can be defined as carrying out a three step process. The first step is identifying with regular classroom teachers and students the types of informal supportive relationships and/or professional supports they would like to have. This includes discussing with and helping teachers and students become aware of the various support options available. The second step is collaborating with teachers and students in determining those supports they would like in their classroom. During these two steps, the support facilitator should listen to and help clarify the perceptions of the teachers and students and *jointly* identify with the teachers and students possible supports. The process of jointly gathering information, defining the problem to be addressed, and identifying supports is fundamental to the third step, which is assisting in organizing and implementing those supports deemed most likely to be appropriate or worthwhile. It is important that teachers and students be inherently involved in the selection, development, and implementation of the supports since ownership of the support(s) by teachers and students is essential for a collaborative venture to work (Conoley & Conoley, 1982; Idol-Maestas, Nevin, & Paolucci-Whitcomb, 1984; Schowengerdt, Fine, & Poggio, 1976).

It should be noted here that "collaboration" means that the support facilitator, teacher, students, and other school personnel work together cooperatively with no one assuming an expert, supervisory, or evaluator role. At any given time any person may assume leadership or be the giver or receiver of information. It depends on who has the expertise at the given time or in a particular situation. Nevin, Thousand, Paolucci-Whitcomb, and Villa (1989) noted:

> The collaborative process is multi-directional, since all members are considered to have unique and needed expertise. At any point in time a member of the collaborative relationship may be the giver or receiver of consultation . . . [or] any member of a group may become a leader by taking actions that help the group complete its task and maintain effective collaborative relationships. (p. 21)

While the authors discuss support facilitation skills and what a support facilitator often does in the following section, it should be kept in mind that the support facilitator is not the only one who has such skills or who may be involved in carrying out some of the tasks discussed.

SUPPORT FACILITATION SKILLS

The skills needed by the support facilitator are similar to those skills needed by educational consultants, which include providing technical assistance, coordinating programs, and communicating with other professionals, parents, and students (Goldstein & Sorcher, 1974; also see Harris, Chapter 9, this volume). However, the difference between the support facilitator and the educational consultant lies in the nature of the technical assistance provided. The technical assistance provided by the educational consultant is based on the premise that the educational consultant has acquired mastery of the educational process (i.e., assessment, planning, implementation, and evaluation) appropriate for mainstream settings (Heron & Harris, 1987; Idol et al., 1986; Idol-Maestas, 1983; Rosenfield, 1987). The technical assistance provided by the support facilitator is based on the premise that the support facilitator knows the structure, how to implement, and the effectiveness of various support options, is informed regarding the availability of support options, and is able to assist teachers and students in selecting the most appropriate option(s) for a given situation. The educational consultant provides support to teachers and students to enhance the instruction of students, while the support facilitator develops a network of supports to enhance the educational success and friendships of students. One support in that network may be the educational consultant.

This implies that there are a number of skills needed to effectively carry out the duties of a support facilitator. First, if a support facilitator is to be of help to teachers and students, he or she needs a *working knowledge of the support models and resources available* that can be utilized to facilitate support networks to provide needed assistance in the mainstream. This involves an understanding of and how to informally facilitate natural supportive relationships among students, teachers, and others, as well as how to effectively use such support models as professional peer collaboration (Pugach & Johnson, 1987) and/or the McGill action planning system (Forest, 1987), as well as those individuals who might be available and willing to participate in these support options or models in a school or school district.

Assessing and matching the needs of students and teachers to applicable support options and resources available is another skill needed to carry out the job of a support facilitator. As in any position that provides support, determining what assistance is required is a critical initial step. To do this, the support facilitator needs experience in and knowledge of regular classroom curriculum, methodology, and programs, and the ability to listen to what support regular classroom teachers and students believe they need to be successful. Johnson, Pugach, and Hammittee

(1988) and Pugach (1988) have pointed out that former special educators working in regular classes must be careful not to assume that they know more about regular classroom problems than regular educators and students in regular classrooms.

Once the needs of a teacher and/or student are determined, a support facilitator needs to work collaboratively with the classroom teacher and students to *organize and operationalize those supports and resources deemed necessary*. The responsibility of a support facilitator to encourage supportive relationships among students and teachers and to help a variety of support people (e.g., vision or hearing specialists) work within predefined schedules, duties, and classroom structures makes the need for organizational skills essential. That is, the support facilitator is called upon not only to organize his or her own activities (e.g., as a team teacher) but also promote supportive relationships and the support activities of others.

Once supports are organized and put into operation, a support facilitator may act as a mediator or catalyst to *promote communication and collaboration among those involved*. Heron and Harris (1987) and Idol et al. (1986) noted that this involves helping others to exhibit behaviors such as sharing information, being a good listener, showing mutual respect, giving and receiving feedback, and employing situational leadership. Inherent in the support facilitator role as a collaborator is facilitating shared responsibility, knowledge, and skills among those involved rather than assuming a supervisory or evaluator role (Friend, 1988).

In summary, special educators can join regular education, become regular educators, and serve as support facilitators in the mainstream. They can be involved in such tasks as locating specialists, team teaching, and/or helping with the organization of assistance teams for teachers; and for students, they can be involved in facilitating peer tutoring, friendship development, and cooperative learning activities. As support facilitators, they can interweave a network of varying supports into a comprehensive and coordinated support system.

POSSIBLE PITFALLS OF USING SUPPORT FACILITATORS

When facilitators were first used in the schools, they were generally employed to work only with students classified as having disabilities. They often followed or shadowed these students around in regular class and school settings. This tended to draw attention to and set such students apart from their peers, interfering with the development of natural networks of supports or friendships. That is, since the student needing assistance always had an adult to assist him or her, natural peer support networks and friendships seldom developed, even when they were encouraged or facilitated by the teacher or support facilitator. Thus, since the mid-1980s, support facilitators have served a broader role. In addition to facilitating networks of support among students, teachers, and others, as team teachers, they often help teachers adapt instruction to meet the needs of a variety of different students and/or directly assist any student, classified disabled or not, who is having difficulty in educational tasks and/or in gaining peer acceptance. Support facilitators are also sensitive about when to help any particular student and when to encourage and allow natural peer supports and friendships an opportunity to develop. It should be stressed that there has been an increased emphasis since the mid-1980s on support facilitators helping classrooms and schools become caring communities that include and support *all* students, rather than focusing on providing support for any particular student or helping him or her "fit into the mainstream."

Finally, it is crucial that support facilitators *not* provide support when it is not needed or be overprotective. The support facilitator also should be viewed as a team teacher, resource, or support person and should *not* assume the role of any particular student's personal teacher in the regular classroom. The teacher maintains responsibility for the education of all the students in the class. The support facilitator acts as a resource to the teacher, family, principal, and the class as a whole in building support networks.

CONCLUSION

Increasing numbers of "special" educators are beginning to informally assume the role of support facilitators as they work as team teachers, consultants, collaborators, and/or resource personnel in regular education classrooms. In this chapter, the authors have tried to provide a rationale for and structure to this emerging role. There is a need for greater awareness, discussion, and study of the support facilitation role so that it does not evolve haphazardly, but rather evolves with forethought, planning, and research.

REFERENCES

Conoley, J., & Conoley, C. (1982). *School consultation.* Elmsford, NY: Pergamon Press.

Falvey, M. (1989). *Community-based curriculum: Instructional strategies for students with severe handicaps* (2nd ed.). Baltimore: Paul H. Brookes Publishing Co.

Forest, M. (Ed.). (1987). *More education/integration.* Downsview, Ontario: G. Allan Roeher Institute.

Friend, M. (1988, November). *Teacher's use of interaction skills in collaboration and consultation: Implications for teacher preparation.* Paper presented at the 11th annual conference of the Council for Exceptional Children's Teacher Education Division, Salt Lake City, Utah.

Fuchs, D., & Fuchs, L. (1988). Mainstream assistance teams to accommodate difficult-to-teach students in general education. In J. Graden, J. Zins, & M. Curtis (Eds.), _Alternative educational delivery systems: Enhancing instructional options for all students_ (pp. 49–70). Washington, DC: National Association of School Psychologists.

Goldstein, A., & Sorcher, M. (1974). _Changing supervisor behavior._ Elmsford, NY: Pergamon Press.

Grenot-Scheyer, M., Coots, J., & Falvey, M. (1989). Developing and fostering friendships. In M. Falvey (Ed.), _Community-based curriculum: Instructional strategies for students with severe handicaps_ (2nd ed., pp. 345–358). Baltimore: Paul H. Brookes Publishing Co.

Haydek, R. (1987). The teacher assistance team: A pre-referral support team. _Focus on Exceptional Children, 20,_ 1–7.

Heron, T., & Harris, K. (1987). _The educational consultant_ (2nd ed.). Austin, TX: PRO-ED.

Idol, L., Paolucci-Whitcomb, P., & Nevin, A. (1986). _Collaborative consultation._ Rockville, MD: Aspen Systems.

Idol-Maestas, L. (1983). _Special educator's consultation handbook._ Austin, TX: PRO-ED.

Idol-Maestas, L., Nevin, A., & Paolucci-Whitcomb, P. (1984). _Facilitator's manual for collaborative consultation: Principles and techniques._ Reston, VA: National RETOOL Center, Teacher Education Division, Council for Exceptional Children.

Johnson, L., Pugach, M., & Hammittee, D. (1988). Barriers to effective education consultation. _Remedial and Special Education, 9,_ 41–47.

Miller, J., & Peterson, D. (1987). Peer-influenced academic interventions. In C. Maher & J. Zins (Eds.), _Psychoeducational interventions in schools: Methods and procedures for enhancing student competence_ (pp. 91–100). Elmsford, NY: Pergamon Press.

Nevin, A., Thousand, J., Paolucci-Whitcomb, P., & Villa, R. (1989). _Collaborative consultation: Empowering public school personnel to provide heterogeneous schooling for all._ Manuscript submitted for publication.

Perske, R., & Perske, M. (1988). _Friendship._ Nashville: Abingdon Press.

Pugach, M. (1988). The consulting teacher in the context of educational reform. _Exceptional Children, 55,_ 273–275.

Pugach, M., & Johnson, L. (1987). Peer collaboration. _Teaching Exceptional Children, 20_(3), 75–77.

Reynolds, M. (1989). Foreword. In R. Gaylord-Ross (Ed.) _Integration strategies for students with handicaps._ Baltimore: Paul H. Brookes Publishing Co.

Rosenfield, S. (1987). _Instructional consultation._ Hillsdale, NJ: Erlbaum.

Sapon-Shevin, M. (1987). The national education reports and special education: Implications for students. _Exceptional Children, 53,_ 300–307.

Schenkat, R. (1988, November). The promise of restructuring for special education. _Education Week, 8,_ 36.

Schowengerdt, R., Fine, M., & Poggio, J. (1976). An examination of some bases of teacher satisfaction with school psychological services. _Psychology in the Schools, 13,_ 263–274.

Stainback, S., Stainback, W., & Forest, M. (1989). _Educating all students in the mainstream of regular education._ Baltimore: Paul H. Brookes Publishing Co.

Stainback, S., Stainback, W., & Harris, K. (1989). Support facilitation: An emerging role for special educators. *Teacher Education and Special Education, 12,* 148–153.

Vandercook, T., & York, J. (1988). Integrated education: MAPS to get you there. *Impact, 1*(2), 17.

Wilkinson, J. (1980). On assisting Indian people. *Social Casework: Journal of Contemporary Social Work, 61,* 451–454.

William Stainback
Susan Stainback |99⁰/

3

The Support Facilitator at Work

In the previous two chapters, the authors provide an overview of the inclusive schooling movement and discuss, in a general way, the emerging role of the support facilitator. This chapter outlines specific responsibilities that a support facilitator can assume to foster integrated schools and classrooms.

As the reader reviews these responsibilities, it will become evident that the support facilitator is involved in assisting and enhancing (i.e., facilitating) a large number of people and activities that support inclusive schooling as well as serving as a team teacher. Also, the support facilitator will likely be needed by teachers and students at various times across a number of classrooms in carrying out the duties described below. Thus, in most cases, being a support facilitator is a full-time job.

ESTABLISH AN INTEGRATION TASK FORCE

The purposes of an integration task force are discussed in Chapter 1. The support facilitator can encourage and help organize a task force for a school moving toward inclusive schooling. In turn, the task force can organize in-service training sessions for students, parents, teachers, and administrators prior to and following initial inclusion.

Establishing an integration task force can help personnel in the school and community assume ownership of any integration plans and activities. In the authors' experiences, once a variety of parents and school personnel become committed and involved, they will help make sure that inclusive schooling is successful.

SEEK EXTRA SUPPORT

When integration first begins, a variety of supports are often needed. This is because segregation of some students, including those classified as having disabilities, has been standard practice for centuries and as a result students and school personnel have had little experience with full inclusion of all students. Thus, any "extra" support, such as a teacher's aide or a small class size, or "extra" resources from the school administration or other sources (e.g., state or federal grants) that can be obtained is likely to enhance the chances of success. The support facilitator can lobby for "extra" support, when it is needed. Once the initial start up and acclimation period is over and routines have been established, the extra support may not be needed and can gradually be faded.

It should be stressed, however, that full inclusion can and should occur whether such support is or is not provided. But, additional support can sometimes make things easier in the beginning stages (and success quicker).

The support facilitator can recruit volunteers to assist and provide support to students and teachers in the mainstream (see Falvey, Coots, and Bishop, Chapter 15, this volume). For example, he or she can contact local groups such as the PTA, the Association for Retarded Citizens (ARC), and/or senior citizen organizations to recruit volunteers who could serve in a variety of situations in which help is needed, such as assisting teachers with clerical tasks, bookkeeping, and routine activities. When the teacher and support facilitator are freed of some routine duties, it allows them more time to adapt and adjust the classroom curriculum and teaching procedures to individual differences among students.

Finally, the recruitment of people who are naturally a part of the school environment to help provide encouragement and support should not be overlooked. For example, students in other classrooms of the school, sports coaches, advisors to various extracurricular activities, custodians, bus drivers, cafeteria workers, school counselors, and others can provide invaluable support and assistance. It is essential to promote the use of peers and people who are a natural part of the school setting whenever possible. An over reliance on "extra" special aides and outside professionals can interfere with students and others developing relationships with each other in natural school environments.

ESTABLISH A PEER SUPPORT COMMITTEE

One of the most worthwhile responsibilities of a support facilitator is to help establish and organize a peer support committee within regular education classrooms. The peer support committee is usually made up of four to six students. The students are charged with the responsibility of being sure that their classroom develops a sense of community where everyone belongs, is supported by and supports his or her peers, and feels welcomed. This differs from peer involvement on teacher and student assistance teams discussed in the next section and in Chapter 7. The peer support committee is classroom based and focused on ways of making the classroom a supportive, accommodating, positive learning environment to help all class members experience success, rather than determining how to solve a problem or difficulty for a particular student or teacher.

The committee often becomes integrally involved in, for example, organizing and participating in buddy systems, peer helpers, study partners, and "circles of friends" within a classroom. They can also be involved in brainstorming ways to help foster friendships and/or supports that allow all class members to successfully participate in classroom programs and activities. School personnel should work closely with the peer support committee to be sure that the classroom environment is arranged so that every student in the mainstream is included and supported.

For any new student being integrated into regular classes, the peer support committee is of particular importance. Having peers who will be a buddy or friend(s) in a new, unfamiliar classroom to provide encouragement, support and/or assistance, when needed, is critical to the success of inclusive schooling. The development of a supportive and friendly classroom can help any student be successful and feel more secure and welcomed in the class.

School personnel can also work with the peer support committee to address the learning as well as social needs of class members. The committee can focus on being sure that the regular classroom curriculum, programs, and activities are flexible enough to foster appropriate instructional objectives for every class member. For example, if any student should need to learn to visually track, follow rules, take turns, grasp, and/or attend to directions, then activities that encourage these skills should be identified within or integrated into the regular overall curriculum, programs, and activities of the class. The peer support committee can assist school personnel in analyzing the school curriculum and other daily activities in inclusive classrooms to see where activities that encourage skills needed by class members can be identified or integrated into the regular classroom routine.

It should be emphasized that the peer support committee should not be a select group with some students always designated as members. Membership on the peer support committee should rotate throughout the year so every student has the opportunity to participate on the committee, whether classified disabled or nondisabled.

Committee involvement has a number of benefits. The students on the committee not only provide a valuable service, but gain practice in "real-life" problem solving and learn important social and civic responsibilities that can carry over into adulthood. Also, by involving the students, they are more likely to take ownership and pride in the development of a classroom where everyone feels welcomed and is provided support and assistance when needed.

ORGANIZE TEACHER AND STUDENT ASSISTANCE TEAMS

Teacher and student assistance teams are usually made up of students, parents, educators, specialists, counselors, and/or administrators. Organization of and participation on such teams is a typical activity of the support facilitator. A major focus of the team is to assist and provide support to a classroom teacher or student. The group is involved in using different expertise and perspectives to brainstorm or problem solve as a way to deal with a situation. It is important to note that the team is not a multidisciplinary assessment and placement committee, but rather a teacher and student support system to serve teachers and students in the regular education classroom (Chalfant, Pysh, & Moultrie, 1979; Haydek, 1987). See Vandercook and York, Chapter 7, this volume for more information on teacher and student assistance teams.

SERVE AS A TEAM TEACHER

A support facilitator can serve as a team teacher. He or she can teach in his or her curricular expertise area (e.g., learning strategies and/or community-referenced instruction) or simply assist the classroom teacher in an area where the classroom teacher has the major expertise.

Bauwens, Hourcade, and Friend (1989) suggested that "former" special educators join regular education and engage in "cooperative" teaching. They explain "cooperative" teaching as follows:

> Cooperative teaching (or co-teaching) refers to an educational approach in which general and [former] special educators work in a coactive and coordinated fashion to jointly teach academically and behaviorally heterogeneous groups of students in educationally integrated settings (i.e., general classrooms). . . . Specifically, in cooperative teaching both general and [former] special education teachers are simultaneously present in the general classroom, maintaining joint responsibility for specified classroom instruction that is to occur within that setting. While some teacher specializa-

tion of subject or content areas and skills may exist, decisions on specific teacher assignments and duties within that classroom are predicated on assessments of individual teachers' skills and strengths, not on artificially determined student categories of presumed disabilities. In this way, specific teacher capabilities are more optimally used.

The cooperative teaching approach most effectively uses the specific and unique skills each professional brings to the school. For example, most general educators are knowledgeable about curriculum and curricular sequencing, especially in the traditional academic areas. In addition, they are also skilled and experienced in large-group management skills. On the other hand, [former] special educators traditionally have developed expertise in targeting areas of difficulty within a curriculum, and analyzing and adopting instructional materials and strategies—skills more in demand in the general classroom as general education teachers face increasingly heterogeneous student populations. . . . Thus, the two professionals working together can bring an impressive combination of skills to the fully integrated classroom. (p. 18)

This is exactly what was done in 1989 at Chaparral Elementary School in Albuquerque, New Mexico. A fourth grade teacher and a teacher of a special class for six students with severe, profound, and multiply handicapping conditions joined their classes and both co-taught _all_ students. The fourth grade teacher noted a number of benefits. While he added six students to his class of 28, he also gained a co-teacher and two aides. He and the former special class teacher stated that all the students benefited from the wide range of expertise and additional assistance that emerged as a result of merging their classrooms (L. Keefe & H. McQueeney, personal communication, September, 1989). While this arrangement does not adhere to the natural proportion principle discussed in Chapter 1, it appeared to work well in their particular situation.

The support facilitator can also foster or enable cooperative or team teaching activities to occur among a variety of teachers in a school. For instance, if expertise in language arts, math, or computers that the support facilitator happens not to have is needed by a teacher for his or her students, a support facilitator may locate another teacher in the school with the required expertise. The support facilitator might then free that teacher to team with the classroom teacher in need of the expertise by working with the principal to arrange a schedule that would accommodate such teaming and/or by possibly covering a study hall or other class or supervision activity for the teacher.

Capitalizing on the expertise of colleagues within a school in a teaming capacity is an important potential resource that a support facilitator can encourage. See Thousand and Villa, Chapter 10, this volume, for additional information about team teaching.

SERVE AS A CURRICULUM ANALYST

What the support facilitator can do as a curriculum analyst is illustrated in the following example centered around a classroom situation cited by Ford and Davern (1989) in which a fourth grade math curriculum was adapted to diverse student needs. (The example given by Ford and Davern has been modified to illustrate several points about curriculum adaptations.) In this example, a fourth grade class was learning how to multiply and divide three and four digit numbers. The teacher used a traditional teaching approach of lecturing and asking the students questions about how to multiply and divide such numbers, worked several problems at the chalkboard to illustrate the concepts and procedures, assigned work sheets for the students to practice, and toward the end of the class discussed and asked the students questions about some "real-life" math problems involving multiplying and dividing three and four digit numbers.

Since there were students with diverse abilities and achievement levels in the class, not all of them were ready to learn how to multiply and divide three and four digit numbers. One of these students, Shawn, was reviewing number recognition, learning how to count from 1 to 100, and matching coins to money cards (graphic representation of a coin).

The support facilitator assisted by analyzing the math lesson to see how students who are at different levels in math would be included. For example, in the case of Shawn, questions such as the following were explored: Could the teacher ask Shawn if he can identify some of the numbers (e.g., six) in the multiplication and division examples given on the chalkboard in the same way that other students are asked if they can tell what eight times nine is or how to regroup numbers? When work sheets are handed out, could Shawn receive one that requires number recognition and coins to be matched with graphic representations of coins rather than a work sheet with multiplication and division problems? When discussing real-life math problems involving three and four digit multiplication and division problems, could the teacher ask Shawn which number is larger—three or five—in the problem written on the chalkboard in the same way another student may be asked what needs to be done to solve the problem?

The support facilitator may want to go on from this point to work with the classroom teacher to help organize a class activity to provide *all* the students in the class a practical real-life experience in applying what they have been learning in the math class. In the illustration provided by Ford and Davern (1989), a "hot chocolate business" was set up similar to what follows. For 6 weeks, each day during math, the class operated the business. Groups of students—five or six at a time—were assigned on a rotating basis following a schedule devised by the classroom teacher and support facilitator.

On Mondays, Tuesdays, and Thursdays the business was held in the classroom and on Fridays the class opened the hot chocolate business for sales during recess to other students in the school. On Wednesdays, the students walked two blocks to a grocery store where they purchased the supplies needed for the business.

Planning the business, keeping records, figuring expenses, prices, profits, and the like provided many opportunities to practice a range of math skills and to learn community-based skills also (e.g., traveling to the grocery store, locating and purchasing the goods). A typical class-room lesson was outlined to accomplish a variety of objectives. These included learning the application of the multiplication and division con-cepts and procedures that many of the students were currently working on in the fourth grade curriculum. Objectives also included learning skills that Shawn and other students needed such as how to count money, how to match real coins to graphic representations of coins on money cards, and some community-based skills. In addition to the math skills all the students learned, it is important to acknowledge that this activity also presented opportunities for the students to develop social and communication skills and, for some students such as Shawn, motor skills. The following excerpt sums up the activity:

> Thus it can be seen that activity-based lessons not only allow teachers to work on a variety of objectives at varying levels of proficiency, but also can make learning much more interesting for all students. They key is not to let the activity dominate the lesson, but to use it as a *backdrop* for achieving specific targeted objectives for each student. Once a student has mastered the objectives, new ones should be built into the lesson. (Ford & Davern, 1989, p. 14)

A variety of different activities such as growing a garden in the spring can be organized to provide learning opportunities at varying levels in a variety of different subject areas, such as science, math, read-ing, motor control, and health and nutrition. The reader is referred to Ford and Davern (1989) for additional examples at different levels of schooling.

Finally, it should be noted that mainstreamed education is moving toward more child centered and holistic methods of education. This means that teachers are increasingly working with small groups of stu-dents rather than lecturing, basing instruction on individual needs rather than arbitrary standards, and facilitating students' learning through real-life projects and activities. This will make it much easier to adapt curriculum and instructional methods to meet diverse needs in integrated classrooms.

LOCATE SPECIALISTS

At times specialists are needed in an integrated classroom to address some difficult or complex educational needs or situations that a student or teacher might encounter. In fully integrated schools and classrooms, there may be students who need counseling, instruction in braille, concept formation, nonverbal communication boards, sign language, mobility and orientation, fine motor movements, and/or how to use hearing aids and equipment or other technological supports. Other students may need intensive help in social skills and/or self-regulation of their behavior. The regular classroom teacher is not likely to have the expertise to deal with all of these areas and will need specialists to work with him or her as well as, in some cases, directly teach or assist the student(s). One or more specialists, who can provide assistance in their area(s) of expertise, can be located by the support facilitator. In addition, the support facilitator can assist with communication and coordination between the specialist and the teacher and/or help organize a student's daily schedule to include time for instruction in braille, sign language, mobility, or whatever might be needed.

WORK WITH FAMILIES

Coordination between the school and the home is often critical to the quality of education that can be provided any student. Since learning occurs both at home and in school, families and teachers need to work in harmony to complement the work of one another. A support facilitator can be instrumental in arranging for sharing of information between the home and the school.

In addition to serving as a school/home liaison, the support facilitator may likewise provide support to parents in finding ways they can help their child(ren) operate effectively in the mainstream. Support to parents might involve assisting in the organization of parent support and discussion groups. Topics such as helping their child develop study skills (Stainback & Stainback, 1989), positive social relationships, and supportive, caring attitudes toward their peers and others in the school and community can be beneficial in the development of inclusive schools. "Including parents in staff development or in-service activities on an ongoing basis and providing written information to parents through newsletters [or by other means] can be used to continue to share information" (Hanline & Halvorsen, 1989, p. 491).

See Bushwell and Schaffner, Chapter 14, this volume, Strully and Strully (1989), and Turnbull, Turnbull, Bronicki, Summers, and Roeder-Gordon (1988) for more information about the importance and involvement of families in the education of their children.

LOCATE MATERIALS AND EQUIPMENT

In almost any school there are materials and equipment that can be useful in a variety of classrooms. However, these materials and equipment often are not accessible, due to organizational arrangements, to all teachers and students who may need them. Generally, books and specific learning materials are assigned to the classroom deemed most appropriate; for example, level four readers are used in the fourth grade. However, too often students in other grades are functioning at a fourth grade reading level, and in order to get needed copies of the readers, teachers are called upon to locate and borrow them from another classroom. A support facilitator can be instrumental in locating materials and equipment needed by various teachers to address the diverse needs of their class members.

FOSTER PROFESSIONAL PEER COLLABORATION

A useful but often overlooked support for teachers is peer teachers (Pugach & Johnson, 1987). Peers can be used as sources of expertise, sounding boards, brainstorming partners, and/or just positive empathetic social interaction partners who can help to relieve the pressure and solve daily problems that can occur in a classroom.

The support facilitator can encourage and foster these types of professional peer relationships. He or she might, for instance, relieve several teachers periodically for short time periods (or arrange for volunteers to do so) in order to provide the teachers with time for professional peer collaboration about particular problems. See Pugach and Johnson, Chapter 8, this volume, for more information about professional peer collaboration.

HELP MODIFY TRADITIONAL LANGUAGE

The support facilitator can assist with the removal of traditional special education labels from students, teachers, classrooms, and programs. The support facilitator might become involved with the director of special education or another administrator to work with school personnel to modify some of the terminology used in the schools. This would include assisting with the modification of the job titles of many "special" edu-

cators. For example, modifying the title of the director of special education to the director of supportive services, teacher of learning disabled
students to cooperating teacher with specialization in learning strategies, or teachers of students with severe disabilities to support facilitators or classroom teachers. In one school district in Canada, the school
administration changed special education teachers into methods and
resource teachers. They help individualize and adapt instruction to individual differences in general education classes. Other special educators
are becoming regular educators and serving as classroom or team teachers, collaborators, and/or consultants in regular education with expertise in community-referenced instruction, behavior management/social
skills development, or specialists in dealing with hearing and visual differences.

Biklen, Ford, and Ferguson (1989) suggested that:

> Instead of terms like "training" or "treatment" [or "special education"] use
> words like "teaching reading," "braille," "community living," "social
> skills," and "social studies." School administrators might refer to class-
> rooms by grade level and classify teachers by subject areas rather than by
> disability categories. A logical result of such new practices may be to elimi-
> nate the need for parallel systems of education (e.g., special and regular]
> and to rid schools of traditional [special education] labels. (pp. 257–258)

STRESS THE IMPORTANCE OF COMMUNICATION SYSTEMS

In integrated schools and classrooms, it quickly becomes apparent that
establishing ways in which all students can communicate with each
other and the classroom teacher(s) is critical. This includes finding ways
students who speak a foreign language, who are deaf, or who have
cerebral palsy can receive and give messages. In some instances, this
may require that students and teachers in a school learn a foreign language, the essentials of sign language, or how to communicate with a
person who uses a computer to send messages, a voice synthesizer, or
various language or picture communication boards.

Communication is so essential to achieving a fully integrated and
quality education for all students, that everybody, including those persons classified as having or not having disabilities or who speak a foreign language, must sit down together to find ways everyone can contribute to developing communication methods for all students. The peer
support committee discussed earlier can become involved also.

The support facilitator can help educators, parents, and students
understand that people who use different communication systems (e.g.,
sign language) should *not* always be the ones who have to adjust their
communication methods. For example, starting in the early grades,

many young children in inclusive schools could learn the essence of sign language. This could happen in integrated schools with some encouragement and guidance from adults. It could lead to people who are deaf being able to more fully participate in the mainstream and being an integral part of school and community life. After studying what happened in a community on Martha's Vineyard in the 18th and 19th centuries where nearly everyone knew sign language and where people who are deaf were fully integrated, Groce (1985) wrote:

> The fact that a society could adjust to disabled individuals, rather than requiring them to do all the adjusting, as in the case in American society as a whole, raises important questions about the responsibilities of those who are not [classified disabled]. . . . The most important lesson to be learned . . . is that disabled people can be full members of a community if the community makes an effort to include them. (p. 27)

In short, finding ways for all students to communicate is essential to achieving inclusive quality education programs and supportive, caring school communities for all students, and should be a priority focus for the support facilitator.

CONCLUSION

While it is true that many schools do not have all the resources they need, there are usually an array of financial, equipment, and people resources available. For example, people resources include specialists or consultants in speech, hearing, vision, behavior management, occupational therapy, computers, reading, science, school psychology, and the like. There are also many teachers with expertise in a variety of areas, as well as the students themselves, volunteers, parents, counselors, and administrators. The job of the support facilitator is to help organize and coordinate all of these different resources into a comprehensive support network for teachers and students in the mainstream.

REFERENCES

Bauwens, J., Hourcade, J., & Friend, M. (1989). Cooperative teaching: A model for general and special education integration. *Remedial and Special Education, 10*(2), 17–22.

Biklen, D., Ford, A., & Ferguson, D. (1989). *Schooling and disability.* Chicago: National Society for the Study of Education.

Chalfant, J. Pysh, M., & Moultrie, R. (1979). Teacher assistance teams: A model for within building problem solving. *Learning Disability Quarterly, 2,* 85–96.

Ford, A., & Davern, L. (1989). Moving forward with school integration. In R. Gaylord-Ross (Ed.), *Integration strategies for students with handicaps* (pp. 11–31). Baltimore: Paul H. Brookes Publishing Co.

Groce, N. (1985). *Everyone here spoke sign language: Hereditary deafness on Martha's Vineyard.* Cambridge, MA: Harvard University Press.

Hanline, M., & Halvorsen, A. (1989). Parent perceptions of the integration transition process: Overcoming artificial barriers. *Exceptional Children, 55,* 487–493.

Haydek, R. (1987). The teacher assistance team: A pre-referral support team. *Focus on Exceptional Children, 20,* 1–7.

Pugach, M., & Johnson, L. (1987). Peer collaboration. *Teaching Exceptional Children, 55,* 273–275.

Stainback, W., & Stainback, S. (1989). *How to help your child succeed in school.* Deephaven, MN: Meadowbrook Press.

Strully, J., & Strully, C. (1989). Family support to promote integration. In S. Stainback, W. Stainback, & M. Forest (Eds.), *Educating all students in the mainstream of regular education.* Baltimore: Paul H. Brookes Publishing Co.

Turnbull, H. R., Turnbull, A., Bronicki, M., Summers, J., & Roeder-Gordon, C. (1988). *Disability and the family.* Baltimore: Paul H. Brookes Publishing Co.

York, J., & Vandercook, T. (1989). *Strategies for achieving an integrated education for middle school aged learners with severe disabilities.* Minneapolis: Institute on Community Integration.

CLASSROOM-FOCUSED SUPPORT OPTIONS

William Stainback
Susan Stainback   *4*

Facilitating Peer
Supports and Friendships

Due to the integration and merger movements, increasing numbers of students with diverse needs are being included in
the mainstream of regular education (Biklen, 1985; Reynolds & Birch,
1988; Stainback, Stainback, & Forest, 1989). Research has shown that
one major problem some students face in regular education classes is
rejection and isolation, that is, they have little peer support and few, if
any, friends (Gottlieb & Leyser, 1981).

Educators and parents who have been extensively involved in integrated schools have noted that a major key to success is the development of informal peer supports and friendships for isolated students in
regular education classes (Discover the Possibilities, 1988; Forest, 1987;
Strully, 1987; York & Vandercook, 1988). Some professionals have gone
so far as to state that peer supports and friendships are not luxuries, but
necessities (Grenot-Scheyer, Coots, & Falvey, 1989; Stainback & Stainback, 1987, 1988; Stocking, Arezzo, & Leavitt, 1980).

When a student enters a classroom such unknowns as schedules,
rules, routines, and student-teacher and student-student interaction
patterns can be intimidating. Classmates can help the student get to
know these and other aspects of the new environment. They also can
make him or her feel welcomed, accepted, and secure in the regular
class. Friends can boost a child's feelings of well-being and foster self-
esteem and self-confidence in integrated situations (Strully & Strully,
1985b). In addition, peers can provide encouragement, understanding,
and support during stressful times in educational and social activities.
Thus, many teachers and parents are beginning to encourage the devel-

51

opment of informal peer support and friendships for students who do not have friends in regular classes (Perske & Perske, 1988; Ruttiman & Forest, 1987; Stainback & Stainback, 1987; Strully & Strully, 1985a; Vandercook, Fleetham, Sinclair, & Tetlie, 1988).

The purpose of this chapter is to suggest strategies that teachers and support personnel can use to promote informal peer support and friendships for students who do not have friends in the mainstream. The strategies are based on what classroom teachers have reported to be effective (Discover the Possibilities, 1988; Forest, 1987; Grenot-Scheyer et al., 1989) and a review of the research literature on friendship facilitation and development in psychology, sociology, education, and related disciplines (Asher & Gottman, 1981; Epstein & Karweit, 1983; Gottleib & Leyser, 1981; Oden & Asher, 1977; Rubin, 1980; Stainback & Stainback, 1987).

STRATEGIES TO FOSTER
PEER SUPPORTS AND FRIENDSHIPS

As discussed in this chapter, supportive relationships and friendships may range from simple, short term events, such as saying hello in the hallway or one student helping another find his or her way to the cafeteria or with a homework assignment during study hall, to more complex, long-term relationships where two or more students "hang out" together, socially interact, and freely help and assist each other inside and outside of school. It should be noted that most people agree that supportive relationships and friendships are highly individualistic, fluid and dynamic, vary according to the chronological age of the participants, and are largely based on free choice and personal preference. They cannot be easily defined and programmed; and they certainly cannot be forced (Perske & Perske, 1988). However, this does not mean that they cannot be facilitated and encouraged by sensitive educators and parents (Stainback et al., 1989).

Proximity

Research has indicated that a critical variable in peer support and friendship development is proximity (Asher & Gottman, 1981). That is, if a student without friends is to gain the support and friendship of other students, he or she must, at the very least, have the opportunity to be with other students.

There are a number of activities that can provide opportunities for a student lacking friends to be with other students. One is to help the student needing friends become involved in extracurricular activities of his or her choice in which other class members participate, such as band, photography club, and/or pep rallies. Arranging peer tutoring, buddy systems, and cooperative learning can also be useful in providing opportunities for an isolated student to get to know classmates. For example, a student without friends can be paired with one or two other classmates or "buddies" to carry the lunch money to the principal's office. Some teachers have been successful by pairing the student without friends with a popular student who others tend to gravitate toward (Forest, 1987). This strategy has been used at the secondary (Strully, 1987) as well as the elementary level (Villa & Thousand, 1988). In this way the isolated student becomes associated with the popular student because of proximity, which potentially might lead to the attention of and interactions with a large number of peers. Simply seating a new or isolated student in close proximity to a sensitive, outgoing, and accepting student might be helpful in some instances.

Another activity for facilitating friendships might be to pair every student in the class with another class member he or she does not know very well and assign the task of writing a paragraph, drawing a picture, or reporting to the class about a positive characteristic of their paired classmate. Another task is to have students attend and report on an event of shared interest such as a ball game or a music concert. Free time and/or class projects can be arranged to allow for these pairs of students to share activities with and get to know one another. In this way all students in the class benefit in the potential for the development of mutual peer supports and new friendships.

School personnel can also communicate with and encourage parents to provide opportunities in the community for their child to be around and interact with other students in the class (Strully & Strully, 1985a). The family can assist their child to actively participate in the community in both formal and informal gatherings. For instance, they might involve their child in a scout troup that other class members participate in, along with swimming or horseback riding classes, neighborhood gatherings, playground time, and/or church youth and teen activities that can all be worthwhile friendship developing opportunities. In addition, parents can invite one or more of their child's classmates to their home or for an outing such as to the zoo or movies. If possible, making an area of the home an enjoyable, safe, and hospitable "hangout" for after school or weekend times can do much for making a student an accepted peer and promote friendship development. It should be noted that in some cases parents may have difficulty creating such opportunities due to time availability, particularly in cases where both parents work, there is only one parent, and/or the parents are experiencing certain hardships. In such cases, it may be necessary for educators to collaborate with social workers and community groups such as "big brothers" (or sisters) to foster opportunities for children to participate with their peers in community programs and activities. A chance for students to be together with their school peers in both school and nonschool activities is critical to the formation of peer support networks and friendships (Rubin, 1980; Strully & Strully, 1985a, 1985b).

Encourage Support and Friendship Development

Along with providing opportunities for peer support and friendship development, there are ways school personnel can encourage students to build peer relationships with one another. One way is to involve students in thinking about supportive relationships and friendships as a part of the curriculum. The goal is to make students more aware of, sensitive to, and accepting of the needs of others. For instance, a topic might be included in a health education class that focuses on the importance of providing support to every person through classmates and friends. Also, differences between paid helpers and friends who provide assistance can be discussed.

When a new student enters a class, whether classified disabled or nondisabled, it is usually a particularly good time to have brainstorming sessions with the class members regarding what can be done to make the new student feel welcome and secure in the class. This is generally much easier at the elementary level than the secondary level because of group scheduling complications, but it can be used with any age group. Helping students recognize how hard it is to come into a new class in which the other students already know one another might increase students' sensitivity and attempts to include the new student in their activities. Also, school personnel can actually work closely with the students in the regular class to help them determine specific ways they can help a new peer feel welcome. This often leads to a number of peer support and friendship facilitation activities such as arranging for a "welcoming committee" of class members to call the new student at night and/or include him or her in games and out of school activities in the neighborhood.

A peer support committee of four or five students can be formed that focuses on ways to be sure all class members are accepted and feel welcome and secure (see Stainback and Stainback, Chapter 3, this volume).

Another way to foster supportive relationships and friendships is to involve class peers on a teacher and student assistance team such as the

McGill action planning system (see Vandercook and York, Chapter 7, this volume). Basically, such teams brainstorm ideas about how a student entering the mainstream can be included, made to feel welcomed, learn classroom routines and rules, and become an integral part of the classroom activities and programs. With the help of school personnel and the students on the team, often a circle of friends can be formed around the student to be sure he or she is included in school and nonschool activities and provided encouragement and support when needed. The reader is referred to the videotape, _With a Little Help From My Friends_ (Forest & Flynn, 1988) and also to Vandercook and York, Chapter 7, this volume, for specific and practical ways "circles of friends" can be formed for isolated students.

Still another way to encourage supportive relationships and friendships is to cue or verbally suggest to students without friends and other students that they work or play together. For instance, a teacher may say to a young student, "John, since you and Stephen are building houses with your blocks, why don't you both work together to make a village that you can use for driving your cars and trucks around?" Or, for older students, a teacher might say, "Mary, since you and Theresa are both interested in the dress of the 18th century for your history project, you could both work together gathering information and helping one another with your presentations."

Finally, it is important to reinforce students when they are exhibiting positive friendship and support behaviors (Stocking et al., 1980). When students approach an isolated peer and engage him or her in an assigned activity, the teacher might say, "The class is doing a good job working together to complete their assignments." Or, when all class members are working cooperatively the teacher might say, "Since everyone is so involved in their art projects the class can have an extra 10 minutes today to work on them." By letting students know that when they include new or isolated peers in their group or activity good things will happen, the chances are that more students will do it more often (Strain & Kerr, 1981).

Teach Peer Support and Friendship Skills

Students who lack friends can display certain behaviors that tend to encourage others to want to be supportive and a friend with them (Stainback & Stainback, 1987). A number of skills or behaviors that students without friends can learn to exhibit that will encourage the development of peer supports and friendships are reviewed in this section. This is followed by a discussion of how such skills might be taught to students without friends. While some students may not be able to become proficient in these behaviors and skills, it is essential that all students learn as many of the skills as they can to whatever degree possible.

Positive Interaction Style   A student's style of interaction or specific behaviors performed during an interaction form the foundation for future friendship and support from others. Individuals who are positive, attentive, approving, encouraging, and appear interested and pleased to be a part of an interaction are more likely to receive support and be included in a group as a friend than individuals who talk about themselves excessively and/or who behave in a grumpy, annoyed, disinterested, or other negative ways (Trower, 1981). People generally like to be around and help others who approve of them, praise their accomplishments, and show concern for their welfare. For a student to be liked and supported by peers, he or she must also like and support others (Rubin, 1980). Thus a student without friends may need to learn how to be positive toward and supportive of others to whatever degree possible.

Establishing Areas of Compatibility   Establishing what a student has in common with a peer can potentially lead to friendship and support (Epstein & Karweit, 1983). Students without friends need to be skilled in how to learn about another individual and compare what is learned with one's own interests, values, and experiences. It is important to share with peers one's experiences and interests to help establish areas of compatibility. More specifically, students who lack friends need to learn how to ask questions about the other person such as: Where do you go to school? Do you like sports? Students also need to learn how to communicate their own preferences about such things as favorite activities, hobbies, or school involvements.

Taking the Perspective of Others   Students who view friendships only in terms of what a friend can do for them are often unable to recognize the attitudes, feelings, and circumstances of others and often do not say the kindest or most fitting thing (Selman, 1981). In order to take the perspective of others, students who lack friends must learn to listen to others, put themselves in the other person's position, and evaluate the impact their behavior has on others. Thus, assisting students to learn to whatever degree possible how to take the perspective of others may help enable them to exercise the tact and sensitivity needed to build friendship and supportive relationships with their peers (Stainback & Stainback, 1987).

Sharing and Providing Support   To develop friendship and supportive peer relationships, students who lack friends must learn to share, comfort, help, and provide support to others, particularly in time of need (Bell, 1981; Berndt, 1986). Often, school personnel go to great lengths to advocate for and provide assistance and help to those students who are new, isolated, and/or without friends; however, such students are often provided little encouragement and/or opportunities to provide comfort, support, assistance, and friendship to others (Stainback & Stainback, 1987). If students are to develop and maintain enduring friendship and supportive peer relationships, all students, including those in particular need of support and assistance, must become supporters, comforters, and helpers of others.

Trustworthiness and Loyalty   To be a good partner in a friendship or supportive relationship, it is important to learn a moral or ethical code to guide one's behavior toward others (Hinde, 1979). Once friendships and supportive relationships begin to develop, loyalty and trustworthiness become necessary components if the relationship is to be maintained. Particularly in close friendships, loyalty and trustworthiness often serve as testing functions to determine the limits or intensity of a relationship, since the existence of a close relationship may be defined in terms of the degree of commitment demonstrated.

Conflict Resolution   The ability to resolve or deal effectively with conflicts that arise is one of the most difficult skills students need to demonstrate in developing and maintaining friendship and supportive relationships (Stainback & Stainback, 1987). Conflict resolution requires a student to be able to make known and protect his or her own rights and needs while being sensitive to and respecting the rights and needs of peers (Stocking et al., 1980). Students who tend to lack friends, often deal with problems in either an overly aggressive or a submissive manner rather than in a constructive attempt to meet their own needs without infringing on the needs or rights of others.

Teaching Friendship Skills   In regard to teaching such skills one approach that has been recommended and used successfully involves coaching (Gottlieb & Leyser, 1981; Oden & Asher, 1977). In coaching, students are assisted in gaining an understanding of the meaning of each of the positive peer support and friendship skills and are then helped to recognize and determine specific actions toward others that represent each of the skills. For example, students without friends are often taught the meaning and importance of establishing areas of compatibility, solving conflicts constructively, and being supportive to others. They also are encouraged to think of specific actions that could be taken to implement the general concepts in the context of real-life activities. This is because often a student's difficulties may come not from lacking a general concept of what is required, but from not knowing precisely how that concept is to be put into action. A student may know that he or she should solve conflicts constructively but may not know what to say or exactly how to do so in a specific situation. Thus, encouraging students to think of specific actions for each general concept is essential. After the

meaning of friendship skills and specific actions that represent the skills
are taught, the students are provided ample opportunities in natural
social interaction situations to practice the skills and then engage in
review sessions with teachers to evaluate their success.

Teaching an understanding of these skills can be included in such
classes as social studies or health as content for themes or projects.
Practice and role playing of the skills might be a focus for class skits or
plays the class develops. Reviews and discussions of these friendship
skills as they were used or practiced by students on the playground or in
the classroom might be used as a focus for general class discussions or in
individual counseling sessions about the value of supporting each other.
See Stainback and Stainback (1987) for more specific information about
how support and friendship skills can be facilitated or coached.

Foster Understanding and Respect for Individual Differences

Many teachers believe that social interactions and potential friendships
tend to develop among students who understand and respect each others' differences and similarities (Stainback et al., 1989). There are a
number of ways to foster this understanding in the classroom. One is to
infuse information about individual differences and similarities into existing reading materials; health and social studies classes; and extracurricular activities such as assembly programs, plays, school projects, service activities, and/or clubs.

A particularly good way to focus on similarities among students at
the elementary school level is to have all students provide information
about their families, summer plans, daily chores, favorite celebrities,
vacations, and the like in special projects, themes, or presentations to be
shared with the class. For older students, interests in sports, teen idols,
music, cars, pet peeves, or jobs may be more appropriate topics in which
to explore common interests and experiences. This can help to foster an
awareness among all students that class members without friends often
have common interests, characteristics, and concerns, and have similar
feelings, anxieties, dreams, and desires that potentially could lead to
friendships.

A method to note differences is to assign tasks based on the individual characteristics of the students, pointing out the differences of each
student as assignments are made. Particular care must be exercised in
seeing that the differences in every student are noted rather than involving only a few of the students. Furthermore, the differences need to be
recognized in a positive way. For instance, the teacher might say, "Judy,
since you have developed good listening skills, would you listen for the

timer to ring so we will know when our clay should come out of the oven." (Judy happens to be blind.) "Jamie, you are tall so would you please take responsibility for watering the plants on the top of the bookcase? Mary, you have a very clear voice so please lead the class in reciting the poem 'Trees'. Michael, since you have a lap tray on your wheelchair, will you take these books back to the library for us?" In this process, teachers can point out the strengths and talents of each of the students in class, which can help to facilitate friendships and supports for all class members, including those who may be without friends.

The basic idea is to establish a classroom atmosphere in which students understand and respect individual differences and similarities among each other so that, to whatever degree possible, the potential for supports and friendships between students is enhanced. Similarly, the unique characteristics of each student can more likely be capitalized on in regard to the advantages the difference has to offer the group.

Be a Positive Support and Friendship Model

Possibly the most important way to promote supports and friendships among students is to be a good model. Teachers must communicate to students through their behavior that every student is an important and worthwhile member of the class. To be a good model, it is essential to be kind, friendly, supportive, and helpful to each student in the class. That is, it is essential to indicate acceptance and positivity toward all class members, including the new and/or isolated student(s).

Another way to provide a model is to request the assistance of fellow teachers to positively interact with some of the students in the classroom. While enlisting the help of fellow teachers is important at the elementary level, at the secondary level such coordination and cooperation among teaching colleagues becomes critical due to the typically complex scheduling arrangements that operate and the myriad of teachers that students have for classes in the higher grades. At all levels, care must be taken to ensure that new or isolated students are included in friendly, supportive encounters with adults. This is important because when some students are new or shy, their chances for being noticed or being known are reduced. Positive attention given by teachers to new or isolated students, along with other students, can indicate that friendly, kind behaviors are appropriate and desirable and that the new and/or isolated students in the class are worthwhile members of the group to include and with whom to build relationships.

Also, the notion that all students have something to offer and should be included can be pointed out by calling upon each student to contribute to the needs of the class and teacher. For example, the students who are typically isolated can be asked, along with other students, to do classroom chores, such as erasing the chalkboard or carrying lunch money to the principal's office, or contributing their talents to the class or school assemblies, student advisory committees, and bazaars.

In addition to modeling positive interactions with each student in the classroom, it is essential to model positive support and friendship behaviors in front of the students toward other peers or colleagues. That is, offering assistance, being courteous, and sharing with fellow teachers, parents, and other adults can provide a positive peer support and friendship model for the students.

WHEN IT DOES NOT WORK

Unfortunately, despite the best efforts of everyone involved, peer support is sometimes slow to develop or does not appear to develop at all. While there are no foolproof ways to ensure that no student will be overlooked or rejected by his or her peers, there are several things to try when difficulties arise.

First, a sociometric assessment can be given to the class that includes questions to ascertain who is being accepted and/or rejected and the *reasons why.* This might provide cues as to what can be done when some students continue to be overlooked or rejected. For example, if a student is being rejected because he or she never initiates social interactions, ways to help the student initiate social interactions can be attempted (Strain & Kerr, 1981). Similarly, if a student is being rejected because he or she is always complaining or "grumpy," then school personnel and possibly the student's parents can work to help the student be more positive. It should be noted that while acceptance of a student is not analogous with friendship, acceptance is a necessary prerequisite to the development of friendships and informal supportive relationships. There are a number of books that provide clear and specific guidelines for designing sociometric assessments for use in classroom and other school settings (e.g., Borg, 1981; Borg & Gall, 1979).

Second, resource and consulting personnel with expertise in social interactions and behavior management available in the school or school district can sometimes be called upon to observe in the classroom and other school and nonschool settings in an effort to detect exactly what is happening, what problems exist, and propose possible solutions. When faced with particularly difficult problems, resource and consulting personnel can often be helpful (Heron & Harris, 1987; Idol-Maestas, 1983).

The support facilitator, discussed in Chapters 2 and 3, can help classroom teachers locate the appropriate personnel.

CONCLUSION

While it is important to help students who are new, isolated, and/or lonely make friends and gain the support of their peers in regular classes, those who have conducted research and written extensively about supportive relationships and friendship development have indicated that the value of having peer supports and friends should not be misinterpreted to imply that having lots of supports and friends is always "good" and having few is always "bad" (Duck, 1983). For some students, one or a few quality friendships may be more satisfying than having a large number of friends. Also, some students who appear isolated may not be concerned or interested in developing friendships. Furthermore, providing excessive support to some students can interfere with the development of skills they need. Too often, particularly for students traditionally classified as having disabilities, others try to "help too much" to the detriment of learning opportunities provided to the individual. As noted by Rubin (1980), it is essential to respect the different social styles and needs of students, including the very real needs that some students have for privacy, solitude, and trying new skills on their own.

Another consideration is that no student should be forced or cajoled into supporting or making friends with any other particular student or group of students. To a large extent, whom students choose to support and make friends with should be their individual choice. That is, while supportive relationships and friendships between two or more students can be encouraged and facilitated, they should be voluntary, based on free choice in the selection of one another as peer supporters and friends. When relationships are based on something other than free choice and personal preference, the relationship is unlikely to be considered one of friendship, thus it is unlikely the individuals will generalize and maintain the relationship beyond the classroom setting (Allan, 1979).

Finally, it should be stressed that along with encouraging others to be supportive of and friends with a new student, it is essential to encourage the new and/or isolated student to be a friend and help other students. This is important because, as stated by Rubin (1980), people tend to like to be helpful and friendly with those who are helpful and friendly to them. It also avoids some students always being the recipient of assistance. Friendships and supportive relationships can and should involve reciprocal giving, although a new or isolated student may require greater support initially.

REFERENCES

Allan, G. (1979). *A sociology of friendship and kinship.* Boston: Allen & Unwin.

Asher, S., & Gottman, J. (Eds.). (1981). *The development of children's friendships.* Cambridge, MA: Cambridge University Press.

Bell, R. (1981). *Worlds of friendship.* Beverly Hills: Sage Publications.

Berndt, T. (1986). Sharing between friends: Contexts and consequences. In E. Mueller & C. Cooper (Eds.), *Process and outcome in peer relationships* (pp. 129–160). New York: Academic Press.

Biklen, D. (Ed.). (1985). *The complete school.* New York: Teacher's College Press.

Borg, W. (1981). *Applying educational research.* New York: Longman, Inc.

Borg, W., & Gall, M. (1979). *Educational research.* New York: Longman.

Discover the possibilities. (1988). Colorado Springs: PEAK Parent Center.

Duck, S. (1983). *Friends for life.* New York: St. Martin's Press.

Epstein, J., & Karweit, N. (Eds.). (1983). *Friends in school.* New York: Academic Press.

Forest, M. (Ed.). (1987). *More education integration.* Downsview, Ontario: G. Allan Roeher Institute.

Forest, M., & Flynn, G. (Directors). (1988). *With a little help from my friends* [Video tape]. Toronto: Center for Integrated Education.

Gottlieb, J., & Leyser, Y. (1981). Friendships between mentally retarded and nonretarded children. In S. Asher & J. Gottman (Eds.), *The development of children's friendships* (pp. 150–181). Cambridge, MA: Cambridge University Press.

Grenot-Scheyer, M., Coots, J., & Falvey, M. (1989). Developing and fostering friendships. In M. Falvey (Ed.), *Community-based curriculum: Instructional strategies for students with severe handicaps* (2nd ed., pp. 345–358). Baltimore: Paul H. Brookes Publishing Co.

Heron, T., & Harris, K. (1987). *The educational consultant.* Austin, TX: PRO-ED.

Hinde, R. (1979). *Towards understanding relationships.* New York: Academic Press.

Idol-Maestas, L. (1983). *Special educator's consultation handbook.* Austin, TX: PRO-ED.

Oden, S., & Asher, S. (1977). Coaching children in social skills for friendship making. *Child Development, 48,* 495–506.

Perske, R., & Perske, M. (1988). *Friendship.* Nashville: Abingdon Press.

Reynolds, M., & Birch, J. (1988). *Adaptive mainstreaming.* New York: Longman, Inc.

Rubin, Z. (1980). Children's friendships. Cambridge, MA: Harvard University Press.

Ruttiman, A., & Forest, M. (1987). With a little help from my friends. In M. Forest (Ed.), *More education integration* (pp. 61–68). Downsview, Ontario: G. Allan Roeher Institute.

Selman, R. (1981). The child as a friendship philosopher. In S. Asher & J. Gottman (Eds.), *The development of children's friendships* (pp. 242–272). Cambridge, MA: Cambridge University Press.

Stainback, S., & Stainback, W. (1988). Educating students with severe disabilities. _Teaching Exceptional Children, 21_, 16–19.

Stainback, S., Stainback, W., & Forest, M. (Eds.). (1989). _Educating all students in the mainstream of regular education_. Baltimore: Paul H. Brookes Publishing Co.

Stainback, W., & Stainback, S. (1987). Facilitating friendships. _Education and Training of the Mentally Retarded, 22_, 18–25.

Stocking, S., Arezzo, D., & Leavitt, S. (1980). _Helping kids make friends_. Allen, TX: Argus Communications.

Strain, P., & Kerr, M. (1981). Modifying children's social withdrawal: Issues in assessment and clinical intervention. In M. Hersen, R. Eisler, & P. Miller (Eds.), _Progress in behavior modification_ (Vol. II, pp. 108–126). New York: Academic Press.

Strully, J. (1987, October). _What's really important in life anyway? Parents sharing the vision_. Paper presented at the 14th Annual Conference of the Association for Persons with Severe Handicaps, Chicago.

Strully, J., & Strully, C. (1985a). Friendship and our children. _Journal of The Association for Persons with Severe Handicaps, 10_, 224–227.

Strully, J., & Strully, C. (1985b). Teach your children. _The Canadian Journal of Mental Retardation, 35_(4), 3–11.

Trower, P. (1981). Social skill disorder. In S. Duck & R. Gilmore (Eds.), _Personal Relationships 3: Personal relationships in disorder_ (pp. 97–110). New York: Academic Press.

Vandercook, T., Fleetham, D., Sinclair, S., & Tetlie, R. (1988). Cath, Jess, Jules, and Ames . . . A story of friendship. _IMPACT, 1_, 18–19.

Villa, R., & Thousand, J. (1988). Enhancing success in heterogeneous classrooms and schools: The power of partnership. _Teacher Education and Special Education, 11_, 144–153.

York, J., & Vandercook T. (1988). What's in an IEP? Writing objectives for an integrated education. _IMPACT, 1_, 16, 19.

Mara Sapon-Shevin   *5*

Student Support through Cooperative Learning

When classrooms are purposively heterogeneous, one clear objective is that students will develop an understanding and respect for one another's differences and will find ways in which to support and nurture each other's learning. Competitive classrooms, in which students attempt to prove to themselves, to their classmates, and to their teacher that they are the best, first, smartest, or fastest, are clearly incompatible with this objective. In renouncing competition and trying to avoid the negative consequences of pitting students against each other in the classroom, some schools and teachers have turned, instead, to individualization, each child doing his or her own thing in isolation from other students. Although some of the negative effects of competition are, in fact, avoided in this way, much is lost. Students are not given the opportunity to learn to work together, to recognize their similarities and their differences, to learn a whole repertoire of teaching and supporting skills. Cooperative learning provides an obvious, and yet often neglected, alternative—a way of structuring the classroom so that students work *together* to accomplish goals, accommodating each other's differences and finding ways to encourage and nourish high levels of achievement and positive social interaction.

This chapter describes how teachers can establish and create *cooperative classrooms* in which every aspect of the structure, organization, and instruction are consistent with creating an environment that recognizes and respects student diversity and allows students to help one another to succeed. It is possible to implement cooperative learning at many levels, from specific cooperative learning group projects to the use of cooperative games. Teachers can examine every aspect of what goes on in their classrooms, reshaping what they say and do, how they teach and what they teach, in order to teach students to be cooperative and to understand the meaning of cooperation in their lives. This chapter explores the implementation of the cooperative classroom at three levels: creating a cooperative classroom environment, using cooperative learning groups and projects, and structuring cooperative instructional and recreational games. Each of these strategies can be used in isolation with considerable success; when implemented as a consistent "package," however, these strategies can do even more for creating supportive school environments in which all students can succeed.

CREATING A COOPERATIVE CLASSROOM ENVIRONMENT

Everything a teacher says or does in the classroom has an effect on how students view themselves and each other. Students can learn to see each other as "enemies" where one's success denotes the other's failure, or as "friends," where one's success contributes to and reinforces the other's. The following strategies represent areas in which teachers can have an immediate impact in creating "friendly classrooms."

Eliminate Competitive Classroom Symbols

To create a friendly, cooperative classroom all competitive symbols should be eliminated. To start, take down the star charts on the walls and any other visual displays of who is doing well and who is not. Do not read student scores aloud, return papers in order of score, or write classroom averages on the blackboard. The teacher should consider the following criterion when determining whether or not a specific act will promote or discourage cooperation: if an outside visitor to the classroom can look around and *see* who is doing well and who is not by looking at the board, the walls, or the seating arrangement, then the classroom atmosphere exemplifies competition.

Another way to eliminate competitive symbols is to create bulletin boards that include the work of all children rather than posting the "five best compositions or drawings." A third grade teacher created an elaborate underwater scene on one wall, with each child's contribution visible—fish, seaweed, skin divers, and so forth. Although there were differences in the complexity of the drawings the children had done, the overall message was one of inclusion, each child's addition improving the quality of the display. Class murals, displays in which every child adds his or her contribution, class books, and other such projects all create a sense of community and belonging with each child viewed as a contributing member of the group.

Use Inclusive Language

The language teachers use carries powerful messages about belonging and cooperation. Teachers should refer to students as "students," "class," or "kids," rather than as "boys and girls" or by reference to specific groups. The commonly advised behavior management strategies in which the teacher calls attention to the exemplary behavior of a single child or a group or explicitly or implicitly compares groups (i.e., "Let's see which row can get quiet fastest," "I like the way Mark and Kevin are raising their hands," or "The red group can go to lunch first today because they're all listening") should not be used. Instead, encourage group achievement or group solidarity by using language such as, "We can go outside when we all have the room straightened up" (and then encourage helping and cooperating) or, "I'm so impressed by all of the reading I saw this morning!". If a particular child or a small group of children present unique problems, the entire class should be engaged in problem solving in an inclusive way; for example, "What can we do about making sure that all the papers get turned in after morning work?" Students should be encouraged to see that they have an important role to play in supporting their peers to be contributing and productive class members.

Build the Classroom Community

A sense of belonging and cohesion can be built by activities that draw the whole class together. Putting on plays, some students writing the script, some painting the scenery, some drawing posters, and others making popcorn, can be a community-building experience that can easily involve students of varying levels of academic proficiency, English-language skill, physical ability, and so forth. Singing together also creates a sense of community; class members can take turns teaching and leading songs or small groups of students can take responsibility for directing the morning's music. The teacher should encourage sharing of all kinds and structure situations in which every child has a chance to speak and be heard. For example, consider allowing students to begin the day by telling a joke, describing a humorous event that happened at home, or just sharing something they have been thinking about.

Encourage Students to Use One Another as Resources

Teachers can create multiple opportunities for students to see each other as sources of information, instruction, and support. One teacher arranges her students' desks in clusters and sets a rule: if anyone in the group has a problem of any sort, they must consult with their group before coming to the teacher for help. The number of questions that the teacher must field is reduced considerably, but, more importantly, all class members get to explain, comfort, and act as miniteachers and committed friends. Additionally, a Classroom Yellow Pages can be developed to include lists of individual students and their skills/talents, and then the class can be encouraged to turn to those people as resources. One teacher reported that when her class found out that Melissa, who was not an exceptional student, was interested in and knowledgeable about cats, they asked questions of her and brought to her attention information and articles that they found. Melissa was validated and the rest of the class saw her as someone who knew a lot about something, even if there were other areas in which she was not proficient.

Another opportunity for students to use one another as resources is to implement peer teaching at many levels. Study partners (two students assigned to work together) are a simple way to begin. The teacher should also think of other students as resources. One fourth grade teacher reported that each year she undertook an elaborate craft project with her students and that it was always chaotic—she found herself being called for help in 20 directions, students became frustrated, and she always ended the project feeling frazzled. After an introductory course in cooperative learning, she implemented a surprisingly simple but greatly underutilized solution: she used a recess period to teach the craft project to six students, and the next day, these students were the resident teachers/experts for all the other students at their table. The project went smoothly, the young teachers felt important and powerful, and all the students felt satisfied. Another teacher, of first graders, got a new record player for her room and was anxious for all the students to learn how to use it properly. Rather than holding a large group lesson, she chose one student and taught him the correct terms (tone arm, spindle, turntable) and utilization of the record player. After she had checked him off on a skills list, he was asked to teach two other students, who then each taught two more until the entire class had received personalized instruction and been checked-off on the skills list.

Encourage Students to Notice Each Other's Accomplishments

In most classrooms, students are attentive to every misdeed and misstep of their classmates, often resulting in tattling, blame, and recriminations. The teacher should try turning around this natural inclination to notice by refocusing the attention to positive acts and achievements. One teacher posted a "Good Deed Tree" in her room and instructed students that any time they saw anyone do or say something nice to another student they were to write their report on a small slip of paper and post it on the tree. On Fridays, the teacher read the notes on the tree, providing positive feedback *both* to the student who had done something nice and to the student who had noticed.

At Christmas time, some teachers implement a Secret Santa program in which students pick the name of another student for whom they do "secret" nice things, leave messages, and so forth. Such a project could be extended for the whole year, encouraging students to be supportive of one another *all year long*. Additionally, when a student accomplishes something, anything—an improved spelling paper, a difficult math assignment, making friends with a former enemy, learning to ride a bicycle—that student should be encouraged to share this with the class, promoting group applause, cheers, or other expressions of support. It needs to be made clear that since it is not a competitive class, everyone can succeed and everyone can be happy for other people's accomplishments without being personally diminished.

Use Children's Literature to Teach About Cooperation

Children's books can provide an excellent way to teach children cooperative skills (Sapon-Shevin, 1986). Teachers can select and read books that have cooperation and/or conflict resolution as a theme and can then extend the book by discussing personal and classroom applications of the book's message. For example, the book, *Two Good Friends* (Dalton, 1974), is about Bear and Duck who are good friends although they are very different. Duck is a meticulous housekeeper with a home that is always clean and neat, but he often has no food in the house. Bear, however, is an excellent cook but a terrible housekeeper, and his house is always dirty. After some initial difficulties in reconciling their differences, they reach a perfect solution: Duck cleans Bear's house for him and Bear bakes delicious things for Duck to eat. Teachers can use this book, and others like it, to begin a discussion of the tremendous variations in talents and skills of class members and ways in which they can support each other. If Bill is wonderful at jump rope but has trouble remembering things (like his homework), perhaps he could give other students jump rope lessons and someone else could remind him to take his books home every day after school. For older students, a book such as *The Blind Man and the Elephant: An Old Tale from the Land of India* (Quigley, 1959) can be the discussion starter for an exploration of the idea that each individual has some information and skills, but that only by working together can the "whole picture" be seen or the best solution devised. Classes can also be encouraged to write their own "Classroom Book of Cooperation" in which they record the things they have accomplished as a class that would not have been possible without collaboration. For younger students, the book might be called "It Takes Two. . ." and could be a picture book with teacher captions. Older students might want to incorporate collaborative writing to produce short stories or poems about cooperation. For more extensive examples of ways for creating overall cooperative classroom environments, see Dishon and O'Leary (1984), Moorman and Dishon (1983), and Prutzman, Burger, Bodenhamer, and Stern (1978).

IMPLEMENTING COOPERATIVE LEARNING GROUPS

In addition to the more generalized, informal approaches described above, teachers wishing to structure cooperative learning in their classrooms can use one or more of the more structured models of cooperative learning. This section discusses two of these, Small Group Learning (Johnson & Johnson, 1975; Johnson, Johnson, Holubec, & Roy, 1984; Sharan & Sharan, 1976) and the Jigsaw Method (Aronson, 1978). These are examples of systematic ways of restructuring academic curricula through the use of cooperative learning techniques. The strengths of these models is their compreheniveness and their adaptability to various subject areas and ages/abilities.

Small Group Learning

Perhaps the most well-known cooperative learning model is the one developed by Johnson and Johnson (1975) usually called Learning Together. In this model, the teacher assigns heterogeneous groups to work on a single product or project as a group, following specific guidelines from the teacher. The teacher's role consists of assigning students to heterogeneous groups, arranging the classroom to facilitate peer interaction, providing the appropriate materials, explaining the task and the cooperative goal structure to the students, observing the student-student interaction, intervening as needed, and evaluating the group products using a criterion-referenced evaluation system. Group members are trained to observe and monitor the social interactions within their own group, and one member, playing the role of "observer," provides feedback to the group concerning the extent to which they engaged in various behaviors, including praising one another, asking questions, clarifying others' statements, giving direction to the group, and so on.

This model can be used with virtually any subject matter or age level. For example, first graders might be grouped and asked to write a sentence together, each member being held accountable for all others in the group being able to read the sentence. A group of high school students might be given information on automobile prices, family income, insurance rates, and loan opportunities, and be asked to come up with a car that a family could afford, how it might be financed, and what the monthly payments would be.

In order for group learning of this kind to be successful there must be individual accountability, some way of monitoring and ensuring that all group members are participating and not simply going along with the answer or product of one or more group members. Careful attention must also be given to teaching the necessary social skills. Rather than assuming that students come to school able to listen, praise, compromise, and negotiate conflict (or bemoaning students' lack of skills in these areas), the teacher must take as his or her responsibility the establishment and improvement of students' interpersonal behavioral skills, providing careful, systematic instruction and feedback of those behaviors necessary for smooth group functioning. One way of structuring and teaching the various social skills necessary for group cooperation is to assign students to various roles within the group; one student might be given the role of observer, one the role of leader, one the role of checker, and one the role of praiser. Each of these roles would be explained and taught and then rotated among group members so that, in time, all students have gotten the opportunity to practice all the different roles.

Sharan and Sharan's (1976) Group-Investigation model involves two to six students working in groups on subtopics that are part of a general area delineated by the teacher. For example, if the students are studying Mexico, one group might investigate the music of Mexico, another group the geography of the area, another group Mexican food, and another group the political system of Mexico. Teachers and students cooperatively plan the goals and expected outcomes of the group, and each group works together on a project that is subsequently presented to the class as a whole. The method stresses having students share their individual perspectives with the group as a whole and having groups broaden the perspective of the whole class through their presentations. This kind of multilevel teaching is particularly conducive to accommodating a range of individual differences within a single class. In one class, a student who was labeled as severely handicapped contributed to the unit on Mexico by planning, shopping for, and preparing a Mexican dinner for the class. This endeavor was consistent with the individual goals of this student (shopping skills, money management, and food preparation), and yet allowed the student to participate as a member of the group and to engage in an activity (making food) that was well-appreciated by *all* the students.

The Jigsaw Method

In the Jigsaw Method (Aronson, 1978; Kagan, 1985), students are assigned to five or six-member teams; the material to be learned is divided into six parts, and each student is responsible for learning and then teaching one part of the material to each of his or her members. Members of different groups who have been assigned to the same section of material meet in "expert" groups to study their sections and become comfortable with their responsibility for teaching their fragment. Each group member is tested on all of the material, so that there is forced interdependence between group members. "Not liking someone," or "thinking that someone looks funny or talks funny," are not reasons for failing to learn or teach one's portion of the material.

As with the other approaches described above, this technique can be applied to a range of subject matters. In one third grade class, students became experts on different parts of pizza—green pepper experts, pepperoni experts, crust experts, and sauce experts. Students learned something about their ingredient, how to prepare it for pizza, and what nutritional value it had. They then returned to their groups and taught other group members what they had learned *and* assembled and ate their pizza! (N. Graves & T. Graves, personal communication, October 23, 1986).

Older students can utilize this technique with written material, each group learning a small section of a chapter, becoming experts on one character in a play, or learning 4 of 20 vocabulary words before returning to teach these to their group. This technique was originally utilized to mitigate the problems and tensions that had developed between students of different racial groups following desegregation, but it has broad applicability in any setting, particularly those in which students are "cliquish" or avoid others whom they perceive as different.

All of these approaches to cooperative learning require sustained observation and teaching of the skills necessary for successful cooperation. The teacher cannot simply put students in groups, ask them to cooperate, and then hope for the best. He or she must plan carefully what kind of interdependence is structured or demanded by the task, monitor individuals' and groups' skills in behaving cooperatively, help students to understand and process their own cooperative skills, and then specifically teach those skills that are absent or inadequately displayed. For example, a teacher might conduct a lesson on listening, involving students in practicing active listening (listening without interrupting, commenting, or judging). If the teacher notices that students have difficulty providing feedback in kind and helpful ways (i.e., "No, you jerk, the answer isn't 12"), then he or she might engage the students in a lesson or discussion of ways of disagreeing without insulting, ways of resolving conflicts by learning to restate the other person's position, and so on. (See Kreidler [1984] for excellent activities for establishing conflict resolution skills in the classroom.)

As cooperative learning methods become more popular and materials and training workshops in this area proliferate, it is important that teachers become critical consumers of programs and activities that are labeled as "cooperative learning." There are tremendous differences in the extent to which such programs are actually cooperative (as opposed to promoting intragroup cooperation with intergroup competition) and the extent to which they actually empower students and teachers to make their own decisions about curriculum, classroom management, and the development of interpersonal skills. *Cooperative Learning, Cooperative Lives* (Schniedewind & Davidson, 1987) provides an excellent model of helping teachers to use the process of cooperation to think about and teach cooperation and competition within the classroom, the community, the country, and the world.

STRUCTURING COOPERATIVE GAMES

One strategy for establishing cooperative behaviors is the use of games that involve students cooperating to overcome an outside obstacle (time, the difficulty of the task, etc.) rather than trying to overcome one another. There are many excellent books of cooperative games now available for teachers to use (Deacove, 1974; Fluegelman, 1976, 1981; Harrison & The Nonviolence and Children Program, 1976; Orlick, 1978, 1982; Weinstein & Goodman, 1980). Games are useful because they represent activities with high appeal for children and because they can structure the environment for a brief period of time according to specific rules. Teachers should not assume, however, that any game will result in positive social interaction or cooperative behavior. Many games provide for social interactions that would be considered highly undesirable in other (nongame) settings (pushing, grabbing, taunting or teasing, monopolizing or excluding other children, tricking other players, hoarding materials or resources, etc.).

Consider, for example, the game of Musical Chairs. In this game, in order for a child to win, he or she must push other children out of the way, grab a chair, and then keep that chair in the face of other students who attempt to share it or take it away. Often there is teasing ("Ha, ha, I was here first") or accusations ("You're a big liar, Michael was there first"). Students' attempts to share the chairs will likely be thwarted by an adult who tells them that they must figure out who was there first and that the student who arrived later must vacate and remove themselves from the game. Lots of social interaction, certainly, but hardly cooperative! And, perhaps worse yet, as children are excluded from the game, some crying, others gloating, the teacher either says, "Aren't we having fun?", thus teaching children that these ways of interacting are not only socially acceptable and adult-approved but also should be considered enjoyable, or chastises the children for their "poor sports-manship," thereby ignoring the role of the teacher in structuring a situation that promotes this kind of behavior.

By contrast, consider the game of Cooperative Musical Chairs. In this game, there are, for example, 10 children and only nine chairs, but the game is presented as follows: all the children walk around the chairs to the music. When the music stops, every child must be on a chair in order for the group to win. When presented like this, the choices are clear—students must figure out ways to share the chairs and must make decisions about who will sit where, who will be supported by whom, and so on. Teachers who play this game with children are likely to observe the following: children holding each other on their laps; children calling, "Come over here, there's room for you," or, "Someone hold up Tanya's leg, she's falling off"; and group problem solving, "Put Jeremy on the bottom and then let Dwayne sit on top."

The relationship between cooperative games and diversity is crucial. In competitive games, such as the Musical Chairs first described, a child who is smaller, shorter, less skilled, does not speak English fluently, is classified disabled, or is simply slower is likely to be the first eliminated. Students are not taught any positive responses to others' differences but learn, rather, to celebrate those differences that contribute to failure. In a cooperative game, such as Cooperative Musical Chairs, even without direct instruction, students realize that in order for the group to succeed they must help each other and that any student whose difference is likely to lead to failure must be particularly supported. In a class with a student with a physical disability, for example, this might mean actually assisting a child who moves slowly; in a class with students who have difficulty following directions or understanding what is going on, this assistance might take the form of informal peer coaching (i.e., "Come on, Miguel, sit over here with us").

Cooperative Instructional Games

Cooperative games can be purely recreational, or they can be designed to have academic content. Some examples of instructional cooperative games follow.

Who Am I?   Who am I is a cooperative game where each student has a card pinned or taped to his or her back with the name of a famous person, an animal, an event in history, or so forth. Participants circulate asking each other only yes/no questions in order to figure out what is on their back. Participants can only ask one question of a person before going on to another player. When players know who they are, they continue to circulate, answering questions from other players. In order to play this game, students must learn how to phrase questions that can be answered by "yes" or "no" that will yield useful information. Because of the one-question-per-person rule, students interact with a range of people. This activity can be adapted to a number of areas and very young children or nonreaders can use pictures of the object to be guessed. One third grade teacher culminated a unit on the United States by putting the name of a state on each child's back and priming them with questions to ask like, "Am I east of the Mississippi?", "Am I a Great Plains State?", "Do I border on another country?"

Concentration-Finding Partners   The teacher prepares a set of cards that contain matches (one card has South Dakota to match another that has Pierre; pictures of animals and their names; math problems and their solution, etc.). Players stand or sit in a circle, each holding one card that they keep hidden against their chest. One player begins by calling on another player to reveal his or her card and then calling on another player (or him- or herself) to reveal that card, attempting to make a match. If the player successfully makes a match (group consensus), the two cards are placed in the center. If no match is found, the next player takes a turn. The players on both sides of the person taking his or her turn are designated as "helpers," and may provide assistance if asked. The game is "won" when all matches have been made and placed in the center. Players continue taking turns even after they are no longer holding a card.

This game combines the skills of regular concentration (being able to read the cards, remember where they are, and determine if they are matches) with a cooperative framework in which students help one another to succeed. This game has been successfully used in preschool classes (children matching colors with color words) and high school physics classes (students matching terms and their definitions). A similar game can also be played with the same cards by giving each child a card and having them circulate around the room trying to find their match. This version actively involves all students who must look at card combinations and determine if they go together.

Sequence Activities   Various cooperative games involve having students put themselves in some kind of order. Students can each be given a letter and asked to put themselves in alphabetical order, they can be given a card with an event from a story and asked to put themselves in the sequence of the story, or they can be given events in history and asked to put themselves in chronological order. In all of these cases, students must talk and discuss the sequence and all agree they are correct before asking each other or the teacher for confirmation.

Sequence games can also be played with cards: cards are prepared in advance with each one containing a clue for what follows next. For example, one card might say, "When a student turns out the lights, you yell, 'Hey, it's dark in here.' " The next card would say, "When someone yells, 'Hey, it's dark in here,' you run around in circles saying, 'I'll generate a little energy,' " and so forth. The cues can be words, actions, gestures, or anything else that would be visible or audible to other players. One card must indicate the beginning, for example, "You go first by _____." The cards are distributed and then each child follows the sequence. This game is infinitely adaptable according to the age, level, or reading ability of the students. More advanced students often enjoy writing their own sequence games for other class members. Cards for nonreaders can have a pantomime on top that is the clue for the pantomime on the bottom. Cards can also have pieces of a story or a rhyme that begins on one card and is continued on another; one card says, "When boating never quarrel, for you will find no doubt," and the next card starts, "A boat is not the proper place to have a falling out," and then continues, "Dr. Brown fell in the well and broke his collarbone" (which in turn, is continued on the next card by, "Why didn't he attend the sick and leave the well alone?"). With children who lack experience in following directions or reading, the teacher can go over all the cards and the sequence as a group, then pair children in reading/acting pairs.

There are several excellent books of cooperative games (Harrison & The Nonviolence and Children Program, 1976; Orlick, 1978, 1982). Creative teachers and students can easily create their own games, implementing the basic principle that students are working together to accomplish something.

Cooperative Recreational Games

Cooperative games can be active or quiet, and they can be played indoors or out. They are generally characterized by the fact that all children are engaged in the activity most of the time, players are not eliminated, and children interact during the game in helpful and supportive ways.

Hug Tag In Hug Tag (Orlick, 1978), one or more children are "huggits" with a red flag (or sock). They try to give their flag to another player, and the other players are only safe when they are in a hug-group of two or three. When the teacher calls "switch," the children must disband their groups and find a new group. At a more advanced level, hug-groups can stay together only as long as all members can hum on one breath. When any member runs out of breath, the group must disband. As one can imagine, the more players run around, the more out of breath they become and the shorter the period of time they are able to stay together. In contrast to many outdoor physical games in which children chase one another, in this game, safety comes from being *with* other people, touching each other. This game is an excellent example of one that can be played and enjoyed by extremely diverse groups. Two-year-olds and 80-year-olds can all participate in the same game.

Frozen Bean Bag   In Frozen Bean Bag (Orlick, 1978) each player moves around with a small bean bag on his or her head. If a player's bag falls off, he or she freezes until rescued by another player who replaces the fallen bean bag without losing his or her own. After players have mastered walking with a bean bag on their head, they can be asked to skip, hop, jump, or run. The salient feature of this game is that students need one another to be rescued; rather than working to get other players out, players are working to keep everyone *in* the game.

Fish Gobbler   In Fish Gobbler (Orlick, 1978), the children all move according to the directions of the Fish Gobbler. When he or she calls "ship," they must all run to one end of the gym (or play area); "shore," to the other end; "fishnet," they all join hands; "waves," they join hands and make waves; "sardines," they get down on the floor and squish together, and so on. Children all remain actively involved in the game, and many of the directions involve them in actions where they must work together and coordinate their movements.

CONCLUSION

There are many ways in which teachers can encourage their students to see themselves as a supportive community; cooperative learning and cooperation are basic principles in establishing a sense of mutual responsibility and caring for other people. Teachers wishing to find out more about cooperative learning are encouraged to join the International Association for the Study of Cooperation in Education (136 Liberty Street, Santa Cruz, CA 95060) and to check resource guides such as the one issued periodically by Graves and Graves (1985, 1987).

Within cooperative settings, students can be supportive of other students who do things differently; the child who talks more slowly, who struggles with language, or who needs his or her fingers in order to count can all be included in the activity because the goal is to get something accomplished, not to do something before someone else or without any support or help. Within cooperative settings, helping people is valued, appreciated, and taught rather than labeled as "cheating" or inappropriate socializing. Students see that praise is not a scarce commodity rationed by the teacher, and so they are free to praise each other. They see that success is not limited to a single student or group, and so they can be supportive of one another's accomplishments.

Cooperative environments nourish and celebrate diversity, epitomizing the poster that reads, "None of us is as smart as all of us." The film "Nicky, One of My Best Friends" (1975), tells the story of a child with cerebral palsy and blindness who is an integrated part of a cooperative classroom. One of Nicky's friends says, "I don't think of Nicky as handicapped. He just needs a little help. We all do." Cooperative learning allows teachers to draw out the best behavior of their students; the most nurturing, supportive, and caring tendencies are nourished and encouraged in cooperative environments.

REFERENCES

Aronson, E. (1978). *The jigsaw classroom*. Beverly Hills: Sage Publications.

Dalton, J. (1974). *Two good friends*. New York: Crown.

Deacove, J. (1974). *Games manual of non-competitive games*. Perth, Ontario: Family Pastimes.

Dishon, D., & O'Leary, P.W. (1984). *A guidebook for cooperative learning: A technique for creating more effective schools*. Holmes Beach, FL: Learning Publications, Inc.

Fluegelman, A. (Ed.). (1976). *The new games book*. Garden City, NY: Dolphin Books.

Fluegelman, A. (1981). *More new games! . . . And playful ideas from the New Games Foundation*. Garden City, NY: Dolphin Books.

Graves, N., & Graves, T. (1985, 1987). *Cooperative learning: A resource guide*. Santa Cruz, CA: International Association for the Study of Cooperation in Education.

Harrison, M., & The Nonviolence and Children Program. (1976). *For the fun of it! Selected cooperative games for children and adults*. Philadelphia: Nonviolence and Children Friends Peace Committee.

Johnson, D., & Johnson, R. (1975). *Learning together and alone*. Englewood Cliffs, NJ: Prentice-Hall.

Johnson, D., Johnson, R., Holubec, E.J., & Roy, P. (1984). *Circles of learning*. Washington, DC: Association for Supervision and Curriculum Development.

Kagan, S. (1985). *Cooperative learning: Resources for teachers*. Riverside, CA: University of California, School of Education.

Kreidler, W.J. (1984). *Creative conflict resolution*. Glenview, IL: Scott, Foresman, and Company.

Moorman, C., & Dishon, D. (1983). *Our classroom: We can learn together*. Englewood Cliffs, NJ: Prentice-Hall.

Nicky, one of my best friends, (1975). New York: McGraw-Hill.

Orlick, T. (1978). *The cooperative sports and games book: Challenge without competition*. New York: Pantheon Books.

Orlick, T. (1982). *The second cooperative sports and games book*. New York: Pantheon Books.

Prutzman, P., Burger, M.L., Bodenhamer, G., & Stern, L. (1978). *The friendly classroom for a small planet: A handbook on creative approaches to living and problem solving for children*. Wayne, NJ: Avery Publishing Co.

Quigley, L.F. (1959). *The blind man and the elephant: An old tale from the land of India*. New York: Charles Scribner's Sons.

Sapon-Shevin, M. (1986). Teaching cooperation. In Cartledge, G., & Milburn, J.

(Eds.), _Teaching social skills to children: Innovative Approaches_ (2nd ed., pp. 270–302). Elmsford, NY: Pergamon Press.

Schniedewind, N., & Davidson, E. (1987). _Cooperative learning, cooperative lives: A sourcebook of learning activities for building a peaceful world._ Dubuque, IA: William C. Brown Company Publishers.

Sharan, S., & Sharan, Y. (1976). _Small group teaching._ Englewood Cliffs, NJ: Educational Technology.

Weinstein, M., & Goodman, J. (1980). _Playfair: Everybody's guide to noncompetitive play._ San Louis Obispo, CA: Impact Publishers.

Alan Gartner
Dorothy Kerzner Lipsky

6

Students as
Instructional Agents

The fact that schools, as currently organized and operated, are not succeeding for large numbers of students is the subject of
almost daily reports. Despite some improvements on the margin, there is
mounting evidence of failure: in terms of drop-out rates, scores on
standardized tests, numbers of graduates, and the knowledge of those
who do graduate. Both cause and effect create large-scale disaffection
among students.

Traditionally, students are seen as the recipients in education. That
is, teachers and other school personnel deliver instruction and students
receive it. This concept implies that when instruction takes place, it
necessarily results in learning. School practices operate as if this were
the reality; however, there are far too many circumstances where the
educators teach but students do not learn. One fundamental reason is
the failure of educators to recognize the unique role of the student as the
producer of her or his learning. It is, therefore, essential for educators to
develop methods to increase the effectiveness of the student in the learning process.

The goal is to make the student a more effective worker in the
production of her or his own learning. The lessons learned from industry's efforts to increase worker productivity indicate that persons are
more productive when they are respected, interested in what they do,
see the purpose of the activity, understand the relationship of the part to
the whole, have some control over the pace and timing of the work, and
have cooperative relationships with their fellow workers. Each of these
factors, true about workers in general, are also true about students as

workers in their own learning. Many of these factors operate in programs where students work collaboratively or teach or tutor other students.

HISTORICAL BACKGROUND

People teaching and learning from each other has been known through the ages. As early as the first century, the great Roman teacher, Quintilian, pointed out that younger children can learn from older children who are in the same class (Wright, 1960). In the 17th century, the Moravian teacher John Comenius wrote: "The saying, 'He who teaches others, teaches himself,' is very true, not only because constant repetition impresses a fact indelibly on the mind, but because the process of teaching itself gives a deeper insight into the subject taught . . ." (Comenius, 1921, p. 47). And, of course, the one-room schoolhouse provided a natural setting for such teaching and learning.

The first modern-era book on tutoring was published in 1971 (Gartner, Kohler, & Riessman, 1971), and it was followed in 1976 by a comprehensive academic survey (Allen, 1976). The first study that focused upon tutoring programs for students with learning problems was written by Jenkins and Jenkins (1981). Throughout the 1980s there were an accelerating number of studies, including a comprehensive meta-analysis of the research (Cohen, Kulik, & Kulik, 1982); an intensive study of the effects on behavior change (Strain, 1981); and Hedin's report (1986) for the Carnegie Commission that recommended tutoring as a component of education for *all* students. In that same year, Osguthorpe and Scruggs (1986) presented the first comprehensive survey of programs using special education students as tutors. Now, cooperative learning programs that include tutoring activities are being widely used to increase student academic success (Johnson & Johnson, 1984; Slavin, 1987a, 1987b; Slavin et al., 1985).

An important aspect of the educational reforms of the 1960s was the development of a range of tutoring programs. Ronald and Peggy Lippitt implemented programs in New York City and Detroit public schools, emphasizing the process of socialization for the older children and the assistance provided to the younger children (Lippitt & Lohman, 1965). At Mobilization for Youth, a pioneering New York City antipoverty program, tutorial centers were set up in neighborhood schools (Cloward, 1967). By the end of the decade there were more than 100 centers serving over 6000 students. Herbert Thelen (1967), as part of a larger effort to address the needs of "problem students" in the Chicago public schools, saw students tutoring each other as an expression of a "caring community." First in Newark, New Jersey, Philadelphia, Pennsylvania, and then in New York City, the National Commission on Resources for Youth, led by Mary Conway Kohler, incorporated Youth Tutoring Youth (YTY) programs as a component of the Neighborhood Youth Corps (Gartner et al., 1971). The most expansive school-based tutoring effort was at Pocoima Elementary School in Los Angeles, where the entire school became a "tutorial community," involving both cross-age and peer tutoring programs (Melaragno & Newmark, n.d.). In the mid-1970s, a program was developed in Central Harlem where students with disabilities tutored other children.

By 1979, it was estimated that some 10,000 schools had used tutoring of one form or another (Goodlad, 1984). A 1983 survey found that 41 states had a variety of local tutoring programs and eight states had some type of statewide program. While a majority of states used adults as tutors, 13 reported use of peer tutoring (Smith, 1983). Hedin (1986) proposed:

> [Reconceiving] tutoring and peer teaching as an integral element in every student's educational experience, . . . [from] the perspective of the classroom teacher, peer teaching could potentially be a great asset to those faced with having to teach large classes of students with widely divergent ability. Here is an inexpensive tool which can individualize instruction, even for large classes. (p. 2)

Citing Slavin's report (1987a) that homogeneous grouping has few if any benefits for students, Stainback and Stainback (1989) also make the case for tutoring programs to foster student interdependence in classrooms consisting of students with diverse abilities.

EFFECTIVENESS OF PEER INSTRUCTION

Tutoring is an old concept with particular value in the modern period of school reform. Collaboration, cooperation, and tutoring fit well with restructured schools that are moving away from the appropriately criticized "factory model," where all students are taught the same material in a lock-step fashion.

Students working together, whether through tutoring or other cooperative modes, provide unique opportunities toward the improvement of education for all students, including those classified "at risk" or labeled as handicapped. These methods are a means of providing individualized instruction and promoting social goals of integration. When "at risk" students are in the role of tutor, it expresses, in practice, the belief that all students, including those labeled as handicapped, are "capable of achievement and worthy of respect" (Lipsky & Gartner, 1987, p. 69). In addition, if all students are "teachers," a pro-learning atmosphere, one which is cooperative and collegial, is more likely to develop in the classroom. Collaborative designs reject deficit-based education models that create segregated dual systems. Instead, they provide the basis for designing education programs of quality that serve and succeed for all students (Gartner & Lipsky, 1987; Lipsky & Gartner, 1989).

Evidence of the instructional, social, and cost effectiveness of tutoring is mounting. A 1981 meta-analysis (Cohen et al., 1982) reported that in 45 of 52 studies analyzed, students who were tutored by older students outperformed those in comparison groups on examinations. The U.S. Department of Education (1986) included it as practice that "works." In a review of instructional programs for "at risk" students, Madden and Slavin (1987) reported, "overall, the results of tutoring studies show this strategy to have strong effects on student achievement" (p. 13). In a study of the cost-effectiveness of various remedial programs, including computer assisted instruction and reduced class size, Levin (1984) reported that tutoring is the most cost-effective.

In one study of what students see as fair in enabling high- and low-achieving students to learn the same things, Thorkildsen (1989) reported that students find peer tutoring the fairest method. Tutoring outranked four other schemes: 1) allowing students who have completed their work to go on to enriched activities, 2) having the slow learners move to new activities when the fast learners were finished, 3) allowing the fast learners to move ahead at their own pace, and 4) having the fast learners do nothing until the others catch up.

For tutees, benefits come about through the individualization and additional time in instructional activities provided. Assessing new psychological theories concerning students with learning disabilities suggests that "reciprocal-teaching" programs may provide what the authors call a "scaffold," a temporary structure to provide support to a novice as he or she learns new materials (Brown & Campione, 1986). Brophy (1986) noted the importance in academic achievement of opportunities for "recitation, drill, practice, and application activities" (p. 1076) offered by tutoring. Jenkins and Jenkins (1981), in a comprehensive study of tutoring programs, stated that, "The major advantages of tutoring programs is their ability to increase academic engaged time and to provide more repetition and practice on important academic tasks" (p. 77). This fits with the research that emphasizes that students need repeated practice on material (Rosenshine & Stevens, 1986). Other research (Hall, Delquardi, Greenwood, & Thurston, 1982) emphasized the importance of "opportunities to respond," including a series of studies that report on the effectiveness of the use of classroom student tutoring teams (Maheady & Harper, 1987; Maheady, Sacca, & Harper, 1987,

1988) and classwide peer tutoring (Greenwood, Maheady, & Carta, in press).

There is an increasing amount of data as to the cognitive and effective benefits for tutors. First, there is the opportunity to practice activities where learning has occurred but mastery is not yet achieved or learning in one setting achieved but is not yet generalized to other settings. The _Harvard Education Letter_ reported that "[t]utors learn at least as much as the students they teach—and tutors who are far behind academically gain even more" ("Big Kids Teach Little Kids," 1987, p. 2). As noted earlier, tutors learn by reviewing, reinforcing, and reformulating the material, as well as from the opportunity to see the learning from a different vantage point, that is, in observing the tutee learn (Gartner et al., 1971).

In the affective domain, tutors gain in self-confidence and self-esteem. Studies report improved student attitudes toward school in general and specific subjects in particular, enhanced self-concepts, increased mutual concern among students, and more appropriate and positive social interactions among students. Featherstone (1987) carried this further, saying "we should think more about ways to help kids learn [so] that they can be powerful enough to help other people." He sees this as "a prerequisite to political character. It starts with a sense that you can matter in someone else's life, that you can make a difference" (p. 36).

Damon (1984) presented an interesting analysis of the benefits of peer interaction from three theoretical perspectives: that of Jean Piaget, Lev Vygotsky, and Harry Stack Sullivan. He concluded:

> Because peer tutoring is of demonstrable value both to tutor and tutee, an ideal school approach would expose children to both roles. Any child has an area of competence that can be imparted to a younger or less sophisticated child. Conversely, all children can benefit from tutoring in areas in which they are relatively novices. In assuming both tutor and tutee roles, children not only gain the benefits of tutee as well as tutor, but also a highly informative experience in role reversal. The child's switching from expert to novice can impart to the child a deeper and more sympathetic understanding of the educational endeavor. (p. 33)

Hedin (1986) echoed some of these same points. "The experience of being needed, valued and respected by another person produces a new view of self as a worthwhile human being" (p. 3). She also noted that cognitively there is particular benefit for the tutors in learning or reviewing material, especially that which is age appropriate for them.

Tutoring has been used across the full range of school subjects and diverse student needs. Tutoring has been successfully implemented from mathematics to spelling, from physical education to vocational education. And, increasingly, tutoring has been used as part of efforts to facilitate mainstreaming.

Beyond those programs where students labeled as having disabilities are tutored by "nonlabeled" students, there are programs where students with disabilities tutor other students with disabilities (Maher, 1986; Stainback, Stainback, & Hatcher, 1983). There are also a number of programs where students with disabilities tutor so-called nondisabled students (Osguthorpe & Scruggs, 1986).

Finally, student collaboration has positive benefits for classroom teachers. A teacher's work becomes of a higher order that includes planning, organizing, and supervising (Hedin, 1986). This new higher order work for teachers, supported by the operation of tutoring programs in the schools, fits well with the growing focus on increasing teacher professionalism.

DESIGNS OF TUTORING PROGRAMS

There is no single way (surely no single best way) to organize tutoring programs. Presented in the following pages are a few examples of different program designs. While some are better suited to student and teacher needs, each can be adapted in terms of student age, subject matter, school organization, and teacher preference.

Classwide Student Tutoring Teams

A synthesis of the classwide peer tutoring design developed at the Juniper Gardens Children's Project, Kansas City, Kansas by Joseph Delquardi and Charles Greenwood and the cooperative learning models developed at Johns Hopkins by Robert Slavin and colleagues has formed the classwide student tutoring teams that have been successfully implemented. Classwide student tutoring teams (CSTT) have been implemented at both the elementary and secondary levels in subjects ranging from spelling to social studies. The key strategy of the CSTT design is to increase students' opportunities to respond and to have those responses affirmed or corrected.

CSTT consists of five major components: 1) small, heterogeneous learning teams, 2) a game format for reviewing weekly instructional content, 3) cooperative goal structures among team members, 4) systematic and proscribed instructional strategies, and 5) daily point earning and public posting of student performance (Maheady & Pernell, 1987, p. 7).

The key ingredient in CSTT is a small (four to five students) heterogeneous learning team, reflecting the ethnic, gender, and achievement composition of the entire classroom (Maheady, Harper, & Sacca, 1986).

Teams include members of both sexes, differing racial backgrounds, and varying achievement levels. Students are assigned either by random selection or by teachers' class ranking in the subject area and then assigning students to teams on a rotating basis. The goal is to establish teams with an equal number of members that are heterogeneous within but homogeneous across the class. This assures both the necessary mixture for the cooperative process to take place and that the competition between the teams is fair. Teams stay together anywhere from one to eight weeks and then new assignments, using the design described above, produce reformulated teams.

Before the tutoring actually begins, training sessions are conducted. This includes the purposes of CSTT (students are told that their "'job' is to help their teammates learn the weekly content presented on the practice sheets. . ." [Maheady et al., 1987, p. 112]), modeling the procedure for students, and providing guided practice. Typically, this can be completed in two or three brief sessions. With careful monitoring in the first weeks of implementation, there usually is little difficulty in the process of establishing the CSTT program.

CSTT sessions generally last about 30 minutes a day and are conducted two to four times a week. On each team, students take turns acting as tutor while their remaining teammates are tutees. After a set period of time, tutor and tutees reverse roles, such that during every period each member of the team has a chance to be both tutor and tutee. The tutors use material, questions and answers, prepared by the teacher. Points are awarded for correct answers. The primary job of the tutor is to examine each tutee's responses so that errors are corrected quickly and appropriate points are awarded for correct answers.

The teacher's primary role, having prepared the tutoring material, is to monitor the process to ensure that the procedures are carried out correctly. Additionally, teachers award "bonus" points for cooperative work habits and correct tutoring behavior.

At the end of each tutoring session, both individual and team points are totaled and recorded. "Winners" are announced weekly. In most CSTT projects, weekly quizzes on the material are conducted, and student scores on the quizzes and the tutoring sessions are combined.

Cross-Age Programs

Cross-age tutoring programs can be divided into two groups: 1) traditional programs that use older tutors who know the subject matter to tutor younger students who do not, with a focus on tutee benefit, and 2) programs where although the tutor may be older or know more than the tutee, the emphasis is upon tutor gain (i.e., "learning through teaching").

Tutee Focused Benefits   Jenkins and Jenkins (1981) have described designs for cross-age tutoring programs that focus on meeting the needs of the younger child with a specific identified learning need. They emphasize that the use of cross-age tutoring does not change the teacher's responsibility for designing an effective instructional program for each child. Rather, cross-age tutoring becomes yet another means to reinforce material for children.

They point out that while not every child with an identified learning need is a candidate to be taught by a cross-age tutor, most students would benefit if the learning situation is appropriately designed. While peer tutoring can be instituted on the teacher's own initiative in her or his classroom, cross-age tutoring, since it involves children from different age groups, requires modifications in school procedures and the support of the principal. Generally, parents of both groups of students are involved in the planning.

Often, the difference in success or failure depends upon the planning. The details to be worked out between the teachers include: 1) where and when the tutoring will take place, 2) which students will be involved and how they will be selected and trained, 3) what material will be used for the tutoring and how it will be prepared, and 4) who will supervise and evaluate the work of the tutors. While in some cross-age tutoring designs the entire classes are involved, in most models only some of the students participate. Generally, only a few tutors at a time will be at work, and most often, tutoring takes place in the classroom of the tutees or in an adjacent area. Usually, tutors are given materials prepared by the teacher of the younger students, generally drawn from the tutee's regular classroom program. The progress of the tutee is most often recorded on simple forms by the tutor.

In cross-age tutoring, tutor training is essential. While it may vary with the subject area in which the tutoring will take place, the types of children to be tutored, and the measurement systems used to assess tutee achievements, it usually will address the following topics: information about the program and the tutor's responsibilities, lesson structure and teaching procedures, measurement and record-keeping procedures, and personal behavior. Training should not be so protracted as to dull the tutors enthusiasm to get on with the tutoring. Generally, three or four tutor training sessions, with careful monitoring and debriefing opportunities during the first weeks of program implementation, are sufficient.

Learning through Teaching Benefits   In cross-age tutoring programs where the focus is on tutor learning as well as tutee learning (learning through teaching), teachers may consider multiple factors in student selection and program design. For example, in selecting tutors, rather than the emphasis being on what the student knows, it is more on what he or she needs to learn. One model may involve students reading below grade level as tutors for students who are reading at a lower grade level. Another alternative would be to involve the entire class of older students as tutors, selecting different tutees depending upon the capabilities of the tutors.

Once the tutors and tutees are selected, there is the question regarding the basis of pairing. The major factor in the pairing is that a level of rapport develop between the students. In this way, the tutoring can go forward, and the sense of confidence on the part of the tutor can develop.

While some training is essential, the amount has varied in different programs. The National Commission on Resources for Youth design, which emphasized maintaining the child's "naturalness," provided little preservice training, while other programs have had lengthier sessions. In any case, it is essential that the tutors be prepared for what it is they are expected to do, particularly in how to present material, how to support correct answers and respond to errors, and the nature of expected personal behavior. In order to strengthen the learning through teaching benefit, tutors should have an opportunity, usually weekly, to meet together with a teacher to review and process their tutoring work. As a result, they can gain the benefits of attending to the learning process, considering alternative approaches for presenting material, reflecting upon another's learning, and then translating that to their own learning. Teachers of such groups play more of the role of facilitator for the tutors than didactic teacher of them.

Students Classified as Having Disabilities as Tutors

Generally, students classified as having disabilities are seen as in need of help, that is, as tutees. Rarely, however, are they viewed as candidates to give help, that is, to be tutors. Sometimes this is called "reverse role tutoring."

As part of a larger school redesign project in a Central Harlem school, personnel conducted a small program where students with disabilities were tutors of students without disabilities. The program was undertaken in the mid-1970s by the New Careers Training Laboratory, then at Queens College and now a part of The Graduate School and University Center, The City University of New York. Both tutors and tutees gained academic, behavioral, and social skills.

A decade later, researchers at Brigham Young University conducted a 3 year research project, *Handicapped Children as Tutors* (1984). Four different tutoring configurations were used: 1) children with handicaps (classified as mentally retarded and learning disabled) tutored their peers without handicaps in sign language, 2) children with handicaps (classified as behaviorally handicapped and learning disabled) tutored younger children without handicaps in reading, 3) children with handicaps (classified as behaviorally handicapped and learning disabled) tutored younger children with handicaps (classified with similar disabilities) in reading, and 4) children with handicaps tutored peers with handicaps (with both groups being classified as behaviorally handicapped and learning disabled) in reading. Research findings on the project are as follows:

> With appropriate training and supervision, handicapped students can function effectively as tutors. They can learn to demonstrate instructional content, monitor tutee performance, and give appropriate feedback.
> Both tutors and tutees experience growth in the topic tutored.
> Socially isolated handicapped students often experience increased social acceptance as a result of tutoring nonhandicapped peers.
> Parents, teachers, and tutees perceive reverse-role tutoring as an effective intervention strategy in special education. (*Handicapped Children As Tutors* 1984, pp. 161–163)

A Peer-Centered School District

Community School District 2, in New York City, has committed to making "[p]eer approaches—peer tutoring, cooperative learning, children helping children—a way of life. . ." (Peer Action, 1988). Working in cooperation with the Peer Research Laboratory, the Center for Advanced Study in Education, The Graduate School and University Center, the City University of New York, the district has developed a series of peer approaches at 19 of its schools. Most interesting, in addition to the fact of the district's commitment to the program and its use of local funds to support it, is the variety of peer approaches used. For example:

Third graders tutor each other in spelling
Fifth graders tutor second graders in science
Sixth graders read to and with kindergarten children
Sixth graders tutor second graders who in turn tutor kindergarten children
Seventh graders are tutored by eighth and ninth graders

Each school has adapted its own focus. In a few, tutoring is primarily a remedial activity; in others, both tutors and tutees are volunteers. In others, tutoring is an integral part of the basic class activity. Overall, there is a commitment to having all children play both the tutor and tutee role.

A new project at two junior high schools will use peer activities to deliver substance abuse prevention and sexuality awareness education.

An elementary school in Chinatown is being developed as an entirely peer-centered school, as well as a training base for the district as a whole. In the collaboration, the central activities of the university involve teacher training and program research, while day-to-day operation is under the leadership of a district coordinator of tutoring programs.

CONCLUSION

While specific to the tutoring designs that they have studied, Jenkins and Jenkins (1987) offer the following summary of the components of successful peer tutoring programs:

> Tutoring proceeds smoothly when tutors have a highly structured and carefully prescribed lesson format.
> Classroom teachers define objectives in terms of their classroom curriculums and evaluate students' competence in relation to success or failure in those materials.
> Teachers select tutoring content carefully and ensure that students master it.
> Frequency and duration of tutoring lessons are given careful consideration.
> Systematic training is essential to sustain an effective tutoring program.
> A positive class climate and active supervision are significant factors in tutoring programs.
> Daily measurement of students' progress is essential. (pp. 65,f.)

In a discussion of tutoring programs, the *Harvard Education Letter* emphasized the following factors as important in creating a good program:

> Training and support, including careful instruction to the student tutors in how to present material, how to applaud success and correct errors, is essential.
> Programs that have brief duration seem to have greater success than those of greater length.
> Mathematics offers a subject of special potential for tutoring. ("Big Kids Teach Little Kids," 1987, pp. 3,f)

Tutoring programs are valuable for students in terms of contemporary research about effective instructional practices, as part of a larger effort to restructure schools as learning communities, in promoting heightened respect for the capabilities of all students (including those considered "at risk"), and as part of the broader societal efforts to promote inclusion and integration. They put the student at the center of the schooling enterprise, not only as the intended beneficiary of education but as the key agent of its achievement.

REFERENCES

Allen, V.L. (1976). *Children as teachers.* New York: Academic Press.

Big kids teach little kids: What we know about cross-aged tutoring. (1987). *Harvard Education Letter, 3*(2), 1–4.

Brophy, J. (1986). Teacher influences on student achievement. *American Psychologist, 41,*(10), 1069–1077.

Brown, A.L., & Campione, J.C. (1986). Psychological theory and the study of learning disabilities. *American Psychologist, 41*(10), 1059–1068.

Cloward, R. (1967). Studies in tutoring. *The Journal of Experimental Education, 36* (1), 14–25.

Cohen, P.A., Kulik, J.A., & Kulik, C.C. (1982). Educational outcomes of tutoring. *American Educational Research Journal, 19,* 237–248.

Comenius, J.A. (1921). *The great didactic.* London: A. and C. Black, Ltd.

Damon, W. (1984). Peer education: The untapped potential. *Journal of Applied Developmental Psychology, 5,* 331–343.

Featherstone, J. (1987). Good teaching. *Instructor,* 4–6, 36.

Gartner, A., Kohler, M.C., & Riessman, F. (1971). *Children teach children: Learning through teaching.* New York: Harper & Row.

Gartner, A., & Lipsky, D. (1987). Beyond special education. *Harvard Educational Review, 57*(4), 367–395.

Goodlad, J.I. (1984). *A place called school: Prospects for the future.* New York: McGraw-Hill.

Greenwood, C.R., Maheady, L., & Carta, J.J. (in press). In G. Stoner, M.H. Shinn, & H.M. Walker (Eds.), *Interventions for achievement and behavior problems.* Washington, DC: National Association of School Psychologists.

Hall, R.V., Delquardi, J., Greenwood, C.R., & Thurston, L. (1982). The importance of opportunity to respond in children's academic success. In E. Edgar, N. Haring, J. Jenkins, & C. Pious (Eds.), *Mentally handicapped children: Education and training* (pp. 107–140). Baltimore: University Park Press.

Handicapped children as tutors. (1984). Salt Lake City, UT: David O. McKay Institute of Education, Brigham Young University.

Hedin, D. (1986). *Students as teachers: A tool for improving school climate and productivity.* A paper prepared for the task force on Teaching as a Profession, Carnegie Forum on Education and the Economy, New York.

Jenkins, J.R., & Jenkins, L.M. (1981). *Cross age and peer tutoring: Help for children with learning problems.* Reston, VA: The Council for Exceptional Children.

Jenkins, J.R., & Jenkins, L.M. (1987). Making peer tutoring work. *Educational Leadership,* 64–68.

Johnson, D.W., & Johnson, R.T. (1984). *Circles of learning: Cooperation in the classroom.* Washington, DC: Association for Supervision and Curriculum Development.

Levin, H. (1984). Lost and cost: Effectiveness of computer assisted instructions. Stanford, CA: California Institute for Research on Educational Finance and Governance.

Lippitt, P., & Lohman, J.E. (1965). Cross-age relationships: An educational resource. *Children, 12*(3), 113–117.

Lipsky, D.K., & Gartner, A. (1987). Capable of achievement and worthy of respect: Education of the handicapped as if they were full fledged human beings. *Exceptional Children, 54*(1), 69–76.

Lipsky, D.K., & Gartner, A. (Eds.). (1989). *Beyond separate education: Quality education for all.* Baltimore: Paul H. Brookes Publishing Co.

Madden, N.A., & Slavin, R.E. (1987). Effective pull-out programs for students at risk. Baltimore: The John Hopkins University, Center for Research on Elementary and Middle Schools.

Maheady, L., & Harper, G.F. (1987). A classwide peer tutoring program to improve the spelling test performance of low income, third- and fourth-grade students. *Education and Treatment of Children, 10*(2), 120–133.

Maheady, L., Harper, G.F., & Sacca, M.K. (1986). *Classwide student tutoring teams: Teacher's manual.* East Lansing, MI: Michigan State University.

Maheady, L., & Pernell, G. (1987). Opportunity to respond and peer-mediated instruction: Implications for teachers of the emotionally handicapped. *Benchmark, 2,* 7–12.

Maheady, L., Sacca, M.K., & Harper, G.F. (1987). Classwide student tutoring teams: The effect of peer mediated instruction on the academic performance of secondary mainstreamed students. *The Journal of Special Education, 21*(3), 107–121.

Maheady, L., Sacca, M.K., & Harper, G.F. (1988). Classwide peer tutoring with mildly handicapped high school students. *Exceptional Children, 55*(1), 52–59.

Maher, C. (1986). Direct replication of a cross-age tutoring program involving handicapped adolescents and children. *School Psychology Review, 15*(1), 53–56.

Melaragno, R.J., & Newmark, G. (no date). *Tutorial community project: Report on the second year.* Los Angeles: System Development Corporation.

Osguthorpe, R.T., & Scruggs, T.E. (1986). Special education students as tutors: A review and analysis. *Remedial and Special Education, 7*(4), 15–26.

Peer action. (1988). *The Peer Tutor, 1*(1), 1.

Rosenshine, B., & Stevens, R. (1986). Teaching functions. In M.C. Wittrock (Ed.), *Handbook on research on teaching* (pp. 376–391). New York: Macmillan.

Slavin, R.E. (1987a). Ability grouping and student achievement in elementary school: A best evidence synthesis. *Review of Educational Research, 57,* 293–336.

Slavin, R.E. (1987b). Cooperative learning and the cooperative school. *Educational Leadership,* 7–13.

Slavin, R.E., Sharan, S., Kagan, S., Lazarowitz, R.H., Webb, C.W., & Schmuck, R. (Eds.). (1985). *Learning to cooperate: Cooperating to learn.* New York, Plenum Press.

Smith, P.K. (1983). *Tutoring: A national perspective.* (ERIC Document No. ED 228722).

Stainback, S.B., & Stainback, W.C. (1989). Classroom organization for diversity among students. In D. Biklen, D. Ferguson, & A. Ford (Eds.), *Schooling and disability* (pp. 195–207). Chicago: University of Chicago Press.

Stainback, S.B., Stainback, W., & Hatcher, L. (1983). Handicapped peers involvement in the education of severely handicapped students. *Journal of The Association for Persons with Severe Handicaps, 8*(1), 39–42.

Strain, P.S. (Ed.). (1981). *The utilization of classroom peers as behavior change agents.* New York: Plenum Press.

Thelen, H. (1967, November). *The humane person defined.* Paper presented at the Secondary Education Leadership Conference, St. Louis, MO.

Thorkildsen, T. (1989). Justice in the classroom: The student's view. *Child Development, 60*(2).

U.S. Department of Education. (1986). *What works: Research about teaching and learning.* Washington, DC: Author.

Wright, B. (1960). Should children teach? *Elementary School Journal, 60*(7), 349–367.

Terri Vandercook
Jennifer York

7

A Team
Approach to Program
Development and Support

What is the purpose of education? What are the available learning opportunities and desired outcomes of participation in public schools? How is an educational system deemed effective? These questions have many responses that can be found in almost any text on education and in school district mission statements and handbooks specifying learner outcomes. In the growing literature on effective schools, one of the identified difficulties in determining whether or not a school is effective lies in the differing expectations that parents, researchers, teachers, and numerous other constituents have for schools or, at least, the different degrees of emphasis placed on various expectations. Despite a lack of uniform agreement, Raiche (1983) has identified the following areas of achievement as ones that most people would promote to some degree for all students: basic skills, higher order thinking and reasoning, psychological development, development of social

Development of this paper was supported in part by the Minnesota Integrated Education Technical Assistance Project (Grant No. 37010-57613) and the Least Restrictive Environment Project (Grant No. G008630347-88). The opinions expressed herein do not necessarily reflect the position or policy of the Minnesota Department of Education or the U.S. Department of Education and no official endorsement should be inferred.

We wish to acknowledge Mary and the circle of caring people associated with Lincoln Elementary School in Fairmont, Minnesota, who participated in her MAPS planning session. They fill us with hope! Also, we thank our colleagues, Sue Wolff, Jan Menke, and Cathy Macdonald, for their assistance in developing the "Regular Classroom Integration Checklist."

95

skills, and vocational preparation. In many states, these major areas of achievement are reflected in legislation. In Minnesota, for example, the legislatively declared purpose of public education reads as follows:

> . . . the purpose of public education in Minnesota is to help all individuals acquire knowledge, skills, and positive attitudes toward self and others that will enable them to solve problems, think creatively, continue learning, and develop maximum potential for leading productive, fulfilling lives in a complex and changing society. (Minnesota Statutes Section, 1988)

This statement applies to all individuals receiving a public education. To a certain extent the curriculum for each individual is tailored, dependent upon his or her needs, interests, and future plans upon graduation. The supports required by individual students to meet identified needs vary also. Some students will require more extensive tailoring and individualized supports than others in order to achieve the educational outcome of community membership and participation. Given the varied and complex needs of some students, educational programs must be carefully designed and implemented by a team of individuals, including both adults and students. The purpose of this chapter is to provide practical teamwork strategies for including students with unique needs in regular school life. Specific emphasis is placed on the invaluable role of same-age peers in program design and implementation and on the appropriate use of support personnel in regular classes. First, general team functions and roles are delineated. Second, a specific team planning process is described and an example provided. Third, strategies for facilitating inclusion in regular classes are discussed.

COLLABORATIVE TEAMWORK

The development of an individualized program for many children, including those with intensive, multiple needs requires the collaboration of a variety of people, including adults and students. Each team member contributes unique perspective and expertise. Together, these contributions provide the information to identify strengths and needs, to analyze performance difficulties, and to design and implement effective curricular and instructional strategies. Collaboration among team members is the key to successful inclusion of all students in a regular class. Collaboration involves a nonhierarchical relationship in which all team members are seen as equal contributors, each adding his or her own expertise or experience to the problem-solving process (Mittler, Mittler, & McConachie, 1987; Sileo, Rude, & Luckner, 1988; Zins, Curtis, Graden, & Ponti, 1988).

In addition to the benefits of collaboration due to the varied perspectives and contributions of individual team members, effective teams yield the benefits of belonging, support, and power. All adults and children have a basic need to belong and to feel that they have some power (Brandt, 1988). In an interview with Glasser conducted by Brandt (1988), Glasser asserted that the need for belonging is supported by the fact that when children are asked what the best part of school is, they invariably respond, "my friends." Glasser felt that students and teachers need to understand that everyone has a built-in need for friendship and belonging and opportunities for satisfying that need should occur as a planned part of learning. Glasser defined the need for power as a continuing sense that "I have some power; I'm somebody; people pay attention to me" (Brandt, 1988, p. 39). At a minimum this means that somebody listens to you. At the next level, an increased sense of power and satisfaction occurs when an individual listens and acknowledges you are right. The ultimate satisfaction and sense of power occurs when a person listens and sometimes concludes that your way is better than his or hers and it should be done your way. Students are not the only ones in the schools who are lacking a sense of belonging and power. Teachers also report a loss of control and a sense that their participation in developing effective schools is not highly valued (Maloy & Fischetti, 1985; Van Meter & Scollay, 1984; Walter & Glenn, 1986). Two organizational structures of the traditional American school that may lead to teachers feeling lonely and powerless are the implicit expectations that teachers work alone and that administrators exercise virtual autonomy in making decisions (Villa & Thousand, 1988).

Glasser (1986) suggested the use of learning teams as a strategy for meeting the needs of belonging and power. In a good team, the need for belonging is satisfied as a sense of caring is developed; the need for power is satisfied when individuals have opportunities to be listened to and affirmed, and when the effect of what he or she could do alone is multiplied. The learning teams that Glasser refers to is his term for the concept of cooperative learning espoused and supported as an effective instructional strategy by the research of Johnson and Johnson (1981); Johnson and Johnson (1987a); Johnson, Johnson, and Maruyama (1983); and Slavin (1977, 1987b). The use of collaborative teaming in the development of educational programs can also lead to a sense of support and empowerment for all team members (Johnson & Johnson, 1987b; Slavin, 1987a).

A final benefit of collaborative teamwork is that of group problem solving. A group has been defined as "a collection of individuals who join together to achieve a goal . . . individuals are not a group unless they are trying to achieve a mutual goal" (Johnson & Johnson, 1987a, p. 6). Use of group problem solving as opposed to individual efforts can yield many benefits. Kruger (1988) put forth several hypotheses in support of group efforts to address complex issues: 1) greater interest in the problem stimulated by group membership, 2) a summative effort of individual contributions, 3) the capacity to recognize and reject poorly conceived solutions, and 4) the availability of greater information. Not only do group efforts frequently yield better and more sustained outcomes, but many people find that the group interaction itself is reinforcing and feel supported within a group construct as opposed to when working in isolation. Groups can provide the supportive environment conducive to the new learning involved in change. In sum, collaborative teamwork can yield many benefits for adults and children by providing a rich forum of varied perspectives and expertise, by fulfilling the needs for belonging and power, and by employing group problem-solving strategies.

Team Members and Roles

The expansion of the planning team beyond the traditional partnership of the classroom teacher and the student's parents is sometimes necessary because no one or two people have the knowledge or skill to meet the varied and complex needs of some students. The composition of the team will depend on the student's needs but typically would include the student, his or her parents or guardians, an administrator or a designee, the classroom teacher, a support teacher with specialized training in curricular and instructional adaptations, and personnel from any related services that are required by the individual student. The inclusion of same-age peers on individual student planning teams is a fairly new practice with benefits that are supported by preliminary data (DiFerdinando, 1987; Scagliotti, 1987; Vandercook, York, & Forest, 1989; Villa & Thousand, 1988). Many adult team members recognize the invaluable contributions that can be made by classmates in terms of identifying age-appropriate needs and providing support throughout the school day. Discussed below are the primary contributions of each team member in developing and supporting an educational program that includes students with high needs in typical school and community environments.

Individual Student In developing an educational program in which an individual student is invested and one based on his or her interests, strengths, and needs, the active participation of the individual student should be encouraged and supported. Sometimes just the presence of the student at meetings assists other team members to remain focused upon the student's needs and sensitive to the importance of the task at hand. The presence of the student serves as a constant reminder that the ability and willingness of the team to problem solve creatively and collaborate will impact the quality of a person's life and that the meeting of a team is not simply an academic exercise or bureaucratic requirement. The extent and manner of the student's participation will vary. Some students can communicate their educational interests and challenges and will be able to make suggestions for addressing social and curricular needs at school. Others may not be able to communicate directly ideas in the format of a group meeting but may be able to communicate in indirect ways by their behavior in different situations. Team members who know the student well and observe him or her in different activities and environments can communicate behaviors displayed that may be indicative of educational strengths, challenges, and needs. The peers of the student will be particularly helpful in this regard.

Parents and Family Members of the Individual Student Parents and other close family members are key members of the team. They communicate not only a picture of the life of the student thus far, but also a vision of their hopes for the student's future. The involvement of family members in addition to parents will be unique for each student. For some, grandparents may be involved in their lives; for others, perhaps a sibling. Professionals will come and go in a student's life, but family members are a constant and have a long-term investment in the quality of life the child is experiencing. Integral involvement of family members can assist in achieving continuity of programming over time. Educational priorities identified by family members, therefore, should receive primary consideration.

Classroom Teacher The classroom teacher has several primary functions, including: 1) to view the individual as a member of the class rather than as a visitor, 2) to contribute information about the classroom curriculum, instructional strategies, management techniques, routines, and rules, 3) to work collaboratively with support personnel, family members, and peers in developing the educational program and in including the individual with his or her peers in typical classroom activities and routines, and 4) to provide a model of appropriate interaction and communication with the student, including recognition and acknowledgement of the positive attributes and contributions of the individual. The classroom teacher sets the expectation for acceptance and inclusion by focusing on what the student can do instead of on areas of difficulty. This mindset leads to building upon an individual's strengths, a proactive and effective educational strategy. Biklen, Corrigan, and Quick (1989) provided some excellent examples of teachers modeling techniques for bringing recognition to a student's unique educational needs, effectively communicating with a student who is nonverbal, and engaging in problem-solving/conflict resolution strategies with a student who is acting out in the classroom.

Support Personnel   The support teacher with training in curricular and instructional adaptations and related services personnel with training in specific functioning areas (e.g., motor, vision, hearing) assume primary responsibility for adapting curriculum, materials, equipment, or instructional strategies such that the educational needs of the student can be met in the context of typical school and community environments. Support from personnel with specialized training could range from primarily consultation with the classroom teacher to a combination of consultation and direct intervention with the student. If the team decides that direct instruction by a professional support person is necessary, in most situations that instruction should occur in regular class settings and other typical school and community environments. In order to develop a new educational system in which all students are assisted to learn in regular class settings (Sapon-Shevin, 1988), the physical and conceptual isolation in which many professionals with specialized training have operated must end (Spodek, 1982). This requires personnel to assist in identifying needs based on student performance in instructional environments and activities (e.g., regular classes) and strategies for implementation in those settings (Giangreco, York, & Rainforth, 1989; York, Rainforth, & Dunn, in press; York, Rainforth, & Wiemann, 1988).

Another potential team member is a paraprofessional support person. Some students with high needs require, at least initially, a support person to be present in the regular class. The role of the support person in class is discussed in greater detail in the last section of this chapter. If it is decided that a support person is required to facilitate inclusion, this person must collaborate as a member of the team.

Building Principal   As is true of the classroom teacher, one of the most important roles of the principal is to model an accepting and welcoming attitude toward all students in the school, conveying the message that each educator and student is valued for his or her unique contribution to the school community. Another critical role of the building principal is to demonstrate support of collaborative teaming by setting an expectation that teachers will collaborate, providing incentives for collaboration, promoting training on efficient team planning, and arranging for the time necessary to plan (Villa & Thousand, 1988; Zins et al., 1988). "The ultimate use of power should be to empower others" (Brandt, 1988, p. 45). This is operationalized when administrators support team recommendations by working with the team to provide the identified resource support.

Classmates of the Individual Student   Classmates are proving to be valuable members of individual educational planning teams. This should not come as a surprise given that a major function of the team is to design strategies to support students with high needs in regular classes and other school environments. Classmates are the experts on the formal and the informal demands and opportunities of regular school life. They provide a fresh perspective on the needs of their classmates related to involvement in typical school environments and activities. Classmates also play a key role in supporting one another throughout their years in public school.

As contributing members of individual educational planning teams, classmates provide the evidence that students with high needs can be accepted, valued, and contributing members of the school community. Many adults grew up in schools and communities that separated individuals who had learning needs or styles different from the norm. This history of separation prevented many from acquiring the attitudes, values, and skills necessary to openly accept and support all individuals in the mainstream of school and community life or the capacity to envision that possibility. This phenomenon is illustrated by the fact that the most frequently heard comment by adults who either have observed an inclusive school community or are involved in creating one is some variation of: "I can't believe the kids, they are great, so accepting and so natural in providing support" (Hanline & Halvorsen, 1989). They go on to marvel at how positively the child responds to classmates, oftentimes more quickly and more agreeably than to adults.

There are many examples of the power of peers in the education of students with high needs (Forest, 1986, 1987; Perske, 1988; Ruttiman, 1988; Strully & Strully, 1985; Vandercook, Fleetham, Sinclair, & Rice Tetlie, 1988). The positive contributions of classmates are acclaimed also in teacher's lounges and living rooms throughout the United States and Canada as more school communities welcome and include all children. To illustrate, the authors share just a few stories about Mary and her classmates. Mary is a third grader who had been educated in a special education classroom for children with the label of severe disabilities until the 1988–1989 school year. Mary began the school year moving very slowly. As a result she was always a good 10 feet behind her classmates as they moved to other settings in the building. With a little coaching from her friends, she has learned to keep up. Once, Mary attempted to make her way to the head of the line before the class headed out for recess. One of her classmates caught her in the act and matter-of-factly explained to her that she could not "cut" and would have to go the end of the line. He pointed to the correct place and she amicably moved to that spot. Mary has also learned the generalized problem-solving skill of watching others around her as a strategy for figuring out what she needs to do. Watching others to determine expected behavior is an important adaptive skill for everyone (Snyder, Apolloni, & Cooke, 1977). At the beginning of the school year when

Mary did not know what to do, she would sit and do nothing and wait for someone to direct her. Now she watches others, and if she needs help, she will ask for it. The acquisition of these skills alone will have a large impact on the adaptive functioning of Mary in current and future environments.

A final benefit of the involvement of classmates on planning teams is that classmates potentially provide consistency across school years. Many classmates remain in the same class as the individual or at least in the same school. The maintenance of these relationships across the years is not only beneficial for the students, but for the adults on the team also. The adult team members, many of whom vary from year to year, profit by having people (i.e., classmates) on the team who know the individual well. In a research study conducted by Turnbull and Bronicki (1989), Turnbull discussed how some adults say they cannot handle Kevin (a 15-year old boy with severe mental retardation who requires dialysis five times a day). Based on the results of her study, she concluded, "They probably could if someone would help them, because the results of my science project show that children can learn what to do and be comfortable. I think everyone can be Kevin's friend. It just takes a little time" (p. 65). Classmates are in a position to provide assistance to new adults on the team, helping them "learn what to do and be comfortable."

Assumptions of Collaborative Educational Teamwork

There have been two major innovations introduced in the individualized planning process. The first innovation is the inclusion and contribution of family and friends in educational planning as evidenced earlier when family members and friends were identified as essential team members. Second, planning sessions are increasingly focused on a vision or image of the individual as a valued, contributing member of the community. From the vision of full inclusion, plans are made on how to realize that vision. This positive and inclusive orientation is in direct contrast to models of planning based on a deficit orientation (Hammill & Bartel, 1975; Kirk, 1972; Salvia & Ysseldyke, 1985).

Several formalized planning processes have been developed that require the participation of family members and friends and base planning upon an assumption that all individuals can be assisted and supported to be fully included in regular school and community life. The "Life-Style Planning" process (O'Brien, 1987; O'Brien & Lyle, 1987) and the "Personal Futures Planning" process (Mount, 1987; Mount & Zwernik, 1988) have been most frequently used with adults. A third process entitled the "McGill Action Planning System" (MAPS) (Forest & Lusthaus, 1987) has been used primarily with school-age children and focuses on their inclusion, participation, and learning in regular education classes and other typical school settings. MAPS provides a planning framework for operationalizing the assertion that each student belongs (Flynn & Kowalczyk-McPhee, 1989; Hanson, 1987). Common to each of these new approaches to individual planning are five assumptions.

Inclusion or Integration   The first assumption asserts that all individuals should be educated in typical school and community environments, including regular classes, and should be provided with the supports necessary to learn and function within these settings successfully. The majority of instruction for elementary aged students should occur in regular classes whereas secondary aged students should receive instruction in both regular education and general community environments (Ford & Davern, 1989; York & Vandercook, 1989). Inclusion is important for two fundamental reasons: 1) each person has a basic need to belong (Brandt, 1988), and 2) it is to everyone's benefit to create schools that welcome and support all individuals as valued members. Diversity enriches "the experience of learning for the children and for those who teach them" (Safford, 1989, p. 11).

Individualization   The assumption of individualization recognizes that each student has unique needs, interests, and abilities and that the educational plan developed for each person should reflect these attributes. The supports required (e.g., adaptations of curricular goals or materials or personal assistance) are individualized also.

Teamwork and Collaboration   Considerable attention is given to the importance of collaborative teamwork in the first section of this chapter and throughout the book. The MAPS process (described in the next section) is an example of a planning strategy that capitalizes on the creativity, perspectives, and experiences of both children and adults who know and care about the individual for whom the planning is to occur.

Flexibility   Flexibility underlies all successful planning efforts and acknowledges that people and environments are not static but continually change and grow. Ongoing problem solving and planning will be necessary as the individual acquires new skills and as members of the school community learn how to better include, teach, and support all children in the school. For example, prior to full inclusion in regular school life, the team can only project needs and adaptations. It is only after the child is actually included in regular school life that performance-based programming decisions can be made.

Natural Supports   A final and unifying assumption of individualized planning is the use of natural supports. Natural supports in the classroom are considered to be the classroom teacher and classmates in that they are the people typically present. Their involvement must be recruited for at least two reasons (York & Vandercook, 1989). First, classmates and the regular education teacher know about the demands, expectations, and opportunities in a regular class. They are in the best position to make these known to another student and to reinforce behavior changes and accommodations made by a student. Second, education and human service systems do not have and will not have the capacity to provide a paid service provider for every individual who needs support in every integrated school, community, and work environment. To some extent, all people are dependent on others around them. As Lynch (1989) stated, "It is a mistake to have independence as a goal because we can not survive without others. We thrive on interdependence, this is community" (p. 1). By promoting the involvement of classmates as natural supports, students with high needs will have a greater probability of inclusion in future community environments also.

MAPS—A COLLABORATIVE TEAMWORK STRATEGY

Team members involved in MAPS planning were delineated previously (see Team Member Roles section). An additional person may be identified to serve as the facilitator. As a point that bears emphasis, the involvement of classmates who know and care about the individual is a unique and essential feature of the MAPS process. Since many students have a history of education in segregated classes, MAPS should not be conducted until the individual has been a member of the class long enough to get to know some of the classmates and for the classmates to get to know the individual. The classmates who participate in the MAPS planning are typically identified by the classroom teacher based upon interest as demonstrated by the amount of interaction the students have with one another. At least two, and preferably three to five classmates, participate in the planning. For kindergarten and first grade children, participation may be limited to select questions, and planning sessions may be broken down to three 1 hour sessions versus two 1½ hour time blocks. Planning usually occurs in one or two sessions and approximately 3 hours should be designated for working through the process.

The MAPS Process

The following overview is reprinted by permission from Vandercook et al. (1989, pp. 207–208):

Participants are arranged in a half-circle with the facilitator positioned at the open end of the circle. The information and ideas generated during the process are recorded on large chart paper which serves as a communication check during the session and as a permanent record when the planning is finished. The facilitator can also serve the role of recorder or an additional person can serve in that capacity. The facilitator needs to be a person who is committed to building an integrated school community in which the individual is valued and provided the support necessary to be a member of the class with same-age peers. The facilitator needs good listening skills and an ability to facilitate interaction among team members in such a way that they challenge one another to broaden their visions of community, and must also make practical suggestions regarding the support and adaptations necessary to meet the needs of the individual in regular class settings and other typical school and nonschool environments. The facilitator must be comfortable interacting with both the adults and the children and able to solicit input from all participants. The best planning will occur for the individual when input is gathered from all participants and conversation is not dominated by a select few. The importance of *each* person's contribution should be clearly communicated by the facilitator before the planning begins. Following are the seven key questions and a final reflection which comprise the MAPS process.

What Is the Individual's History?   Aside from the individual for whom the planning is occurring, family members are the most important members of the circle because they typically know the individual better than anyone else. Because of this, family members, and the individual to the greatest extent possible, are asked to spend a few minutes talking about the individual's history, including some of the key milestones in the person's life.

What Is Your Dream for the Individual?   The question, "What is your dream for the individual?" is intended to get people to think about their vision for the individual's future. They are encouraged to think about what they want and what they think the person would want for his or her future. This vision should not be based solely on current realities. Dreams can become reality if there is a shared vision and commitment to strive for that vision. In the realm of dreams, the only certainty is that if you cannot dream it, you will not achieve it. The dream question forces the team to think about the direction in which the individual is heading. This allows concrete plans to be made for realizing the vision. This is not to say, however, that the vision or the plans for achieving the dream are set in concrete. The visions and resulting expectations will be challenged continually as more is learned about how to facilitate inclusion in the school community and as positive outcomes are realized. Depending upon the age of the individual, it may be difficult to think about the dream for the individual as an adult. If that is a problem, team members can be encouraged to think about the person 5 years from the present time or perhaps when the individual is in high school. The important factor is not how far into the future the vision projects, but simply that a dream exists for an integrated future, thereby providing direction and goals to strive toward.

What Is Your Nightmare? The question, "What is your nightmare?" is a difficult question to ask the parents of any child, yet an extremely important one. Parents frequently relate the nightmare as a vision of their child being alone. The nightmare presents the situation that the members of the individual's team and others who care for him or her must work very hard to keep this from happening.

Who Is the Individual? Everyone in the circle participates in responding to the question, "Who is the individual?" The participants are asked to think of words that describe the individual (i.e., what comes to mind when they think of the person?) There are no right or wrong words. Participants take turns going around the circle until all thoughts have been expressed. Participants can pass if nothing comes to mind when it is their turn to supply a descriptor. When the list is complete, the facilitator asks certain people to identify the three words from the list that they feel best describe the individual. Frequently, family members and classmates are asked to identify key descriptors.

What Are the Individual's Strengths, Gifts, and Abilities? So often when educational teams get together, they dwell upon the things that the individual cannot do as opposed to identifying and building upon the strengths and abilities of the individual. The facilitator asks the participants to review the list that described the individual as a way to identify some of his or her strengths and unique gifts. In addition, they are instructed to think about what the individual can do, what he or she likes to do, and what he or she does well.

What Are the Individual's Needs? "What are the individual's needs?" is a question that provides an opportunity for all the team members to identify needs from each of their unique perspectives. When the list of needs is complete, family, friends, and educators are asked to prioritize the identified needs.

What Would the Individual's Ideal Day at School Look Like and What Must Be Done to Make It Happen? MAPS is a process that is intended to assist teams to plan for the full inclusion of students who have typically been excluded in regular age-appropriate classes. The framework used in addressing this issue will depend upon what the individual's current day at school looks like. If the schedule of activities for the individual is discrepant from that of his or her peers, initial planning would begin by delineating the schedule of each and, as a team, reviewing the rationale for those differences. For instance, if a student is being sent to a special education classroom for a certain subject such as math, the team should consider whether the individual's needs in math could be addressed in the regular class or in another typical school setting such as the school office or library. The bottom-line question to be asked is, "Does the individual need special, separate space shared only with others who are ascribed similar labels to meet his or her educational needs?" (York & Vandercook, 1989, p. 24). For some students there may not be large discrepancies between their schedule and that of their peers. However, the quality of their involvement may not be adequately meeting their unique needs. This presents a second area for team brainstorming: how is the individual participating in various activities, what educational goals are being addressed, and is the individual's participation in the activity of benefit to them? Planning for the supports needed to achieve successful inclusion must be an overarching question that team members frequently address. One final question for the team to consider in contemplating the ideal day is, "Are the priority needs of the individual able to be addressed in the school community?" As an example, as individuals reach secondary age, some needs may be best addressed via instruction in general community environments and vocational settings outside of the school.

MAPS in a Word   The last request by the facilitator provides an opportunity for feedback specifically related to the process itself and as such, should always be included. The facilitator asks each person to describe, in one word, the MAPS process. The adjectives supplied by team members are usually positive and affirming of the process and the time they have spent planning together. However, this is also an opportunity to share impressions or feelings that may not be completely positive. A classroom teacher once put forth the word "pressure" when asked to describe MAPS in a word and then went on to explain that she considered herself a Type A personality and as a result, was feeling that all of the wonderful ideas generated during the process should be implemented right away. This provided the opportunity for other team members to assure the teacher that it was not their intention for everything to be in place by the end of the week. Together the team immediately prioritized actions to be initiated, identified persons responsible, and established reasonable timelines for implementation.

Mary's MAPS

An example of the MAPS planning process is provided to clarify and enrich the previous description of the process. A more detailed discussion of the MAPS process, including modifications that have been used for secondary age students, can be found in Vandercook et al. (1989). Mary is an 8-year-old child who attends the regular elementary school in her home town. Prior to the 1988–1989 school year, Mary was served in a self-contained special education class in a neighboring community. As part of a school district effectiveness project designed to increase the inclusion of students into their school community, Mary was enrolled in the third grade in her home school this year. Toward the middle of the school year, Mary's educational team participated in the MAPS process in an effort to collaborate more effectively in addressing Mary's needs in typical school activities and environments.

For Mary's MAPS, the team included Mary, her mom (Linda), dad (Mike), three third grade friends (Nick, Sara, Alisha), third grade classroom teacher (Ellie), music teacher (Ray), special education teacher and integration facilitator (Cheryl), speech and language therapist (Bill), teaching assistant (Vonnie), certified occupational therapy assistant (Karen), exercise consultant (Marilyn), and building principal (Gary). The facilitator and the team met after school and into the evening (with a pizza break halfway through) and worked their way through the questions that comprise the MAPS process. The planning session began by having each person in attendance introduce themselves and state their relationship with Mary. Following is a summary of the discussion and information generated related to Mary for each specific question in the MAPS process.

What Is Mary's History? Mary's dad, Mike, identified the members of Mary's family and then continued by sharing some major events in Mary's history. Mary was thought to be progressing normally until age 2. Following a couple of examinations at medical centers, it was communicated to Mary's parents that she had limited intellectual capabilities. Mary began attending a special preschool when she was 3 years old. This school year Mike said the family had really seen Mary "opening up" and acting much more cheerful. He attributed that to Mary's classmates and the modeling they provided. In contrast, Mary's models in the self-contained classroom had been limited and consisted primarily of adults. Mike also related how nice it was for Mary to be in her *home* school.

What Is Your Dream for Mary as an Adult? Mike and Linda's dreams for Mary included that she be as self-sufficient as possible, learn how to speak better and be able to communicate with more people, be happy, and be more active both in and outside of school. Other team members also shared dreams such as friends calling Mary and asking her to go to a movie with them or out for a burger. They also envisioned Mary initiating inclusion with her friends and participating in community education offerings, such as recreation swimming or T-ball, with natural community supports. Increased communication between Mary and her friends and greater participation in general community activities was a consistent theme throughout the dream discussion.

What Is Your Nightmare? Mike and Linda's nightmare was Mary returning to a separate program, apart from her peers; an event they thought would lead to her being alone. Other members of the team also shared some of their nightmares regarding Mary's future—being called a name, retreating into a shell, not developing her full potential, being ignored, and ending up in an institution.

Who Is Mary? Mary's team generated an extensive list of descriptors: neat person, does what she's told, easy going, helpful, third grader, animal lover, warm smile, loves her friends, enjoys her classroom, loving, enjoys the bus, excited, screamer, enjoys Mrs. Anderson, bossy, fun, cute, headstrong, likes babies, follower, shy, stubborn, manipulator, book lover, hearty giggle, easily frightened of things she can't see, likes to eat, and a friend.

What Are Mary's Strengths, Gifts, and Abilities? Mary's planning team identified the following strengths, gifts, and abilities: likes to be read to, likes to eat, likes gym, likes fishing with dad, likes her brother—talks about him a lot—learned to use the public library, likes to play outside (chase boys), likes to laugh, likes to listen to audiotapes, loves outdoors, likes to draw, has a way with animals and with friends, likes to look at pictures, likes to swing, likes art, likes to watch other kids, likes music class, likes to use scissors, likes to have fun, likes to hug, likes her friends, likes to help and is good at following directions, likes being in her reading group, likes to walk, and likes to go home at the end of the day. Reviewing the responses to this and the previous question underscores one of MAPS most valuable features; a focus upon the person's capabilities and an appreciation of his or her unique characteristics. Such a positive orientation assists in designing a hopeful future.

What Are Mary's Needs? The discussion was first opened up for general responses from all of those present. Family, friends, and educators were then asked to identify the needs from the list that they considered priorities. Priority needs identified by family members, friends, and educators are listed in Table 1.

What Would Mary's Ideal Day at School Look Like and What Must Be Done to Make It Happen? Mary's team briefly reviewed and discussed her schedule of activities and that of her third-grade classmates. Based upon that discussion, several recommendations were made. The first recommendation was for the team to identify alternative goals and activities for Mary to engage in while her classmates did independent, quiet seatwork (e.g., taking spelling tests, completing work sheets). The primary concern was that Mary be as productive and learn as much as possible during the school day. The two key questions addressed by the team were: 1) during which activities could Mary work on alternative

Table 1. Mary's priority needs identified by family, friends, and educators

Family	Friends	Educators
Needs directions from classmates as well	Needs responsibility	Needs responsibility
Needs more friends	Needs directions from classmates as well	Needs love
Needs love	Needs more friends	Needs more independence
Needs to learn more appropriate ways of initiating communication	Needs *fun* things	—getting dressed
	Needs teachers to help her	—taking bath
	Needs love	—more communication
Needs positive rein-forcement (to cheer her on when she does something right)	Needs a lot of attention	—running
	Needs to learn more ap-propriate ways of initiat-ing communication	Needs to learn how to say more words
Needs to learn that money has value	Needs goals and guidelines	Needs to respond physically to music—keep the beat and use instruments
Needs to learn how to say more words	Needs positive reinforce-ment (to cheer her on when she does some-thing right)	Needs discipline—consistent expectations
Needs to be in a reg-ular third grade class	Needs more independence —getting dressed —taking bath —more communication —running	
Needs to learn how to write name and address	Needs to learn that money has value	
Needs homework	Needs to learn how to say more words	
	Needs to stay steady when walking	
	Needs to respond physically to music—keep the beat and use instruments	
	Needs to be in a regular third grade class	
	Needs to learn how to write name and address	
	Needs homework	
	Needs discipline—consistent expectations	

goals while maintaining the same format (e.g., individual seatwork) as her classmates?, and 2) during which activities should Mary engage in an alternative activity in the classroom or elsewhere in the school?

The second recommendation was to determine appropriate speech therapy consultative and direct intervention strategies related to Mary's communication needs in her regular class. Much of the discussion centered around communication needs because Mary only uses a few words and has no augmentative system in place to expand her repertoire. The team decided that use of a picture communication system would be explored for Mary. Reading time was identified as a good time for the speech therapist to observe Mary and her interactions with both the teacher and her classmates. During reading, Mary functions in a group (her assigned reading group), with a partner (looks and listens to story tapes with a classmate), and independently (looks at a book or magazine at her desk and practices writing her name). Additional communication development ideas included selecting a "word of the week" that would be communicated to members of Mary's class and others in the school with whom she had frequent contact. The principal suggested that words such as "please" and "thank you" might be good words because there is a strong emphasis on using good manners in the school and because they are expressions that engender positive feelings toward the person using them. Mary would not necessarily learn how to verbalize those words, but could be taught to point to a card with the words written on them or learn the sign language expression for certain words. The team also thought Mary should be assisted to contribute during class sharing time on Monday and Friday.

Finally, the team recommended that efforts to connect Mary with her peers outside of the regular classroom be continued. Arrangements had already been made to get Mary on the regular bus schedule and the team suggested that joining a Girl Scout troop should now be explored.

MAPS in a Word   The last request of the facilitator was to ask everyone to describe in a word what they thought of the MAPS process. The following list of descriptors was generated: creativity, thought-provoking, programmability, helpful, informative, sharing, challenging, collaboration, caring, and encouraging. In closing Mary's MAPS session, the facilitator wrote the following words at the bottom of the last sheet of paper: "No man is an island." These are the words of the title of a song sung by the third-grade class as part of their end of the school day routine. The last stanza of the poem written by John Donne is as follows:

> We need one another,
>   So I will defend
> Each man as my brother,
>   Each man as my friend.

It is the collaboration of those on Mary's team and the connections she is making with those in her home school community that will work to ensure that she not become a person stranded upon an isolated island.

Concluding Thoughts on the MAPS Process

The MAPS process provides a common vision and road map for all team members. Following the MAPS planning, parents have reported a sense of renewed hope in hearing team members share dreams and visions of a life of inclusion for their child. One parent was thrilled to hear the principal describe his child as 1 of 356 important and special children in the school! The fear and hurt expressed by parents in relating their nightmare is poignant and seems to deepen the commitment of all team members to work diligently to avoid its realization. The adults on the team often communicate a sense of relief at having the opportunity to openly communicate their nightmares, their perspective on the student's needs, and their ideas on priorities for creating the "ideal" school day. There is reassurance in acknowledging openly that the "ideal" day will never live up to its name, but rather will always be in a state of evolution as different priorities are targeted over time.

The inclusion of classmates in MAPS sessions consistently receives the largest amount of positive comment. In addition to ideas and offers of support to better connect the student in school activities, numerous opportunities for connecting with classmates outside of school have been suggested and implemented by classmates. Reports of reciprocal home visits, party invitations, and telephone calls are increasing in frequency and graphically illustrating the importance of relationships. When outlining the needs of the individual during the MAPS process it has been peers and siblings who have identified the following needs not typically heard in traditional individual planning meetings: the need for love, more friends, teachers' acceptance, others to know the individual is not helpless, and a good life!

FACILITATING INCLUSION IN REGULAR CLASSES

To the greatest extent possible, supports that are typically available in regular classes (e.g., classmates) should be used if students require individualized adaptations. However, in order for some students to be included in a regular classroom and to have their needs met in that setting, additional adult support may be necessary. When an adult provides physical support to a student in the classroom, a great deal of caution must be exercised to prevent conveying the message that if the student needs help, the support person always will provide the assistance. This can prevent interactions with natural support personnel, build dependence, and prevent skill acquisition by the classmates and classroom teacher. The support person should be viewed as an adaptation to the environment and like all adaptations, should be faded if and when it is appropriate. This is not to say that additional support is not needed but that natural supports exist and should be utilized to the greatest extent appropriate. If needed, the responsibility of the adult who provides additional support is to facilitate the membership, participation, and learning of all students in regular classes and other integrated school settings. To serve effectively in this role, several guidelines are offered.

Guidelines for Facilitating Inclusion

Know Why the Student Is in the Regular Classroom   It is important to know why the student is in the regular classroom and to communicate why to students and fellow professionals. First, in order to support effectively the learning and participation of an individual in a regular class, one must be cognizant of both the overall and the student specific educational goals. Second, the majority of adults and students will have a history of separation from some individuals, particularly those with significant disabilities, and will not automatically understand the rationale for the movement from education in separate environments to education in regular classes. Students are included in regular classes because by growing up and learning together those with disabilities and their peers without disabilities have the opportunity to learn the skills, values, and attitudes necessary for positive interdependence. Through participation in integrated schools and communities, students with and without disabilities can experience the richness of a society that values and includes all its citizens.

Know Why the Additional Support Person Is in the Regular Classroom   It is also important to know why the additional support person is in the regular classroom and to communicate why to students and fellow professionals. This applies to any person who provides additional support to the classroom above that typically available. The reason for his or her presence is to facilitate inclusion and learning in the class. The ultimate goal is to recruit natural supports so that the additional support person can be faded, at least intermittently.

Empower the Student to Be an Active Participant in All Classroom and Other School Activities   Being included in the regular class does not mean that all students in the class have the exact same goals for each learning activity. As an example, when playing a math facts game in the classroom, the questions asked of students could be individualized and might include number recognition for some, addition facts for others, and multiplication facts for still others. The important point is that each child is actively involved in a way that is educationally beneficial for him or her.

Do Things with Instead of for the Individual   When the student needs assistance, do things with instead of for him or her. This is a difficult practice with any child, but especially with a student who has high needs. The tendency is to do the activity or skill for the student rather than to modify the activity and assist the child to participate as independently as possible. Doing for instead of doing with the student may be more expedient in the short run but does not provide the student with an opportunity to acquire skills and become proficient. Team decisions are made regarding how to provide assistance so that active participation is achieved. This practice not only benefits the individual student, but provides a model of interaction for the individual's peers to follow. Sometimes classmates lend too much assistance also.

Include the Student in Conversations and Never Talk about a Student in Front of Him or Her The student should be included in conversations. Furthermore, never talk about the student in front of him or her. This is not to say that it is unacceptable to talk about a student when he or she is present, but just not in a manner that discounts his or her presence and treats the student as if he or she were invisible and incapable of contributing to the conversation. Many students understand to a greater degree than they are able to communicate.

Consider the Age-Appropriate Expectations of Classmates and Treat the Student Similarly It is important to consider the age-appropriate expectations of classmates and treat the student similarly. This item does not refer to academic expectations. The fact that most third graders learn cursive writing does not mean that expectation must be met by each child in order to be considered a member of the third grade. Rather, this guideline refers to the social mores and ways of interacting with a student that are consistent with those used with the same-age peers of a student. Social mores include adhering to the same school and classroom rules, as well as the way that adults interact with children. If the school rules say no running in the hallway and a student who uses a wheelchair is caught racing down the hallway, the consequence should be the same (e.g., go back and try it again, slowly this time). If high school age students are typically referred to as Joe, Sam, and Sue, as opposed to Joey, Sammy, and Susie, then that same practice should be followed with all students.

Provide Ways for Classmates and Teachers to Interact with the Student The additional support person who may spend time in the classroom working directly or indirectly with a student should be a model for classmates and teachers. When a student first becomes a member of a regular class, the support person may know the student better than the classroom teacher or the student's classmates. Demonstrating ways to communicate with the student and setting up situations that require interaction between classmates can help to facilitate interactions so that the student is participating actively.

Know School and Classroom Rules   The support personnel operating in the school community needs to know school and classroom rules and abide and enforce them as any staff person would. The importance of all children being expected to follow the school and classroom rules was discussed previously. This item refers specifically to the importance of support personnel knowing, following, and enforcing school and classroom rules that are in place for both students and staff. Following and enforcing a common set of rules promotes membership in the school community.

Be a Part of the Class by Working with All Students   Although support personnel (professional and paraprofessional) are in the classroom because the unique needs of an individual student require consultation and additional support, it is not necessary for that service to be provided only in a one-on-one fashion. In fact, a group lesson is a much more effective structure in which to teach certain skills. By working with other students, the paraprofessional may make it easier for the classroom teacher to work directly with the student as well. For example, a teaching assistant might give a spelling test to a large group of students in the classroom, thereby freeing the classroom teacher to work with a small group of students (including a student classified as having disabilities) on a new computer program.

Watch Classmate and Teacher Reactions to Disruptive Behaviors by the Student   In facilitating the inclusion and learning of an individual in the regular class, the support person must be sensitive to any behaviors displayed by the student that might disrupt the teaching or the learning taking place in the classroom. Then the support person should respond accordingly and problem solve on the spot. If a student engages in behavior discrepant from that of classmates (e.g., whining or verbally protesting when he or she must physically move from one place to another), the reason for this behavior should be explained to the other class members (e.g., Tim protests when he has to move from his desk to the reading table because it is hard work for him to walk and it is also scary because he has to count on people to do a good job of helping him so that he doesn't fall). Once classmates understand why the discrepant behavior occurs, frequently they can ignore it. In fact, when several students were asked whether the noise of their classmate was disruptive, they responded, "Oh Tim makes those noises because walking is hard for him and kind of scary but he's getting better at walking so someday it won't be so scary." There are times when a student's behavior may be disrupting others and depending upon the situation, the classroom teacher, classmates, or a support person should deal with that behavior in a manner instructive for the individual while at the same time stopping the disruption. In responding to discrepant behaviors, the support person should be cognizant of others' reactions. In many situations, the behavior may be disconcerting to the support person but of seemingly little interest to classmates.

Regular Classroom Integration Checklist

In an effort to operationalize, in an easy to access format, the guidelines for facilitating inclusion in regular classes, the authors and their colleagues developed a checklist (see Figure 1) that delineates components reflective of regular class membership. The checklist has been used by adults on planning teams to assist in identifying ways to include classmates with high needs in regular class activities and routines. The checklist is divided into four sections, each of which questions a different aspect of inclusion. The questions in the first section, "Go With The Flow," are intended to examine whether the student is following the regular sequence of events and routines (i.e., is the student in step with his or her classmates?). The items that ask whether the student enters and exits the classroom at the same time as his or her peers are particularly critical for older students who switch classes regularly. Classes are disrupted when someone always arrives late. Furthermore, if always arriving late, the student is deprived of the opportunity to engage in the all important socializing that takes place right before the bell rings. If it takes a student longer to change classes, arrangements should be made to leave class a few minutes early or to get some help from a friend in moving more quickly between classes.

The second section is entitled, "Acting Cool" and refers to how the student participates in classroom activities. Is he or she actively involved? When necessary, how is assistance provided? An important aspect of every student's social learning is the opportunity to "deal appropriately with helping, being helped, or indicating that no help is needed" (Safford, 1989, p. 312). The point to be emphasized is the need for each student to not only receive assistance, but also to provide it to others. A necessary condition for the successful inclusion of any individual in an educational program is that he or she is able to contribute to the program and the program is able to contribute to the individual (Meisels, 1977).

"Talking Straight" designates the third section that focuses on the communication between a student and his or her classmates and teachers. Interpersonal communication is essential for emotional development (Dupont, 1989) as well as general functioning and participation in the school and general community. For students who communicate in ways other than verbal language, classmates and teachers may need assistance in learning how to communicate using a different system consider whether any changes should be made and what those changes might be. [partial text cut off at top: "...of the blank preceding each item. If the answer to any of the items is 'no' your team may wish to"]

GO WITH THE FLOW:

____ Does the student enter the classroom at the same time as classmates?

____ Is the student positioned so that she or he can see and participate in what is going on?

____ Is the student positioned so that classmates and teachers may easily interact with him or her (e.g., without teacher between the student and his or her classmates, not isolated from classmates)?

____ Does the student engage in classroom activities at the same time as classmates?

____ Does the student make transitions in the classroom at the same time as classmates?

____ Is the student involved in the same activities as his or her classmates?

____ Does the student exit the classroom at the same time as classmates?

ACTING COOL:

____ Is the student actively involved in class activities (e.g., asks or responds to questions, plays a role in group activities)?

____ Is the student encouraged to follow the same classroom and social rules as classmates (e.g., hugs others only when appropriate, stays in seat during instruction)?

____ Is the student given assistance only as necessary (assistance should be faded as soon as possible)?

____ Is assistance provided for the student by classmates (e.g., transitions to other classrooms, within the classroom)?

____ Are classmates encouraged to provide assistance to the student?

____ Are classmates encouraged to ask for assistance from the student?

____ Is assistance provided for the student by classroom teachers?

____ Does the student use the same or similar materials during classroom activities as his or her classmates (e.g., Tom Cruise notebooks, school mascot folders)?

(continued)

117

Figure 1. (continued)

TALKING STRAIGHT:

_____ Does the student have a way to communicate with classmates?

_____ Do classmates know how to communicate with the student?

_____ Does the student greet others in a manner similar to that of his or her classmates?

_____ Does the student socialize with classmates?

_____ Is this facilitated?

_____ Does the student interact with teachers?

_____ Is this facilitated?

_____ Do teachers (e.g., classroom teachers, special education support staff) provide the same type of feedback (e.g., praise, discipline) for the student as for his or her classmates?

_____ If the student uses an alternative communication system do classmates know how to use it?

_____ If the student uses an alternative communication system do teachers know how to use it?

_____ Is the system always available to the student?

LOOKING GOOD:

_____ Is the student given the opportunity to attend to his or her appearance as classmates do (e.g., check appearance in mirror between classes)?

_____ Does the student have accessories which are similar to his or her classmates (e.g., oversize tote bags, friendship bracelets, hair jewelry)?

_____ Is the student dressed similarly to classmates?

_____ Is clothing that's needed for activities age appropriate (e.g., napkins instead of bibs, 'cool' paint shirts)?

_____ Are personal supplies or belongings carried or transported discreetly?

_____ Is the student's equipment (e.g., wheelchair) kept clean?

_____ Given the opportunity (and assistance as needed):

_____ Is the student's hair combed?

_____ Are the student's hands clean and dry?

_____ Does the student change clothing to maintain a neat appearance?

_____ Does the student use chewing gum, breath mints, breath spray?

118

(e.g., communication board, sign language, or facial expressions and gestures).

The last section is titled "Looking Good" and is an acknowledgment of the importance that an individual's appearance plays in the acceptance by classmates (Hallinan, 1983) and adults in the school. Appearance is judged by good personal grooming habits as well as wearing clothes and using accessories that are in style.

The primary use of the checklist is as a tool for facilitating team discussion about inclusion in regular classes. A "y" for yes and an "n" for no are placed in the blank preceding each question. The blank lines following the item are to be used to record examples of compliance or lack of compliance for each item. These brief notes are helpful to the team when they complete the checklist and reexamine the results to determine if there are priority items to address. When using the checklist related to specific students and classes, team decisions are made as to the applicability of individual items on the checklist.

CONCLUSION

As noted at the beginning of this chapter, the purpose of public education is ". . . to develop maximum potential for leading productive, fulfilling lives in a complex and changing society" (Minnesota Statutes Section, 1985). The Minnesota Legislature was quite astute in recognizing that "developing maximum potential" was not only a matter of acquiring knowledge and skills, but also developing a positive attitude toward self and others. This is a key concept precisely because society is so complex and ever changing. Interdependence is a fact of life. Everyone needs one another, each with individual abilities and needs, in order to function in the community and feel a sense of belonging and power. The development of positive attitudes and the recognition of the strengths and value of each individual can only occur when students have the opportunity to grow up together with the expectation and modeling of acceptance and support for each member of the school community.

As school communities become more inclusive, a greater degree of collaboration will necessarily develop. Expanding traditional team planning approaches to include classmates of students in need of assistance and support marks an important point in the evolution of program development and implementation. Presented in this chapter are several strategies intended to capitalize on the involvement of classmates as team members. The classmates and friends of today are the community members, co-workers, and friends of tomorrow. By promoting interdependence among peers in schools today, there is greater hope for more inclusive communities tomorrow.

REFERENCES

Biklen, D., Corrigan, C., & Quick, D. (1989). Beyond obligation: Students' relations with each other in integrated classes. In D.K. Lipsky & A. Gartner (Eds.), *Beyond separate education: Quality education for all* (pp. 207–221). Baltimore: Paul H. Brookes Publishing Co.

Brandt, R. (1988). On students' needs and team learning: A conversation with William Glasser. *Educational Leadership, 45*(6), 38–45.

DiFerdinando, R. (1987, October). *An administrator's perspective on the value of peer support networks.* Paper presented at Vermont's Least Restrictive Environment Conference, Burlington.

Dupont, H. (1989). The emotional development of exceptional students. *Focus on Exceptional Children, 21*(9), 1–10.

Flynn, G., & Kowalczyk-McPhee, B. (1989). A school system in transition. In S. Stainback, W. Stainback, & M. Forest (Eds.), *Educating all students in the mainstream of regular education* (pp. 29–41). Baltimore: Paul H. Brookes Publishing Co.

Ford, A., & Davern, L. (1989). Moving forward with school integration: Strategies for involving students with severe handicaps in the life of the school. In R. Gaylord-Ross (Ed.), *Integration strategies for students with handicaps* (pp. 11–31). Baltimore: Paul H. Brookes Publishing Co.

Forest, M. (1986). Sabrina and Adrian. *entourage, 1,* 111–115.

Forest, M. (1987). Just one of the kids. In D. Schwartz, J. McKnight, & M. Kendrick (Eds.), *A story that I heard* (pp. 55–58). Harrisburg, PA: Pennsylvania Developmental Disabilities Planning Council.

Forest, M., & Lusthaus, E. (1987). The kaleidoscope: Challenge to the cascade. In M. Forest (Ed.), *More education/integration* (pp. 1–16). Downsview, Ontario: G. Allan Roeher Institute.

Giangreco, M.F., York, J., & Rainforth, B. (1989). Providing related services to learners with severe handicaps in least restrictive educational settings. *Pediatric Physical Therapy, 1*(2), 55–63.

Glasser, W. (1986). *Control theory in the classroom.* New York: Harper & Row.

Hallinan, M.T. (1983). Commentary: New directions for research on peer influence. In J.L. Epstein & N. Karweit (Eds.), *Friends in school: Patterns of selection and influence in secondary schools* (pp. 219–231). New York: Academic Press.

Hammill, D.D., & Bartel, N.R. (Eds.). (1975). *Teaching children with learning and behavior problems.* Boston: Allyn and Bacon, Inc.

Hanline, M.F., & Halvorsen, A. (1989). Parent perceptions of the integration transition process: Overcoming artificial barriers. *Exceptional Children, 55,* 487–492.

Hanson, J. (1987). Each belongs. In M. Forest (Ed.), *More education/integration* (pp. 95–100). Downsview, Ontario: G. Allan Roeher Institute.

Johnson, D.W., & Johnson, F.P. (1987a). *Joining together: Group theory and group skills* (3rd ed). Englewood Cliffs, NJ: Prentice-Hall.

Johnson, D.W., & Johnson, R. (1987b). Research shows the benefit of adult cooperation. *Educational Leadership, 45*(3), 27–30.

Johnson, D.W., Johnson, R., & Maruyama, G. (1983). Interdependence and interpersonal attraction among heterogeneous and homogeneous individuals: A theoretical formulation and a meta-analysis of the research. *Review of Educational Research, 53*, 5–54.

Johnson, R.T., & Johnson, D.W. (1981). Building friendships between handicapped and nonhandicapped students: Effects of cooperative and individualistic instruction. *American Educational Research Journal, 18*, 415–423.

Kirk, S.A. (1972). *Educating exceptional children.* Boston: Houghton Mifflin Company.

Kruger, L. (1988). Programmatic change strategies at the building level. In J.L. Graden, J.E. Zins, & M.J. Curtis (Eds.), *Alternative educational delivery systems: Enhancing instructional options for all students* (pp. 491–512). Washington, DC: National Association of School Psychologists.

Lynch, B. (1989, March). Barriers to community. *ARC News for Colorado*, p. 1.

Maloy, R.W., & Fischetti, J.C. (1985). School improvement teams: A qualitative perspective. *Educational Horizons, 63*, 164–168.

Meisels, S.J. (1977). *Programming for atypical infants and their families: Guidelines for program evaluation.* Monograph No. 5 of the Nationally Organized Collaborative Project to Provide Comprehensive Services for Atypical Infants and Their Families. New York: United Cerebral Palsy Association.

Minnesota Statutes Section. (1988). As originally passed by Minnesota law 1985, Chapter 240, Section 1, 120.011.

Mittler, P., Mittler, H., & McConachie, H. (1987). Family supports in England. In D.K. Lipsky (Ed.), *Family supports for families with a disabled member* (pp. 15–36). New York: World Rehabilitation Fund.

Mount, B. (1987). *Personal futures planning: Finding directions for change* (Doctoral dissertation, University of Georgia). Ann Arbor, MI: UMI Dissertation Information Service.

Mount, B., & Zwernik, K. (1988). *It's never too early, it's never too late.* St. Paul, MN: Metropolitan Council, Publication No. 421-88-109.

O'Brien, J. (1987). A guide to life-style planning. In B. Wilcox & G.T. Bellamy (Eds.), *A comprehensive guide to the activities catalog* (pp. 175–189). Baltimore: Paul H. Brookes Publishing Co.

O'Brien, J., & Lyle, C. (1987). *Framework for accomplishment.* Decatur, GA: Responsive Systems Associates.

Perske, R. (1988). *Circles of friends: People with disabilities and their friends enrich the lives of one another.* Nashville: Abingdon Press.

Raiche, J.J. (Ed.). (1983). *School improvement: Research-based components and processes for effective schools.* Minneapolis: Educational Cooperative Service Unit of the Metropolitan Twin Cities Area.

Ruttiman, A. (1988, May). She's right where she belongs. *ARCHtype Newsletter*, pp. 12–13.

Safford, P.L. (1989). *Integrated teaching in early childhood.* White Plains, NY: Longman.

Salvia, J., & Ysseldyke, J.E. (1985). *Assessment in special and remedial education.* Boston: Houghton Mifflin Company.

Sapon-Shevin, M. (1988). Working towards merger together: Seeing beyond distrust and fear. *Teacher Education and Special Education, 11*, 103–110.

Scagliotti, L. (1987, December 20). Helping hands: School works to overcome student's handicap. *Burlington Free Press*, Sec. B, pp. 1, 10.

Sileo, T.W., Rude, H.A., & Luckner, J.L. (1988). Collaborative consultation: A model for transition planning for handicapped youth. *Education and Training in Mental Retardation, 23,* 333–339.

Slavin, R.E. (1977). Student team approach to teaching adolescents with special emotional and behavioral needs. *Psychology in the Schools, 14,* 76–84.

Slavin, R.E. (1987a). Ability grouping and student achievement in elementary school: A best-evidence synthesis. *Review of Educational Research, 57,* 293–336.

Slavin, R.E. (1987b). Cooperative learning and the cooperative school. *Educational Leadership, 45,* 7–13.

Snyder, L., Apolloni, T., & Cooke, T.P. (1977). Integrated settings at the early childhood level: The role of nonretarded peers. *Exceptional Children, 43,* 262–266.

Spodek, B. (1982). What special educators need to know about regular classrooms. *Educational Forum, 46,* 295–307.

Strully, J., & Strully, C. (1985). Friendship and our children. *Journal of The Association for Persons with Severe Handicaps, 10,* 224–227.

Turnbull, K., & Bronicki, G.J. (1989). Children can teach other children. *Teaching Exceptional Children, 21,* 64–65.

Van Meter, E.J., & Scollay, S.J. (1984). Excellence and accountability through school site management. *Educational Horizons, 63,* 19–21.

Vandercook, T., Fleetham, D., Sinclair, S., & Rice Tetlie, R. (1988, Winter). Cath, Jess, Jules, and Ames . . . A story of friendship. *IMPACT Newsletter, 1*(2), 17.

Vandercook, T., York, J., & Forest, M. (1989). The McGill Action Planning System (MAPS): A strategy for building the vision. *Journal of The Association for Persons with Severe Handicaps, 14,* 205–215.

Villa, R.A., & Thousand, J.S. (1988). Enhancing success in heterogeneous classrooms and schools. *Teacher Education and Special Education, 11,* 144–154.

Walter, L.J., & Glenn, C.L. (1986). Centralized decision making threatens teacher autonomy. *Educational Horizons, 64,* 101–103.

York, J., Rainforth, B., & Dunn, W. (in press). Training needs for physical and occupational therapists who work with school aged students with severe handicaps. In A. Kaiser & C. McWhorter (Eds.), *Critical issues in preparing personnel to work with persons who are severely handicapped.* Baltimore: Paul H. Brookes Publishing Co.

York, J., Rainforth, B., & Wiemann, G. (1988). An integrated approach to therapy for school-aged learners with developmental disabilities. *Totline, 14*(3), 36–40.

York, J., & Vandercook, T. (1989). Strategies for achieving an integrated education for middle school aged learners with severe disabilities. In J. York, T. VanderCook, C. Macdonald, & S. Wolff (Eds.), *Strategies for full inclusion* (pp. 1–20). Minneapolis: University of Minnesota, Institute on Community Integration.

Zins, J.E., Curtis, M.J., Graden, J.L., & Ponti, C.R. (1988). *Helping students succeed in the regular classroom.* San Francisco: Jossey-Bass.

Marleen C. Pugach
Lawrence J. Johnson

8

Meeting Diverse Needs through Professional Peer Collaboration

Teaching has always been an extremely complex and demanding job, but the heterogeneous student population of the 1980s has greatly intensified the demands placed on teachers. Although the different experiences and backgrounds students bring to the classroom can provide a rich foundation on which good instruction can be built, it also challenges a teacher's ability to be effective for all students. Diversity introduces the need for flexibility; teaching routines that have previously been successful for a less diverse group may no longer be effective for one that is more so, and teachers need to be given opportunities to consider flexible, alternative ways to accomplish their goals.

The structure of the typical teacher's work day, however, provides few opportunities for them to reflect on alternative strategies to address the diverse needs of students within their classrooms. Teachers engage in thousands of interactions a day with their students, see students throughout the day with few breaks, and have little, if any, time to talk with their colleagues about issues of educational substance. It is precisely this lack of time to engage in collegial dialogue that has traditionally been cited as one of the most problematic aspects of teaching (Goodlad, 1984; Lortie, 1975). Such complexity often prevents teachers from having the opportunity to step back from challenging classroom situations and adopt a reflective attitude about what might be problematic and what aspects of their practice they might be able to change. Also, the immediacy of a particularly frustrating situation is often so prominent in teachers' minds that it is difficult to break away from the frustration itself.

In the midst of teachers' complex work, colleagues are usually ready to offer support and advice, reminding others of similar situations they have experienced in the past and sharing ideas that have worked for them. This kind of advice giving can be especially useful when the immediate frustrations of working with students who "just aren't making it" are prominent. However, support alone is not always enough. In teachers' lounges, in lunchrooms, or hunched over in twos in a classroom, good, sound advice is often exchanged, but it is the complaints that sometimes dominate and resound.

In an attempt to break from this cycle and encourage teachers to utilize their expertise through collegial support, these authors have developed a structured problem-solving process entitled *peer collaboration*. Peer collaboration is a specific conception of teacher support that builds upon the natural relationships many teachers have already established in their schools and facilitates the development of alternative classroom practices for students who are having difficulty. It extends these collegial relationships into a structured, interactive dialogue between teachers, setting the stage for a focused consideration of the limitations of routine practice based on a teacher's knowledge of his or her own classroom, teaching and management routines, and students. Through the dialogue embedded in the peer collaboration process, teachers are provided with a structure to reflect with their peers on problems of classroom practice, to reconstruct the nature of problematic situations based on a more complete understanding, and to develop specific plans for trying new approaches. With peer collaboration, the energy between teachers is directed toward clarifying the frustrating situation, not toward the frustrations of the situations themselves. In many teacher interactions, and in fact in many meetings designed to solve problems, it is this kind of specific structure that is typically lacking, structure that may provide an effective framework for approaching the problem at hand and dealing with it in a clear and thoughtful manner. It is hoped that collaboration provides such a structure in the context of collegial interaction, thereby blending two important aspects, support and focused attention, in dealing with problems of classroom practice and their solutions. In working with teachers using peer collaboration, these authors have often heard teachers say that the structure of the dialogue encourages them to use their time constructively and that they probably spend less time solving problems using peer collaboration than they previously did complaining about them!

HOW DOES PEER COLLABORATION WORK?

Three assumptions underlie peer collaboration. They are as follows:

1. Teachers have a great deal of expertise in developing novel and creative approaches to problems of classroom practice. They also possess a great deal of information about their students that can be brought to bear on problem resolution. But given the complexity of their work and working conditions, teachers need time and a specific structure to access their expertise and creativity. It is this time and structure that allows teachers to stretch the limits of their understanding in creating new responses to problems of practice.
2. Learning to access teacher expertise is a function of metacognitive, or strategic, thinking. By learning to use strategies associated with active thinking, teachers can become skilled in constructing the meaning of challenging classroom situations in such a way that they more easily develop creative and flexible alternatives for working with diverse student needs. This set of skills encourages teachers to step back from the daily frustrations of their teaching and gain some objectivity about the challenges they are facing.
3. The disposition to be flexible in developing solutions to challenging classroom situations is best enhanced in a supportive situation in the context of collegial problem solving.

Peer collaboration usually occurs in pairs and begins when teachers identify a problem of practice they wish to change. Two distinct roles characterize the dialogue based on peer collaboration: teacher initiator and teacher facilitator. The initiator is the teacher who brings the problematic situation to be considered and the facilitator is the teacher who guides his or her colleague through the strategies of the dialogue. In this way, one teacher can practice the strategic skills identified below and the partner can assist his or her peer in following each step of the process to maximize the benefits of their time together. When teachers are learning the steps of peer collaboration, they learn the role both of initiator and facilitator. The four steps that make up peer collaboration include: clarifying problems, summarizing problems, generating and predicting outcomes, and developing an evaluation strategy.

Problem Clarification

The first step, problem clarification, is the heart of peer collaboration. This is the step where teachers do the critical work of constructing a new, extended understanding of the problem through consideration of aspects that have not previously been fully considered. After writing down a brief (one or two sentence) description of the problem, the initiating teacher spends a few minutes setting the scene for his or her facilitating partner by talking about the description. The strategy used for clarification is a self-questioning format on the part of the initiating teacher; this means that the initiating teacher begins to ask him- or herself questions about various aspects of the situation and then answers those questions. The facilitator's role is to provide guidance in suggesting or extending the topics about which such questions are asked.

For example, if the problem described focuses on a bilingual student who does not appear to be motivated, the facilitator might begin the dialogue by saying, "What could you ask yourself about your strategies for motivating Tina?" The initiating teacher would then respond with a question stimulated by his or her partner's suggested question and answer it. That question might take the form, "Do I do anything special to motivate Tina?" By creating a question from the facilitator's suggestion, the initiating teacher gives thought to that aspect of the situation he or she believes to be important rather than simply answering the question of a collaborating partner; in this case, it is a direct consideration of the teacher's techniques. By asking and then answering one's *own* question, a teacher practices the dynamic of thinking about the classroom dilemma from an internal frame of self-questioning and responding, a critical skill if teachers are eventually to internalize the ability to consider alternatives to their routine responses in the classroom.

In responding to one's own question about techniques for motivation, the initiating teacher (IT) mentions that he or she uses those techniques that seem to work with the rest of the class. The facilitator (FT) responds with:

FT: What question can you ask yourself about the motivational techniques that do work with the rest of the class?

IT: What motivation works with the whole group? I allow them to do role playing activities that they like, I let them take turns being teacher if we play games or something like that, and I don't always make them do every question.

FT: What about the materials you are using in class?

IT: Are the class materials motivating? For the most part they are, because there is not a lot of written work; we use a variety of things—puzzles, games.

FT: What question can you ask about why Tina has problems being motivated?

IT: How can I tell that Tina is unmotivated? She stalls in completing her written work, she seldom raises her hand, she seldom volunteers in giving information, she depends heavily on work written on the board instead of doing anything on her own. She waits for assistance. . .

FT: Is there a question you can ask about Tina's ability?

IT: Are Tina's abilities at the same level as the other students? I would say yes, because she is in the same reading group as the other children. Her reading and writing in class is at a comparable level. She worked with the same group of children last year, and did OK. On days that she does try, on good days, her work is a little bit below the others, but it is acceptable.

FT: What about Tina's perceptions of her work?

IT: How does Tina see herself doing? I guess I'm going to have to say I don't really know.

This brief excerpt shows the movement of questions and the transition from questions suggested by the facilitating teacher to those self-questions posed by the initiating teacher. It also illustrates the important role the facilitator has in suggesting a logical direction for follow-up questions when the initiating teacher ends a thought. Sometimes a question is asked for which a teacher does not know the answer; two responses can occur. First, the dialogue may stop temporarily until the information can be located. Alternatively, the teachers may continue their dialogue but not finalize plans for interventions until the needed information is available. What is important to remember is that it is all right to take a break, as long as notes are kept from the initial session for use later on.

Later the conversation moves on to Tina's perceived need for English class. In response to self-questioning on that subject, the initiating teacher mentions that Tina knows she needs help but does not realize that her English is weak. The initiating teacher then says:

> I could ask myself if Tina thinks that she just can't read. Maybe sometimes if we don't go through with it [the material] first, Tina is intimidated by the reading part of it . . . [intimidated] to read what she has written and won't volunteer because of that.

Rather than wait for a question from the facilitating partner, the initiating teacher had come up with a logical follow-up question of his or her own, asked it, and then responded. As it turned out, the issue of reading became the focal point for this particular dialogue and finding ways to encourage Tina to volunteer in class became the center of one of the interventions.

As teachers begin to internalize the process of self-questioning, they easily begin to come up with questions that stretch their own thinking, much in the same way the facilitator's questions did the "stretching" for them at first. What begins as a self-conscious step in the dialogue becomes more natural. When this movement begins to occur, teachers appear to be taking an active voice in considering their own classroom situations and an active role in seeking greater understanding through the process of self-questioning.

The problem clarification phase of peer collaboration often takes between 20–30 minutes to complete. It ends when both the initiating and facilitating teacher sense that a much greater understanding of the

problem has been reached. Sometimes this is signaled by moving un-
aware into the development of solutions (that is part of the next step of
the process); sometimes there appears to be a kind of "aha" experience
in which it is clear to both participants that enough progress in constructing new meaning for the problem has taken place for solutions to
be discussed.

Problem Summarization

In this step of peer collaboration, a three-part summary is developed.
Usually the facilitating teacher recognizes the pair's readiness for the
next step by saying, "Do you think you've clarified the problem enough
to summarize it?" Or, he or she might ask, "Do you see a pattern in the
problem?" The first part of the summary is a description of a pattern of
student behavior that emerges from the previous clarification process.
Typically, this pattern differs from the brief written description that stimulated the dialogue at the start; it is essential to understand the importance of restating the pattern, since what may first have appeared to be
the problem might look different as a result of the new understandings
to which problem clarification has led. This pattern summary allows an
initiating teacher to consolidate his or her reconceptualization of the
situation before launching into possible interventions and encourages
the facilitator to check the new pattern against the issues that were
raised in or during the process of clarification. In Tina's case, the pattern
was as follows:

> She doesn't participate if it feels like it is not going to be fun for her. She is
> not motivated if it is not fun or if it is going to be too difficult. Another
> pattern that I'm beginning to notice is that if it involves her volunteering to
> talk to someone who is not her friend [she will not volunteer] . . .

In the second step, the facilitator asks the initiator to describe his or
her feelings about the problematic situation. This step enables the initiating teacher to acknowledge any immediate frustrations and air them
prior to considering specific interventions.

The third, and perhaps most important, summarization step includes an identification of variables that are under the control of the
classroom teacher who has initiated the peer collaboration session.
Since it focuses attention on things that can be done by the teacher, this
step is essential in establishing a mindset of potentially successful interventions for the teacher. Often, the things teachers are frustrated about
are aspects of the student's life that seem to be out of the teacher's
control, for example, a difficult home situation. In peer collaboration,
the teacher is encouraged to give attention to what can actually be
changed within the classroom. Tina's teacher identified the following as
things that could be controlled: materials, expectations, the amount of

written work, teacher's assistance, difficulty of assigned work, and with whom she works in her group.

This set of variables, once identified, logically leads to the third step of peer collaboration, generating interventions and predicting outcomes. During the summarization, the facilitator again guides the initiating teacher through each step, modeling as necessary and reminding his or her partner to consider any issues that had been discussed earlier that might lend themselves to helping in the identification of controllable variables.

Interventions and Outcomes

With an identified list of potential variables in hand around which interventions might be constructed, the initiating and facilitating partners then engage in developing at least three potential alternatives, or interventions, to address the problematic situation. For each possible intervention, the initiating teacher also predicts potential outcomes. In this way, he or she can consider the possible effects of a particular change on the student in question, on other individuals who might be affected by the new routine, on the class as a whole, and on the teacher. The reason for requiring more than one possible alternative is to emphasize that the first idea may not necessarily be the most effective, that new nuances of interventions may emerge as one makes multiple plans, and that flexibility is developed through multiple considerations of a single situation. One caveat is that any intervention should be as practical as possible and be seen by the initiating teacher as reasonable for implementation.

In this phase of peer collaboration, the facilitator has an extremely important role, that of ensuring that interventions selected are consistent with the pattern established earlier as well as with the variables identified as being in the teacher's control. Should the initiating teacher have difficulty coming up with interventions, it is the role of the facilitating partner to model their development by suggesting specific areas on which to focus or variables that might have been neglected.

It is common in this step of the dialogue for the initiating teacher to choose to combine various elements of the three or more alternatives developed. A second common outcome is to plan to use the various alternatives sequentially. Finally, if a single alternative is selected and is not successful, the initiating teacher has a ready-made follow up intervention to utilize.

Evaluation Strategy

To encourage systematic implementation, a two-part evaluation strategy is set up before the dialogue is over. First, the initiating teacher identifies a plan for how he or she will keep track of his or her own implementation of the intervention. Then, he or she identifies how to account for the student's progress. Before they complete the session, the teachers plan to meet again in about 2 weeks to review progress and discuss new interventions, if needed. This time period is set to emphasize the important fact that often it may take at least 2 weeks for a change to be visible or convincing; teachers are encouraged further to "stick with it" and not give up if improvement does not seem immediate. Although anxious for an immediate change in a student's behavior, teachers need to acquire a sense of patience in anticipating results even in what may be a highly frustrating situation where such waiting is difficult.

TRAINING TEACHERS TO USE PEER COLLABORATION

Training in peer collaboration consists of a 2-hour group session and two 1-hour individual training sessions. The *Peer Collaboration Training Manual* (1987) is used to design training specific to the individual needs of the participating school or district. This manual contains a step-by-step outline for conducting group training and includes handouts or overheads that provide excerpts from teachers who have used the process with kindergarten, elementary, junior high, and high school students. (Peer collaboration training materials can be obtained from the authors.)

The group session is conducted for all individuals participating in the training at the local school or district. During this session participants are first provided with a description of the evolution of the peer collaboration process and its potential for helping teachers develop alternative strategies for addressing the needs of students in their classes who are having difficulty being successful. The *Peer Collaboration Guidelines* (1987) is then distributed; it contains definitions of peer collaboration terms, descriptions of each step in the process, illustrative samples from real sessions, and guidelines for completing each step in the process.

After this background information is provided, a brief videotape of two teachers engaging in peer collaboration is shown. The videotape is 15 minutes in length; the teachers in the tape work on a real, rather than a simulated, problem. As the trainer explains each step, reference is made to the process presented in the videotape and described in the *Peer Collaboration Guidelines*.

At the end of the session the *Peer Collaboration Booklet* (1987), used when teachers implement the process, is distributed and discussed. The booklet is structured to provide both a place for teachers to record relevant information from the peer collaboration session and to guide teachers through the process by providing reminders on how to complete each of the four steps.

After group training, the pairs of teachers schedule at least two individual meetings with the trainer. At these follow-up sessions, each teacher uses the process as an initiator to solve a real problem under the guidance of the trainer. As the teachers implement the process, the trainer monitors their progress, utilizing a minimum number of prompts and only intervening when teachers deviate from the steps. It is critical that at least two such sessions occur so that each individual teacher learns the role of both initiator and facilitator. If at the end of these sessions teachers are not able to use the process without making errors, additional meetings are scheduled with the trainer.

RESEARCH ON PEER COLLABORATION

Research on peer collaboration has proceeded in three stages. In the 1986–1987 school year a small pilot study was conducted to refine the process and develop training procedures. In the 1986–1987 school year peer collaboration was examined comparing a group of teachers trained in the process to a group that did not receive training at sites in Illinois and Wisconsin. In the 1987–1988 school year, this was expanded to sites in Alabama, Illinois, and Wisconsin.

To examine the impact of this project the following sets of data have been collected: 1) the number of referrals made to special education; 2) descriptions of classroom problems prior to and after peer collaboration training; 3) interventions developed to remediate identified problems and their outcome; and 4) four paper and pencil instruments measuring teachers' tolerance for diversity in students, teachers' affective outlook toward their classrooms, teacher efficacy, and teacher confidence in developing alternative classroom interventions.

The data from these studies are extensive and a full discussion of these findings is beyond the scope of this chapter. However, a brief summary of major findings, including relevant citations for the interested reader, follows. Classroom teachers who received peer collaboration training:

1. Tended to shift the focus of problems away from the child toward changes the teacher could make (Johnson & Pugach, in press; Pugach & Johnson, 1988a)
2. Were able to generate interventions for all problems targeted through a peer collaboration session (Johnson & Pugach, in press)
3. Successfully resolved over 85% of the problems targeted (Pugach & Johnson, 1988a)

4. Had a significant reduction in referrals compared to the previous year (Johnson & Pugach, 1989)
5. Had significantly fewer referrals to special education than comparison group counterparts (Johnson & Pugach, 1989)
6. Became significantly more confident in their ability to handle classroom problems and were significantly more confident than their comparison group counterparts (Johnson & Pugach, 1989; Pugach & Johnson, 1989a)
7. Had an increased positive orientation toward their class whereas the comparison group became less positive (Pugach & Johnson, 1989a)
8. Significantly expanded their tolerance for students with cognitive deficits (Johnson & Pugach, in press; Pugach & Johnson, 1988a, 1989a)

IMPLEMENTING PEER
COLLABORATION AS A SCHOOLWIDE ACTIVITY

Collaborative dialogue for purposes of developing alternatives to routine classroom practice is best supported when an entire school staff learns to participate in peer collaboration in roles of both initiating and facilitating teacher. In this way, all professionals in a school building can assist in the process of reflecting on problems, and all can take on the role of receiving assistance from their peers. At times one might be on the initiating end of a collaborative dialogue and at other times be on the facilitating end. It is the authors' position that having teachers learn both roles is essential, not only because it operationalizes the assumption of parity among all school-based professionals—classroom teacher and specialist alike—but because it fosters sensitivity to the teacher who at any given time is receiving support in a challenging situation as well as sensitivity to the importance of learning the restraint required of a facilitator.

It is not often feasible to teach an entire staff a process like peer collaboration. However, it has proven successful to train a small group of teachers and the building principal and have them serve as a core who then train others in the building. Another method for introducing and supporting peer collaboration at the local level is facilitative consultation in which a part of the role of the consultant is redefined to focus on facilitating the acquisition of collaborative problem-solving skills among classroom teachers (Pugach & Johnson, 1988c).

When implementing peer collaboration, the commitment of school principals is essential, since without their support such collaborative endeavors can quickly be perceived as only a function of special services personnel. What is critical in beginning collaborative partnerships through structured dialogue is communicating the assumption that such collaboration is part of the daily work of all professionals in a school building, teachers and specialists alike; it is especially important as a support mechanism for helping teachers to be successful in challenging classroom situations. Furthermore, the principal has a major role to play in helping develop structures and organize schedules so activities like peer collaboration can take place in meaningful ways on a regular basis. However, it is equally important to gain the interest and support of a core of teachers, since it is teachers who face the daily challenges of working with students whose instructional and management needs are so diverse.

When everyone in a school is knowledgeable as both an initiator and a facilitator, many potential partnerships exist. In some schools, partners formed during the training continue to work together over time; in fact, in one school teachers changed rooms in order to work in closer proximity to their partners. The question of who makes the "best" partner in peer collaboration is often raised. There are no hard and fast rules, but a few guidelines should provide some direction. First, it is not essential for teachers at the same grade level to be partners; however, the authors have found that sometimes teachers feel more comfortable in terms of their curricular and developmental orientations if they work with teachers from the same or near-same grade level. Next, it is possible to work in triads, or even in a small group of four, with one teacher as the initiator and the balance of the group as co-facilitators. In this configuration, co-facilitators must be sure not to dominate the strategic thinking of the initiating teacher. Finally, teachers should be encouraged to choose their own partners whenever possible.

Once teachers learn to use the strategies of peer collaboration successfully, the challenge lies in finding time to work together. Time is one of the most valuable resources of the schools, and without identified time in which to collaborate, the benefit of shared expertise will be difficult, if not impossible, to reap. When two classroom teachers wish to engage in supportive collaboration, finding time is perhaps most difficult of all. Planning time, especially at the elementary level, is not always available. However, with careful coordination of the schedules of specialists (e.g., art, music, physical education, guidance counselors), principals can facilitate partnerships among teachers for the purpose of engaging in peer collaboration. If partnerships are developed at the same or near-same grade level, such planning time serves multiple purposes.

Another option is to reserve time at faculty meetings on a regular rotation for peer collaboration to take place. While this approach neatly solves the time problem, it detracts from teachers being able to engage in such dialogue when it is needed; some of the immediacy is traded for the security of available time. Yet another option is to incorporate peer collaboration into existing constructs for addressing problematic students, for example, informal problem-solving teams (often known as teacher assistance teams). While such teams are often structured soundly, the content of their deliberations is often less structured and a team's effectiveness may benefit from some of the strategic thinking approaches upon which peer collaboration is founded. Likewise, at the middle-school level, a process like peer collaboration would fit neatly into the concept of house meetings. Finally, if grade level teams are structured at the elementary level, grade level chairpersons could become the first source for locating or serving as a facilitator for teachers.

The Scope of Problem Solving with Peer Collaboration

Peer collaboration was originally designed as a support system for teachers in developing interventions for specific students who were not having successful school experiences. However, teachers and principals have found it to be effective for solving an array of problems not limited to individual students. Teachers have engaged in structured dialogue over problems of small group management and instruction to problems involving the whole class. Principals have worked with other building administrators to consider problems of staff development. It appears that this process has the potential to be applied to many problem situations in which guidance through teamwork is appropriate.

Furthermore, when all staff in a school are skilled in such a support system, other schoolwide situations can also be addressed using strategic dialogue. These might include, for example, curricular issues, schoolwide management issues, coordinated scheduling of specialists, and the use of resources. From the outset collaboration needs to be characterized and presented as a schoolwide commitment to increased professionalization among teachers and school staff. In this way, the notion of reflective consideration of problematic situations becomes the norm rather than an activity that is added on as an "extra" responsibility.

Special Education and Peer Collaboration

Where does special education fit into a schoolwide plan for peer collaboration? Since many programs designed to promote individual intervention in schools have been developed in the context of serving students who are labeled as having disabilities, this is a reasonable consideration.

The authors' response is that special educators, school psychologists, administrators, and classroom teachers should all have access to collaborative strategies and use them as needed. In the case of special educators, it is imperative that such collaborative skills be incorporated into various informal structures that exist for assisting teachers with difficult cases. However, it should be clear from the description of the process of peer collaboration in this chapter that the expertise of classroom teachers is often sufficient for addressing many of the problems they encounter. The problem is finding the time and structure to do so. Maximizing the use of teacher expertise can free specialists to provide, assist, or facilitate a range of support for students whose difficulties are more persistent or more severe.

Ideally, in a collaborative school, dialogue would occur continuously among all staff members. When a specialist and a classroom teacher interact, with the teacher asking for advice, a specialist's knowledge of peer collaboration should provide the classroom teacher with the skills to facilitate, rather than to prescribe, the development of reasonable alternatives. Thus, training of a whole school staff should encourage more collaboration among members of the staff and more effective collaboration between teachers and specialists. Similarly, since a whole school can be trained, the notion that specialists have important knowledge to gain from their classroom teacher peers should be emphasized. To underscore this particular point, it is preferred to teach classroom teachers to use peer collaboration first, and they in turn are the trainers for their specialist peers.

Furthermore, as suggested earlier, processes like peer collaboration can be especially useful in increasing the effectiveness of existing structures for problem solving that have been developed explicitly for the purpose of reducing referrals to special education. In particular, informal teaming options like teacher assistance teams (Chalfant, Pysh, & Moultrie, 1979) sometimes mistakenly function much like expert teams and fail to provide the facilitative support that distinguishes peer collaboration (Pugach & Johnson, 1989b). Learning to take on a facilitative role may be a challenge specifically for specialists who are used to playing an information-dispensing role, and peer collaboration can foster the development of strong working relationships between specialists and teachers based on common understandings of what it means to give and receive advice.

CONCLUSION

The face of teaching is changing as the students who enter schools change. Teachers need to enter their careers understanding that students will be diverse in their educational needs and abilities. This diversity is both a resource to be celebrated and a challenge to be mastered. Finding techniques to serve students well, and finding ways to alter teaching techniques when they are not successful, will be the hallmarks of good teaching.

There are many levels of change that must occur in the nation's education system if schools and classrooms are to accommodate the educational and social needs of a diverse student population successfully. For teachers to work effectively with the heterogeneous groups of students they now instruct, schools need to reassess their use of resources and their approaches to curriculum, and teachers need to reassess their approaches to teaching. These represent major initiatives in the movement to develop schools that are responsive and attentive to all students, and particularly to students who may have difficulty learning under typical classroom conditions. Building on the richness a diverse student population brings to a class, while at the same time developing methodological expertise and flexibility in working with heterogeneous groups of students, is likely to be the major professional issue that teachers face in the 1990s.

To meet this challenge, supports need to be created at the district level, the school level, and within individual classrooms. Support for students who are not succeeding is now conceptualized as a series of unrelated pull-out programs; it is evident that this kind of approach has not been effective in assisting teachers with the numbers of students who are finding it difficult to achieve success in school. Particularly in the area of professional relationships, substantial shifts will have to occur to build the kinds of supportive networks needed among teachers when they are faced with complex classroom situations. Across the specializations in schooling, teachers need to interact with their colleagues to a far greater extent than in the past in order to develop mutual support and utilize the expertise various professionals bring to the school.

In a collegial school climate, teachers will depend upon each other for the support needed to develop this professional flexibility. It will be critical to work jointly, across various specializations, for the common goal of educating all students successfully. In this chapter, the authors present one method of promoting such collaboration: structured dialogue based on strategies associated with active, reflective thinking on the part of teachers. In the presence of such supports among teachers, the challenge of creating responsive instructional and management approaches is shared, and the expertise of all teachers is maximized. It is this kind of professional environment that all teachers should strive to create in their schools.

REFERENCES

Chalfant, J.C., Pysh, M.V., & Moultrie, R. (1979). Teacher assistance teams: A model for within-building problem solving. *Learning Disability Quarterly, 2*(3), 85–96.

Goodlad, J.I. (1984). *A place called school.* New York: McGraw-Hill.

Johnson, L.J., & Pugach, M.C. (1989). *Enhancing instructional options for students with mild learning and behavior problems.* Final Project Report. Unpublished manuscript, University of Alabama, Area of Special Education, Tuscaloosa, AL. University of Wisconsin, Department of Curriculum and Instruction, Milwaukee.

Johnson, L.J., & Pugach, M.C. (in press). Accommodating the needs of students with mild learning and behavior problems through peer collaboration. *Exceptional Children.*

Lortie, D. (1975). *School teacher: A sociological study.* Chicago: University of Chicago Press.

Peer collaboration booklet. (1987). Unpublished manuscript. Tuscaloosa, AL: University of Alabama, Area of Special Education. Milwaukee: University of Wisconsin, Department of Curriculum and Instruction.

Peer collaboration guidelines. (1987). Unpublished manuscript. Tuscaloosa, AL: University of Alabama, Area of Special Education. Milwaukee: University of Wisconsin, Department of Curriculum and Instruction.

Peer collaboration training manual. (1987). Unpublished manuscript. Tuscaloosa, AL: University of Alabama, Area of Special Education. Milwaukee: University of Wisconsin, Department of Curriculum and Instruction.

Pugach, M.C., & Johnson, L.J. (1988a). *Peer collaboration: Enhancing teacher problem-solving capabilities for students at-risk.* Paper presented at the annual convention of the American Educational Research Association, New Orleans.

Pugach, M., & Johnson, L.J. (1988b). Peer collaboration: Helping teachers help themselves. *Teaching Exceptional Children, 20,* 75–77.

Pugach, M.C., & Johnson, L.J. (1988c). Rethinking the relationship between consultation and collaborative problem-solving. *Focus on Exceptional Children, 21,* 1–14.

Pugach, M.C., & Johnson, L.J. (1989a). *Peer collaboration: Unlocking expertise in general education through teacher dialogue.* Paper presented at the annual convention of the American Educational Research Association, San Francisco.

Pugach, M.C., & Johnson, L.J. (1989b). Prereferral interventions: Progress, problems, and challenges. *Exceptional Children, 56,* 217–226.

Kathleen C. Harris   9

Meeting Diverse Needs through Collaborative Consultation

As all students are educated in the mainstream, there
will be more diversity in the classroom. Though students may still be
grouped by age, there will be children of various abilities, languages,
and ethnic groups in classrooms. For example, students with differing
reading abilities will be learning together as will students with differing
physical abilities. In addition, with the changing demographics in this
country, children of different cultural heritages and native languages will
be learning together. It is projected that between 1980 and 2000, the
Asian and Hispanic populations in this country will almost double
(Bouvier & Davis, 1982). Because of this diversity among the student
population, it will be difficult for a single teacher to meet the needs of all
the students in the classroom. Therefore, educational services will need
to be provided to students in a different way. Instead of one teacher
providing instruction to all students, many individuals with various
areas of expertise will need to work together to plan and provide instruction for the diversity of students that will exist in classrooms. To
work together effectively, these individuals will need to consult with one
another.

Consultation has been defined in a number of different ways, de-
pending upon the purpose of the consultation (cf. Bergan, 1977; Bergan
& Tombari, 1976; Brown, Wyne, Blackburn, & Powell, 1979; Conoley &
Conoley, 1982; Friend, 1985; Heron & Harris, 1987; Idol, Paolucci-
Whitcomb, & Nevin, 1986; Parsons & Meyers, 1984; Robinson, Cam-

eron, & Raethel, 1985). In this chapter, consultation is defined as a process that will enable individuals with differing areas of expertise to work together to plan and conduct educational programs for diverse students who are learning together in mainstream settings. This chapter discusses generic consultation skills needed by all individuals who are providing educational services to students in the mainstream. These generic skills include: technical expertise, effective communication, and the ability to coordinate instructional services so that the student's educational program is well-integrated (Goldstein & Sorcher, 1974).

GENERIC CONSULTATION SKILLS

Technical Expertise

As mentioned previously, when diverse students are educated together in mainstream classrooms, a variety of services will be needed to meet their needs. No single educator will have all the skills necessary to meet the needs of all students; therefore, it will be necessary for a variety of individuals to work together. For example, in a mainstream elementary classroom, one may find a specialist in reading instruction, a specialist in behavior management, a specialist in English as a second language (ESL), and a physical therapist all working together to develop educational programs and provide direct instruction for the students in that classroom. The skills that each of these individuals has represent different areas of technical expertise. Each person who is involved in developing and/or implementing an educational program for a student has some technical expertise. The people who consult with one another share their technical expertise with one another and with the student when they develop and implement educational programs together. Table 1 provides a listing of individuals and areas of technical expertise. This list is not meant to be exhaustive; rather, its purpose is to *suggest* the possible areas of technical expertise that may be required when serving diverse students in mainstream classrooms.

Communication

Though many individuals have written extensively on the specific communication skills that are necessary when individuals collaborate with one another in developing and implementing educational programs (e.g., Conoley & Conoley, 1982; DeBoer, 1986; Gutkin & Curtis, 1982; Heron & Harris, 1987; Idol et al., 1986; Rosenfield, 1987; Speece & Mandell, 1980; Tombari & Bergan, 1978), in essence, when providing a service in collaboration with another, it is important that there is professional respect based on a recognition of each other's technical expertise.

Table 1. Areas of technical expertise

Technical expertise	Providers
Alternative communication	Sign language instructors
	Braille instructors
Assessment of learning style/ achievement	School psychologists
	Educational diagnosticians
Basic life skills	Elementary teachers
	Occupational therapists
Behavior management	Behavior management specialists
Community living skills	Orientation and mobility specialists
Computer literacy	Computer educators
Corrective speech and language	Speech and language specialists
General education curriculum	Elementary teachers
	Middle school teachers
	High school teachers
Identification of resources	Support facilitator
Instructional grouping	Cooperative learning specialists
	Peer tutoring specialists
Language instruction for non-native English speakers	Bilingual educators
	English as a second language (ESL) instructors
Motor skills	Physical education teachers
	Physical therapists
Remedial reading	Reading specialists
Student reinforcers	Parents
	Teachers
Vocational skills	Vocational educators

Individuals must be willing to listen and learn from one another. They must realize that it is necessary to understand the nature of each person's technical expertise so that each person can be most effective in serving students. It is also essential that effective communication skills are used to identify and resolve problems as well as provide clear feedback regarding program implementation. Table 2 lists some important conditions and activities for establishing and maintaining communication. All individuals should strive to create these conditions when working together to provide educational services for students. For an extensive discussion of these conditions and activities, see Heron and Harris (1987) and West, Idol, and Cannon (1989).

Coordination

Coordination is defined as the process by which individuals work together to provide educational services for all students in mainstream

Table 2. Selected conditions and activities for establishing and maintaining effective communication

Condition	Activities
Gain acceptance and establish rapport	Treat others with respect Shift credit for ideas to others Share information Learn with and from others Participate in activities with others
Provide feedback	Listen to others Analyze nonverbal cues of others Respond appropriately to message of others —Acknowledge —Paraphrase —Summarize
Engage in collaborative problem solving	Establish common goals Use brainstorming techniques Assign priorities Develop action plan

settings. A process is suggested so that each student receives a well-integrated program. If several individuals are providing educational services to a single student, it is quite possible that, without coordination, those educational services will be fragmented and the student's total program will not be unified.

Coordination is discussed within a framework of problem-solving strategies. Individuals, with diverse areas of technical expertise, should engage in this process when working together to develop and implement educational programs in mainstream settings. The process discussed in this chapter is derived from theory (cf. Kurpius, 1978; West et al., 1989) and practice (cf. Harris et al., 1987). Though components of the process are discussed sequentially, they may actually occur simultaneously. However, it is suggested that all components in the process be addressed so that a well-integrated educational program for each student can be developed.

Table 3 outlines an application of the coordination process for individuals who wish to design and implement a program for a heterogeneous group of upper elementary students. The components discussed below are reflected in Table 3.

Assess the Situation In developing any collaborative activity it is necessary to clearly determine the need to be addressed (Kurpius, 1978; West et al., 1989) as well as the practicality of implementing proposed activities. Therefore, collaborators should carefully identify the problem

Table 3. Application of the coordination process

Situation: The design and implementation of upper elementary instruction for heterogeneous groupings of students.

Component	Activities
Assess the situation	Principal announces to the upper elementary teachers (i.e., teachers of grades 4, 5, & 6) that all upper elementary students should be grouped by grade level, not by abilities or disabilities.
	Chair of upper elementary teachers asks support facilitator for assistance in designing a program to teach students with special needs.
	Support facilitator identifies characteristics of upper elementary students: reading skills—nonreader to 6th grade; sensory skills—hearing impaired to average hearing acuity; language skills—limited English proficient (LEP) to fluent English proficient (FEP).
	Support facilitator identifies resource people to address student needs: upper elementary teachers, reading specialist, sign language instructor, ESL instructor.
	Support facilitator arranges meeting with resource people to discuss situation.
	Resource people decide to conduct a pilot program and limit scope of situation. Goal is to design and implement program in social studies for one group of sixth grade students (a sixth grade student is defined as any student enrolled in the school who is 12 years to 12.8 years as of September 1).
Establish objectives	All sixth grade students in the pilot program will participate in a social studies unit on the geography of the neighborhood.
	All sixth grade students in the pilot program will learn the physical layout of the streets in the neighborhood and the location of relevant buildings (e.g., home, school, public library, public park, food markets, theatres).
Identify program content	Instructional area: mapping skills
	Instructional activities: sheltered English techniques, sign language interpretation, multimodal presentations, cooperative learning groups, peer tutoring
	Evaluation activities: Support facilitator will observe instruction once a week and discuss program implementation with sixth grade teacher. Sixth grade teacher, reading specialist, sign language instructor, ESL instructor, cooperative

(continued)

Table 3. (continued)

Component	Activities
	learning specialist, and peer tutoring specialist review student work produced at end of unit.
Identify program participants	All sixth grade students in the pilot program will participate in the social studies unit.
	Sixth grade teacher will develop lesson plans, teach the social studies unit, and collect student work samples.
	Sign language instructor will provide sign language interpretation.
	Cooperative learning specialist will facilitate group instruction.
	ESL instructor, reading specialist, and peer tutoring specialist will modify instructional strategies and materials.
	Support facilitator will monitor program implementation, collect evaluation information, and organize meeting at the end of the unit to review evaluation information.
Develop program schedule	Direct instruction: The social studies unit is taught third period, Monday through Friday, by the sixth grade teacher. Cooperative learning specialist facilitates groups during third period Monday through Friday. Sign language instructor provides sign language interpretation during third period Monday through Friday.
	Materials/instruction modification: ESL specialist, reading specialist, cooperative learning specialist, peer tutoring specialist, sign language instructor, and sixth grade teacher meet every Friday during fourth period to develop/modify lessons and materials for the following week.
	Evaluation: Support facilitator observes third period class 1 day per week (observation day varies each week) and talks with sixth grade teacher 1 day a week during fourth period.
Articulate program	Support facilitator arranges meeting of program participants to discuss/agree upon program.
Implement program	Participants conduct activities as described under content, participants, and schedule.
Conduct summative evaluation/ redesign program	Support facilitator arranges meeting to review evaluation information. Program participants review log of activities to ascertain if the first objective was met and reviews student work samples to determine if the second objective was met. Program participants develop plans to revise and expand the program.

or need they want to address and assess the adequacy of the resources to meet that need.

The nature of the assessment is one that includes an assessment of the environment as well as the skills of all participants. In the situation outlined in Table 3, the support facilitator identified the characteristics of the students and resource people who could assist in addressing the situation. Before conducting the needs assessment, all should understand that the _situation_ is being assessed, not the competence of any individual.

Establish Objectives   Once the need and resources to meet that need are identified, it is feasible to develop objectives. Without clearly defined and measurable objectives, it is conceivable that the purpose of the activity will become obscured and this may affect program refinements. With clearly defined objectives, it is possible to evaluate the effectiveness of the program and thereby provide feedback for future program refinements (Kurpius, 1978). Establishing objectives also helps individuals to determine the range of their collaborative program. In the example in Table 3, the scope of the program was limited to a pilot program in one subject area for one heterogeneous group of sixth grade students. The teachers felt that a pilot program should be developed and implemented before a plan was implemented for all upper elementary students.

Identify Program Content   Program content includes the areas of instruction, the activities conducted to instruct in those areas (i.e., the technical expertise needed to meet the objectives), and the evaluation plan. Frequently, establishing the objectives and identifying program content are completed simultaneously. Program content should clearly address program objectives. For example, in Table 3, one of the objectives was that all sixth grade students in the pilot program would participate in the social studies unit. Therefore, it was decided that if sheltered English techniques (e.g., use of concrete terms, simple sentences), multimodality presentations (e.g., visual and auditory cues), and an interpreter were used for large group instruction, the content would be comprehensible to all the sixth grade students in the class, whether those students were fluent or nonfluent English speakers, good or poor readers, or hearing impaired. Also, in the example in Table 3, it became apparent that additional resources would be needed. As the sixth grade teacher was not sure how to group all students in this class for guided and independent practice of the content introduced in large group instruction, the cooperative learning specialist and the peer tutoring specialist were asked for assistance in designing small group activities.

In addition to identifying instructional areas and instructional techniques, it is also necessary to decide how to measure the impact of the instruction. Therefore, the evaluation plan is an essential aspect of the program content. Evaluation information provides input for program change and documentation of program success. As suggested by Idol-Maestas, Nevin, and Paolucci-Whitcomb (1984), it is one of the basic principles of collaborative consultation.

The evaluation plan should be simple but include formative and summative evaluation (Gersten & Hauser, 1984), the consumers of the program as a source of evaluative information, and data collection activities that are as nonintrusive as possible. The author has found it useful to be familiar with data that are already collected in the school and use that data whenever possible to answer evaluation questions about the program.

Ongoing or formative evaluation is conducted during the implementation of the program and should answer two questions about the program: Is the program being implemented as it was designed? Is the program generally producing the intended effects? (Heron & Harris, 1987). Formative evaluation allows for "midcourse correction." If the program is being implemented as intended, yet the desired effect is not occurring, modifications in the program can be initiated. In the situation outlined in Table 3, the support facilitator monitored the implementation of the pilot program and identified, with the sixth grade teacher, any changes that needed to be made as well as any additional resources that were needed to implement the program.

Outcome or summative evaluation is conducted at the end of the program and should specifically measure desired outcomes of the program. In the example in Table 3, the monitoring activities conducted by the support facilitator also served as a summative evaluation of one of the program objectives (i.e., the level at which all sixth grade students in the pilot program participated in the social studies unit). In keeping a log of the program implementation, the support facilitator described the activities, concerns, and decisions made. It was possible to document, through this description, if any students were excluded for any reason and what activities were conducted to deal with that exclusion.

It is important to keep in mind that whatever evaluation activities are conducted, they should be as noninstrusive as possible. In an effort to conduct nonintrusive summative evaluation activities, the student data collected in the example in Table 3 were data that were already collected as part of the instructional activities (i.e., student work). However, it is important for the student work to be well documented, that is, dated, identified by student, and notations made on work samples regarding difficulties the student may have experienced and the activities conducted to remedy those difficulties.

Identify Program Participants   Program participants are often identified in conjunction with the previous components, but they are seldom finalized until the previous components have been completed. It is useful if all program participants are identified and their level of involvement specified. Clearly identifying the individuals and their roles facilitates the evaluation of program effects. In the example in Table 3, participants were identified as were their responsibilities for instruction, materials, and evaluation.

Develop Program Schedule   To develop a schedule, it is necessary to have completed the above components, as schedules are developed in consideration of content and participants. The initial schedules that are developed should meet the needs of the participants and should also be flexible since schedules may need to be modified depending upon the ongoing feedback (i.e., formative evaluation) received about the program. In the example described in Table 3, it was found that, by the second week of the unit, the cooperative learning specialist was not needed every day because the sixth grade teacher became more skilled in facilitating cooperative learning groups.

In addition to the content, features considered important to the participants are incorporated within these schedules. In the example described in Table 3, the program was designed to support the sixth grade teacher. Therefore, it was felt that program planning activities should be conducted during the normal preparation time of the sixth grade teacher, not during times when the sixth grade teacher may have scheduled other activities. As the schedules of the specialists were more flexible than the sixth grade teacher, the specialists modified their schedule so that all participants could meet during the sixth grade teacher's preparation period (i.e., fourth period) every Friday.

For collaborative programs to work, it is essential that time for planning/collaboration occurs (Idol, 1988; Speece & Mandell, 1980). Without time to plan, it is possible for intentions to become obscured and problems to develop and fester.

Articulate Program   Program content and schedules are usually not developed in committee. However, all participants in a program should agree to the program and should have the opportunity to provide input into all aspects of the program. In the example in Table 3, the support facilitator, after the initial meeting with resource people, outlined the program. The support facilitator then arranged a meeting of resource people to discuss the program outline. It was at this second meeting that the program as defined in the content, participants, and schedules components was developed and agreed upon by all participants.

Team ownership is essential for a program to be implemented as designed (Idol-Maestas et al., 1984; West et al., 1989). The purpose of this component is to provide the opportunity for key participants to examine the initial draft of the program, provide input for program changes, and agree upon a program to be implemented. It is essential that effective communication skills be used by participants so that the collaborative program is clearly described and understood by all participants, potential problems are identified, and agreeable resolutions are formulated.

Implement Program The reader is advised not to implement the program until the previous components have been completed. While implementing the program, instruction and formative evaluation activities are often conducted simultaneously as formative evaluation data provide information that is useful for program change. For example, in the situation described in Table 3, it was discovered through observation of lessons and interviews with the sixth grade teacher that the services of the cooperative learning specialist were not needed daily after the second week of program implementation.

Conduct Summative Evaluation/Redesign Program At the completion of the program, summative evaluations should be conducted, their results analyzed, and plans made to redesign the program. In the example in Table 3, program participants noted that all students in the pilot program participated most of the time. When students were not participating, it was generally due to disruptive behavior. Participants decided to involve the behavior management specialist to help work with those students who tended to be disruptive.

Program participants also noted that many students in the pilot program achieved more than reflected in the program objectives. Participants decided to develop a range of objectives based upon the skills and needs of the students in the class.

Finally, program participants decided to extend the program. The sixth grade teacher decided to teach heterogeneous groups of sixth grade students in the following content areas: social studies, science, and arithmetic. Plans were also made to share the results of this program with the other upper elementary teachers and offer support to those teachers should they wish to replicate the pilot program.

CONCLUSION

This chapter discusses the need for collaboration in schools and the generic consultation skills that collaborators need to work well together. The author has found collaborative activities to be "never-ending" (i.e., collaboration is dynamic and the possibilities for the improvement and expansion of programs are identified as an ongoing process of the collaborative activity). Readers who participate in collaborative programs are encouraged to proceed slowly and deliberately and to give themselves time to engage in the process of collaboration. Without time to coordinate the activity, the possibility for misunderstandings, resistance, and undesirable effects magnifies. In addition, participants deny themselves the reinforcement inherent in engaging in a dynamic activity. Collaborative planning and implementation of educational programs offers the opportunities for educators to be involved and thinking about their work and for students to receive the best that a school, not a single teacher, can offer them. Therefore, it is the author's opinion that the potential effects of collaborative education far surpass the time and effort required to provide it.

REFERENCES

Bergan, J.R. (1977). _Behavioral consultation._ Columbus, OH: Charles E. Merrill.

Bergan, J.R., & Tombari, M.L. (1976). Consultant skill and efficiency and the implementation and outcomes of consultation. _Journal of School Psychology, 14_ (1), 3–14.

Bouvier, L.F., & Davis, C.B. (1982). _The future racial composition of the United States._ Washington, DC: Demographic Information Services Center of the Population Reference Bureau.

Brown, D., Wyne, M.D., Blackburn, J.E., & Powell, W.C. (1979). _Consultation: Strategy for improving education._ Newton, MA: Allyn & Bacon.

Conoley, J.C., & Conoley, C.W. (1982). _School consultation: A guide to practice and training._ Elmsford, NY: Pergamon Press.

DeBoer, A.L. (1986). _The art of consulting._ Chicago: Arcturus Books.

Friend, M. (1985). Training special educators to be consultants. _Teacher Education and Special Education, 8_(3), 115–120.

Gersten, R., & Hauser, C. (1984). The case for impact evaluations in special education. _Remedial and Special Education, 5_(2), 16–24.

Goldstein, A.P., & Sorcher, M. (1974). _Changing supervisor behavior._ Elmsford, NY: Pergamon Press.

Gutkin, T.B., & Curtis, M.L. (1982). School-based consultation theory and techniques. In C.R. Reynolds & T.B. Gutkin (Eds.), _The handbook of school psychology_ (pp. 796–828). New York: John Wiley & Sons.

Harris, K.C., Harvey, P., Garcia, L., Innes, D., Lynn, P., Muñoz, D., Sexton, K., & Stoica, R. (1987). Meeting the needs of special education high school students in regular education classrooms. _Teacher Education and Special Education, 10_(4), 143–152.

Heron, T.E., & Harris, K.C. (1987). _The educational consultant: Helping professionals, parents, and mainstreamed students_ (2nd ed.). Austin, TX: PRO-ED.

Idol, L. (1988). A rationale and guidelines for establishing special education consultation programs. _Remedial and Special Education, 9_(6), 48–58.

Idol, L., Paolucci-Whitcomb, P., & Nevin, A. (1986). _Collaborative consultation._ Austin, TX: PRO-ED.

Idol-Maestas, L., Nevin, A., & Paolucci-Whitcomb, P. (1984). *Facilitator's manual for collaborative consultation: Principles and techniques.* Reston, VA: National RETOOL Center, Teacher Education Division, Council for Exceptional Children.

Kurpius, D. (1978). Consultation theory and process: An integrated model. *Personnel and Guidance Journal, 56,* 335–338.

Parsons, R.D., & Meyers, J. (1984). *Developing consultation skills.* San Francisco: Jossey-Bass.

Robinson, V.M., Cameron, M.M., & Raethel, A.M. (1985). Negotiation of a consultative role for school psychologists: A case study. *Journal of School Psychology, 23,* 43–49.

Rosenfield, S. (1987). *Instructional consultation.* Hillsdale, NJ: Erlbaum.

Speece, D.L., & Mandell, C.J. (1980). Interpersonal communication between resource and regular teachers. *Teacher Education and Special Education, 3*(4), 55–60.

Tombari, M., & Bergan, J. (1978). Consultant cues and teacher verbalizations, judgments, and expectancies concerning children's adjustment problems. *Journal of School Psychology, 16,* 212–219.

West, J.F., Idol, L., & Cannon, G. (1989). *Collaboration in the schools: An inservice and preservice curriculum for teachers, support staff, and administrators.* Austin, TX: PRO-ED.

Jacqueline S. Thousand
Richard A. Villa

10

Sharing Expertise and Responsibilities through Teaching Teams

Traditionally, American schools have sorted and separated students into high, medium, and low groups through heavy reliance upon segregated or pull-out special and compensatory education service models, ability groupings, and tracking (Slavin, 1987). With the growing recognition of the inefficiency of these segregated educational service delivery models (Reynolds, Wang, & Walberg, 1987; Wang, Reynolds, & Walberg, 1988) and the movement toward merging general and special education (Stainback & Stainback, 1984; Will, 1986), a growing need has arisen to identify instructional arrangements and technologies that enable all students to be educated successfully together.

There are schools and school districts that *do* educate all students in general education environments (Porter, 1988; Thousand et al., 1986; Thousand & Villa, 1989). What have these schools done to merge the instructional staff and resources of general and special education to meet the diverse educational and psychological needs of a heterogeneous student body? Some schools have dropped professional labels and distributed traditional job functions across a number of school personnel. All such schools have had to create opportunities for teachers to meet and plan collaboratively on a regular basis. Some have created an in-service agenda expressly designed to build among *all* school staff a *common* conceptual framework, language, and set of skills regarding the instruction of a heterogeneous group of students (Villa, 1989; Villa & Thousand, 1988). Most schools also have established some types of team teaching arrangements among the faculty. For example, Bauwens, Hourcade, and Friend (1989) described a "cooperative teaching" model for including students with a variety of educational needs within the general education classroom. In this direct service delivery system option, all "former" special educators are simultaneously present in the classroom with the "regular" educators, and each teacher is responsible for particular classroom instructional activities. Bauwens and associates described three instructional arrangements within cooperative teaching (i.e., team teaching, complementary instruction, and supportive learning activities) that hold promise for including students with diverse needs in general education settings as described and differentiated.

The purpose of this chapter is to familiarize the reader with instructional teaming practices that are emerging in fully inclusionary schools. These practices incorporate elements of and expand upon the general education "team teaching" arrangements (Bair & Woodward, 1964; Beggs, 1964; Pumerantz & Galano, 1972) popularized in the mid-1960s and special/general education cooperative teaching arrangements (Armbruster & Howe, 1985; Bauwens et al., 1989) of the 1980s. The authors have selected the term "teaching teams" to refer to the various instructional teaming arrangements that are being employed in schools that educate *all* students, including students with severe disabilities, in local school general settings.

In this chapter the authors define the term "teaching teams," identify the critical elements of an effective teaching team, present examples of teaching teams in action, and discuss the potential benefits of employing teaching teams in schools. In preparing for this chapter, the authors constructed a 20-item structured interview regarding teaching teams. One or more members of 30 teaching teams operating in *fully inclusionary* schools in Vermont were interviewed. The content of this chapter represents an integration of the results of these interviews; the authors' firsthand experiences observing teaching teams; and the authors' reading of the literature regarding team teaching (Bair & Woodward, 1964; Olsen, 1968), cooperative teaching (Armbruster & Howe, 1985; Bauwens et al., 1989), collaborative consultation (Idol, Paolucci-Whitcomb, & Nevin, 1986; Polsgrove & McNeil, 1989; Tindal, Shinn, Walz, & Germann, 1987), adult cooperation (Brandt, 1987; DeBevoise, 1986; Hord, 1986; Johnson & Johnson, 1987b; Lieberman, 1986; Trumbowitz, 1986), and group theory (Johnson & Johnson, 1987a).

DEFINITION OF AND RATIONALE FOR TEACHING TEAMS

A teaching team is an organizational and instructional arrangement of two or more members of the school and greater community who distribute among themselves planning, instructional, and evaluation responsibilities for the same students on a regular basis for an extended period of time. Teams can vary in size from two to six or seven people. They can vary in composition as well, involving any possible combination of classroom teachers, specialized personnel (e.g., special educators, speech and language pathologists, guidance counselors, health professionals, employment specialists), instructional assistants, student teachers, community volunteers (e.g., parents, members of the local "foster grandparent" program), and students themselves.

The overall purpose for assembling teaching teams is to increase the potential for individualizing instruction and enabling all students to be educated with their same-age peers within local school general education settings. With multiple instructors, there is increased grouping and scheduling flexibility (Olsen, 1968), greater opportunity to capitalize upon the unique, diverse, and specialized knowledge, skills, and instructional approaches of the team members (Bauwens et al., 1989), and a higher teacher/student ratio that allows for more immediate and accurate diagnosis of student needs and more active student participation in a variety of learning situations.

CRITICAL ELEMENTS OF AN EFFECTIVE TEACHING TEAM

An examination of the literature on team and cooperative teaching, collaborative consultation, adult collaboration, and group theory yields more than 100 specific, yet overlapping, characteristics of effective teams or groups. The characteristics identified by members of Vermont teaching teams were strikingly consistent with those presented in the literature. As the definition of teaching teams (offered above) reflects, central to the concept of teaching teams is _the distribution of responsibility among team members for planning, instruction, and evaluation for a common set of students._ In attempting to categorize the other identified characteristics, the authors, ardent advocates of cooperative learning instructional models (Johnson, Johnson, Holubec, & Roy, 1984; Slavin, 1987), were drawn to the same conclusions as researchers and teachers in the area of group theory and cooperative group learning (Brandt, 1987; Johnson & Johnson, 1987b). Fundamentally, effective teaching teams are the adult analogue of student cooperative learning groups; they are optimally effective when five basic elements are in place. These five elements are: 1) frequent face-to-face interactions; 2) a positive "sink-or-swim-together" sense of interdependence; 3) small group social skills in leadership, communication, trust building, decision making, and conflict management; 4) periodic assessments of how well the group is functioning and how the group might do better in the future; and 5) clear individual accountability for personal responsibilities.

Face-To-Face Interaction

Some of the questions most frequently raised when teaching teams are initiated to support all students in heterogeneous classes relate to time. When and how often will the team members meet? How much time will meetings take during or outside of school hours? When should any of the other people used to support students in the classroom (e.g., teaching assistants, specialists, psychologist, physical therapist, other consultants) attend meetings? Do team members have a system for quickly communicating information among themselves when they are not scheduled for a formal team planning meeting (e.g., communication log book located on the instructors' desk, "post it" notes stuck to the inside of a storage door in the classroom)?

Face-to-face interaction involves collaborative decision making on the part of all team members regarding each of the above questions. It involves the structuring of time for team members to plan for and evaluate the effectiveness of their instruction. Face-to-face interaction also concerns the outside limits of effective team size. The literature on student learning teams recommends a maximum group size of six members (Johnson et al., 1984). The authors recommend the same size limitation for adult teams, as this allows for adequate "air time" during meetings for each team member.

Positive Interdependence

For teaching teams, positive interdependence involves the recognition among the team's membership that no one person can effectively respond to the diverse psychological and educational needs of the heterogeneous group of students for whom they are responsible. It involves the creation of a feeling among members of the teaching team that they *all* are responsible for the learning of *all* students to whom they now are assigned and that they can best carry out their teaching responsibilities by pooling their diverse knowledge, skills, and material resources. Methods for creating positive interdependence include: 1) the establishment of a common group goal (i.e., a school mission of full inclusion for students; an expectation that teaching staff will collaborate in curriculum development, planning, and teaching); 2) the creation of rewards for team success with students (e.g., public recognition of the team at a faculty or school board meeting, arranging for a team to present their successes at a conference); and 3) the distribution of "classroom leadership" responsibilities and decision-making powers (i.e., the who, what, where, when, why, and how of teaching) across all members of any given teaching team.

One of the respondents to the authors' interview stated that "a teaching team does everything that a 'normal' teacher would do except that now there are two or more people doing it" (N. Keller, personal communication, March 17, 1989). What is important about this statement is the implicit recognition that teaching teams must make numerous decisions about how their former "classroom leadership" responsibilities and decision-making powers will be redistributed. Most of the questions and issues regarding teaching teams concern this role clarification. Some of the questions that each team must answer for themselves include the following:

Who plans for what content?

Who adapts the curriculum and instructional procedures for select students?

How will the content be presented—will one person teach and the other(s) arrange and facilitate follow-up activities, or will all members share in the teaching of the lesson?

Who evaluates which group of students—do team members collaborate in evaluating all students' performances, or is each team member primarily responsible for evaluating a subset of students?

Who decides on the disciplinary procedures?

Who carries out the disciplinary procedures and delivers the consequences?

How do team members arrange to share their expertise—do they observe one another and practice peer coaching?

Do team members rotate responsibilities?

Who communicates with parents and administrators?

Who completes the paperwork for students identified as needing special education?

How is the decision made to expand or contract the team membership?

How will a balance of decision-making power be maintained among group members?

Small Group Social Skills

The last question regarding role clarification listed above concerns not only the distribution of leadership authority, but also the social skills needed to communicate effectively and resolve the conflicts that will arise naturally in team work. The most effective teams are those that employ a consensual (i.e., all members must agree) rather than a democratic (i.e., the greatest number of votes wins) decision-making process. To behave in a consensual fashion, however, requires the development of a great many small group social skills including trust, active listening, perspective taking, questioning for deeper understanding, and skills in giving and receiving criticism (Johnson & Johnson, 1987a). The mastery of these and other needed social skills does not occur overnight. Every group progresses through stages of group growth (Johnson & Johnson, 1987a; Trumbowitz, 1986) in which mutual trust is built (i.e., the forming stage), communication and leadership behaviors for achieving the task and maintaining positive personal relationships are acquired (i.e., the functioning stage), problem-solving strategies are settled upon (i.e., the formulating stage), and conflict and controversy come to be viewed as proactive methods for generating the most creative solutions (i.e., the fermenting stage).

A major issue for all beginning teacher teams is how to acquire these basic teaming skills. David and Roger Johnson recommend two approaches, one direct and the other indirect. With the direct method, collaborative skill training is arranged as part of an ongoing in-service agenda. The indirect method, the Johnsons' preferred method, engages teachers in the act of teaching their students social skills as part of cooperative learning or basic skills lessons. Teachers acquire the same skills as their student through the instructional process and come to recognize the importance of these skills to their own team's functioning (Brandt, 1987).

Processing of Team Effectiveness

Research on staff development points out the importance of creating frequent opportunities for teachers to process and receive coaching and feedback regarding the new skills they are attempting to acquire (Showers, Joyce, & Bennett, 1987). This is particularly true for teaching teams, whose members may have little or no previous experience in planning and teaching with others or exercising small group skills. Consequently, it is important for teaching teams to structure, as an integral part of team meetings and the teaching day, time for processing task and relationship achievement and selecting personal and team social growth goals (Thousand et al., 1986). Outside observers (e.g., the supervising administrator, a colleague from another teaching team) also may be invited to observe meetings or lessons and share their observations, as a regular professional development activity or as an intervention when members feel that the team is functioning less than optimally.

Individual Accountability

Collaborative norms reinforce traditional methods of accountability. . . In the collaborative school, teachers monitor one another's performance, set limits on one another's behavior, and take responsibility for helping their colleagues to improve. The self-policing efforts are a measure of a faculty's true professionalism. (Smith, 1987, p. 6)

Collaboration, including the use of teaching teams, has the potential for increasing teachers' accountability (Smith, 1987). The use of teaching teams has the natural consequence of introducing additional pairs of instructional eyes in the classroom to observe each team member's agreed upon planning, teaching, and evaluation activities.

Clearly, working as a team *does* take away some of the freedom and autonomy that teachers enjoy when they operate independently as free-standing one-room schools, housed under a single roof (Johnson, 1979; Skrtic, 1987). However, a major purpose of a teaching team situation is to maximize the potential teaching and collaborative teaming performance of each individual instructor through teammates' modeling, coaching, and provision of regular feedback (Johnson et al., 1984). For team members to provide appropriate assistance to one another, it is necessary for them to observe and ask questions of one another in an atmosphere of trust and professionalism. The potential freedom that teaming may threaten is balanced by the potential for survival and power in dealing with a diverse group of students, the freedom of not being solely responsible for the learning of these students, and the fun and sense of belonging that comes with successfully problem solving with others (Glasser, 1986).

CASE STUDIES EXEMPLIFYING THE
CRITICAL ELEMENTS OF TEACHING TEAMS

What follows are descriptions of several teaching team arrangements that exist in the Winooski School District, one of Vermont's fully inclusive school districts. The examples have been selected to illustrate differences among teaching teams in terms of composition, size, and strategies for implementing the critical elements discussed above.

Situation #1—Team in Formative Stage

At 3:30 P.M. one Friday in November of 1988, 15 teachers, administrators, teaching assistants, and students "pitched in" and moved all of the contents of a first grade classroom to another wing of the elementary school. The teacher in this classroom had been discussing with another first grade teacher the advantages they both would reap if they were to join as a teaching team. Both teachers shared the same support personnel (i.e., speech and language pathologist, special educator, teaching assistant), all of whom practiced an "in class" rather than "pull out" service delivery model. The teachers were interested in having the flexibility of mixing their two classes of students in various instructional groupings throughout the day to increase individualization of instruction. They also recognized that by pooling their classes, they would increase the amount of time that resource personnel were available to them and increase the teacher/student ratio during the reading and written language segment of the day, a time when resource support was provided. In this elementary school building, some rooms have folding walls between them. One of the two teachers had such an arrangement with the adjoining room being a multiage classroom.

In early November, the two teachers approached their principal and the supervisor of support personnel to propose that the following year they trade rooms with the multiage teacher so they could physically join classrooms as desired throughout the day. The administration was impressed with the educationally sound rationale for this move. Within one week the principal had spoken with the multiage teacher, who agreed to the move, and the classrooms were rearranged immediately rather than waiting until the following year.

General educators have been in the practice of forming teaching teams for decades (Bair & Woodward, 1964), recognizing the increased grouping and scheduling flexibility that the practice allows (Olsen, 1968). What these two general educators also recognized was that, given the specialized educational support services available to students since the implementation of PL 94-142, their establishment of a teaching team increased the number, diversity, and intensity of instructional supports available to them and to their students. This teaching team is at the forming stage of team development, engaged in making decisions about the distribution of their planning, teaching, and evaluation responsibilities.

Situation #2—Elementary Teacher Team

Another pair of first grade teachers have not closed the divider between their rooms for 2 years. Three years ago, these two teachers occasionally brought their classes together. As they expanded the time they jointly planned and taught together, both teachers began to notice a feeling of isolation when they returned to their separate rooms. They also noted that they felt more creative and effective when they were collaborating. As a consequence, this teaching team made the decision to plan and teach every lesson together.

This team has arranged weekly and daily planning meetings that occur before, during, and after school hours. One teacher stated that when they first started this arrangement, she felt she needed to be prepared for every lesson of the week before she could go home on Friday. With a successful collaborative history behind her, she now feels more relaxed and "trusts that it will come together" (R. Whitehouse, personal communication, February 24, 1989). In the beginning, joint planning was quite time consuming. Now they spend substantially less time planning together, aided by a planning format that they designed on their own. Each teacher maintains individual preparation time and is careful to be respectful of one another's need for this personal time and space.

One of the teachers in this team has a master's degree in reading, the other has a bachelor's degree in elementary and special education and special talents in the areas of music and art. They bring these complementary skills to their planning and teaching and consider their unique skills when arranging for accommodations or modifications of lessons. They share a lesson plan book and rotate large group and small group responsibilities for each subject area on a daily basis.

Even though these two teachers plan and instruct as a single unit, when it comes to assessing student progress and communicating with parents, they have made the decision that each of them is responsible primarily for the students (including all students with special education needs) who technically are listed on their respective class rosters. It should be noted that they do collaborate with one another and specialized support personnel to design or select the assessment instruments to be used with students.

This teaching team considers collaborative planning and teaching as the *vehicle* for teaching professionals the social skills of openness and honesty in communication, flexibility, compromise, and acceptance of difference. They stress the importance of feeling that they do not always need to be "perfect," that they can make mistakes in front of one another. "It is OK to fail now. I am more likely to try new things. It is easier to try new things if you have someone to take the risk with—someone to laugh with" (R. Whitehouse, personal communication, February 24, 1989).

When asked how their teaming situation could be improved, one teacher expressed the desire to acquire new content and instructional skills to share with her partner. The other teacher noted the need to create a more structured planning format so that the support personnel who teach in the room could be *equally* involved in the planning and teaching of all students.

Situation #3—Junior High Teacher Team

The Winooski Junior High School core content area teachers (i.e., math, science, social studies, English, and reading teachers) have functioned as a teaching team for 3 years. During their daily preparation period, they jointly plan for the assessment and monitoring of students' academic and social progress across content areas; meet with parents, students, and support personnel; coordinate the content of their student advisory periods; plan for assemblies and field trips; and integrate curriculum for particular units.

Two of the teachers on this team formed a smaller teaching team. One of the teachers was trained in science and the other in special education. They jointly plan, teach, and evaluate student performance for one period of the day. They have chosen to be a teaching team for philosophical and educational reasons. In the words of the teacher trained in special education, "The content of science is difficult. If we want to serve students in the least restrictive environment, we need to give them support in the classroom" (L. Cravedi-Cheng, personal communication, March 27, 1989). The science teacher describes their partnership as "a more appropriate way to teach children. We integrate our services so we can mainstream our students effectively" (N. Keller, personal communication, March 17, 1989).

This teaching team does not have a regularly set time during which they plan for their weekly or daily lessons. They mutually decide, week to week, when and where they will conduct their planning. What does remain constant is their commitment to making this time "sacred," a time when no interruptions are tolerated.

This teaching team has been in operation for 2 years. In the first year, the teacher trained in special education functioned largely as a teacher assistant, but contributed significantly to the class by individualizing and adapting instruction to accommodate for individual differences among students. At that point in time, she did not have content mastery, and the two teachers had different philosophies and approaches to teaching and classroom management. In the second year, the role of the teacher trained in special education evolved to that of an equal partner in planning, teaching, and student evaluation. The team attributes this change in their working relationship to three things. First, having worked together for nearly 2 years, the team now has developed a climate of trust and an effective communication system. Second, the teacher trained in special education has acquired more content mastery and is more competent to instruct science. Finally, both team members have participated in a yearlong, districtwide intensive in-service training effort to provide all instructional staff with common knowledge and skills in effective teaching, assessment, classroom management, social skills development, and peer coaching (Villa, 1989). As a consequence, these teachers now share a common language and approach to instruction and discipline and are better able to hold one another accountable for effective teaching and discipline. They also share peer coaching skills that enable them to assist one another in continued professional development.

For this team, the social skill of perspective taking, being able to "walk in the shoes of someone else," has been a key to their success. The teacher trained in special education states that, by being placed in the role of a classroom teacher, she now has a greater appreciation and understanding of the difficulty of instructing large groups of students. The science teacher, who prefers a discovery learning approach to science, has come to value more structured learning and discipline approaches that have been modeled by her teaching peer.

Situation #4—Multiple Team Membership

Second Grade Six-Member Teaching Team   Nadine, a teacher at the elementary school who is trained in special education, is a member of six very different teaching teams. One of her largest teams includes six members: a second grade teacher, a graduate student intern, an undergraduate student teacher, a compensatory education teaching assistant, a volunteer from the community "foster grandparent" program, and Nadine. This team works together primarily to coordinate reading and written language services for all of the students in this second grade class and select students from other classes who are eligible for Nadine's services and who join reading and written language groups in this class at times during the morning.

Planning for reading and written language activities is done primarily by the classroom teacher, Nadine, and the two student teachers during regularly scheduled meetings that occur before and after school. This core of four provides the other team members with the curriculum objectives, materials, and training in how instruction is to be delivered. All six members of this team provide direct instruction to small groups of students, and all are involved in monitoring student progress. The classroom teacher shares responsibility for evaluating students with the special and compensatory education personnel, but considers herself and the school district ultimately responsible for the quality of education that the students in this classroom receive.

Periodically, time is structured for team "processing"—for giving one another positive feedback and constructive criticism and for assessing the team's instructional effectiveness. The team also discusses the current division of labor and reassigns roles and responsibilities as needed.

The second grade classroom teacher considers the students as the primary beneficiaries of the teaching team arrangement. Students receive supportive, specialized, and intensive instructional services without having to be evaluated, categorized, labeled, and pulled out of the classroom. "I have very positive feelings about working with my team. It is great! All children in the room benefit" (M. Steady, personal communication, April 10, 1989).

Students as Members of a Teaching Team Nadine also is a member of a fourth grade classroom team. The fourth grade teacher has six additional support people, including Nadine, who rotate in and out of her classroom throughout the day. In this class, the teacher and Nadine have developed a peer tutor/partner learning system for delivering individualized instruction. Nadine provides no direct instruction in this classroom. Instead, she and the classroom teacher collaborate in training and supervising the peer tutors and instructional assistants. Through the use of cooperative learning groups and peer tutor/partner learning arrangements, this fourth grade teacher has included the students as members of one of the teaching teams operating in the classroom.

A few months after the peer tutor program was initiated, a first grade teacher asked if some of the fourth grade tutors could become cross-age tutors in her classroom. Recognizing the potential positive outcomes of such an experience (e.g., content mastery, practice in the use of higher level thinking skills, enhanced self-esteem), an arrangement was made for six tutors to form a teaching team with the first grade teacher and Nadine for the purpose of providing math review in the first grade for 30 minutes on every other Wednesday.

Each tutor works with a group of three to four first graders, allowing all students in the class to receive this individualized instructional experience. Nadine initially provided tutors with support in delivering effective teaching and correction procedures. This support was gradually faded, and within 2 months of the initiation of the project, the cross-age tutors became responsible for creating their own instructional materials and for reinforcing and correcting their tutees' work. Supervisory responsibilities also were shifted from Nadine to the classroom teacher. Nadine, however, continued to conduct brief post-instructional conferences with the tutors, tutees, and the classroom teacher.

When questioned as to her feelings about being a member of multiple teaching teams, Nadine responded:

> I always liked the idea of collaborating with other professionals and para-professionals. It holds people accountable and generates new ideas which no one person would come up with alone. The biggest advocates of teaching teams are the cooperative and open-minded general educators who truly have students' best interests as a top priority. Our teaching teams work because our administration supports innovation and allows us to make educational decisions. (N. Zane, personal communication, April 10, 1989)

WHY USE TEACHING TEAMS?

Some insights as to what may motivate school personnel to teach as members of a team is provided by the existing literature concerning group theory, adult cooperation, collaborative consultation, and cooperative and team teaching. Members of teaching teams operating in Vermont's fully inclusionary schools provide additional insights.

Table 1 summarizes some of the rationale, potential benefits, and motivating factors for establishing teaching teams cited by the literature and Vermont educators. As illustrated in the table, each of the identified factors can be categorized into at least one of the five basic human need categories described by Glasser (1985, 1986) in his "control theory" of human behavior. According to the theory, people choose to do what they do because it satisfies one or more of five basic human needs: survival, power or control in one's life, freedom of choice, a sense of belonging or love, and fun. Cooperative group learning models have been considered particularly attractive learning structures for children because, more than competitive or individualistic learning structures, they allow students to meet basic human needs (Glasser, 1986). If teaching teams may be considered the adult analogue of cooperative learning groups, it seems that collaboration in teaching may yield the same benefits for instructional personnel in terms of personal and professional need satisfaction as collaboration in learning may yield for children (Johnson et al., 1984). As Table 1 suggests, the autonomy (freedom) that educators may lose when they decide to share students and instructional responsibilities should be well compensated by an enhanced potential for survival and power in dealing with a diverse group of students, freedom in not being solely responsible for the learning of these students, and the fun and sense of belonging that comes with successfully problem solving with others. Clearly, intensive and systematic research is needed to verify the proposed positive effects and critical attributes of teaching team arrangements in all of their forms.

CONCLUSION

Teaching need not be a "lonely profession" (Sarason, Levine, Godenberg, Cherlin, & Bennet, 1966, p. 74); and the small group pull-out and special class arrangements of special and compensatory education need not be the solution to increasing teacher/student ratios, individualizing instruction, and accommodating for student differences. When members of the school community choose to pool their resources in creative combinations such as teaching teams, both teachers and students should more fully experience educational success and satisfaction of their basic

Table 1. Rationale, potential benefits, and motivational factors for establishing teaching teams

Survival/power	Freedom	Sense of belonging	Fun
Provides critical resources to regular education (Reynolds, Wang, & Walberg, 1987; Tindal, Shinn, Walz, Germann, 1987; Will, 1986)	Increases flexibility in scheduling and grouping (Olsen, 1968)	Alleviates isolation (Bauwens et al., 1989; Fox & Faver, 1984)	Allows for adult stimulation, professional talk, and interaction (Lieberman, 1986)
Promotes professional growth through peer coaching (Brandt, 1987)	Allows for more effective and efficient use of each team member's skills (Armbruster & Howe, 1985; Bauwens, Hourcade, & Friend, 1989)	Motivates commitment to others (Fox & Faver, 1984)	Provides someone to laugh with
Promotes acquisition of trust, communication, leadership, and conflict resolution skills (Johnson & Johnson, 1987a)	Allows for division of labor (Fox & Faver, 1984)	Develops positive interpersonal relationships (Johnson & Johnson, 1987b)	Enables creativity
Increases adult self-esteem (Johnson & Johnson, 1987b)	Facilitates sharing of responsibility for all children	Increases social support (Johnson & Johnson, 1987b)	Creates a positive learning environment
Increases the number of students who get help from specialized services (Armbruster & Howe, 1985)	Provides an opportunity to work with a variety of students	Promotes students' inclusion with peers through elimination of pull-out programs (Armbruster & Howe, 1985; Bauwens et al. 1989)	Improves staff morale
Decreases the number of students referred for specialized services through increased individualization (Gelzheiser, Shepard, & Wozniak, 1986)	Reduces the amount of direct support needed from an administrator	Allows for integration of specialists in classroom settings	
Allows for sharing of skills			
Provides access to technical assistance			
Promotes perspective taking			
Increases student-teacher direct contact time			

Note: All items in the table without citations were identified by Vermont teaching team members through a structured interview developed by the authors.

human needs in a learning environment that is more inclusive for all concerned.

REFERENCES

Armbruster, B., & Howe, C. (1985). An alternative instructional approach: Educators team up to help students learn. *National Association of Secondary School Principals Bulletin, 69*(479), 82/86.

Bair, M., & Woodward, R.G. (1964). *Team teaching in action.* Boston: Houghton Mifflin.

Bauwens, J., Hourcade, J.J., & Friend, M. (1989). Cooperative teaching: A model for general and special education integration. *Remedial and Special Education, 10*(2), 17–22.

Beggs, D.W., III (Ed.). (1964). *Team teaching: Bold new venture.* Indianapolis: Unified College Press.

Brandt, R. (1987). On cooperation in schools: A conversation with David and Roger Johnson. *Educational Leadership, 45*(3), 14–19.

DeBevoise, W. (1986). Collaboration: Some principles of bridgework. *Educational Leadership, 43*(5), 9–12.

Fox, M.F., & Faver, C.A. (1984). Independence and cooperation in research: The motivations and costs of collaboration. *Journal of Higher Education, 55*(3), 43–49.

Gelzheiser, L.M., Shepherd, M.J., & Wozniak, R.H. (1986). The development of instruction to induce skill transfer. *Exceptional Children, 54,* 125–129.

Glasser, W. (1985). *Control theory.* New York: Harper & Row.

Glasser, W. (1986). *Control theory in the classroom.* New York: Harper & Row.

Hord, S.M. (1986). A synthesis of research on organizational collaboration. *Educational Leadership, 43*(5), 22–26.

Idol, L., Paolucci-Whitcomb, P., & Nevin, A. (1986). *Collaborative consultation.* Austin, TX: PRO-ED.

Johnson, D.W. (1979). *Educational psychology.* Englewood Cliffs, NJ: Prentice-Hall.

Johnson, D.W., & Johnson, R.T. (1987a). *Joining together: Group theory and group skills* (3rd ed.). Englewood Cliffs, NJ: Prentice-Hall.

Johnson, D.W., & Johnson, R.T. (1987b). Research showing the benefits of adult cooperation. *Educational Leadership, 45*(3), 27–30.

Johnson, D.W., Johnson, R.T., Holubec, E., & Roy, P. (1984). *Circles of learning.* Arlington, VA: Association for Supervision and Curriculum Development.

Lieberman, A. (1986). Collaborative work. *Educational Leadership, 45*(3), 4–8.

Olsen, C.O. (1968). Team teaching in the elementary school. *Education, 88,* 345–349.

Polsgrove, L., & McNeil, M. (1989). The consultation process: Research and practice. *Remedial and Special Education, 10*(1), 6–13.

Porter, G. (1988, June). *School integration: Fad, fantasy, or the future?* Paper presented at the International Conference on Special Education, Beijing, China.

Pumerantz, P., & Galano, R.W. (1972). *Establishing interdisciplinary programs in the middle school.* West Nyack, NY: Parker.

Reynolds, M.C., Wang, M.C., & Walberg, H.J. (1987). The necessary restructuring of special and regular education. *Exceptional Children, 53,* 391–398.

Sarason, S., Levine, M., Godenberg, I.I., Cherlin, D., & Bennet, E. (1966). *Psychology in community settings: Clinical, educational, vocational and social aspects.* New York: John Wiley & Sons.

Showers, B., Joyce, B., & Bennett, B. (1987). Synthesis of research on staff development: A framework for future study and a state-of-the-art analysis. *Educational Leadership, 45*(3), 77–87.

Skrtic, T. (1987). An organizational analysis of special education reform. *Counterpoint, 8*(2), 15–19.

Slavin, R.E. (1987). Ability grouping and student achievement in elementary school: A best-evidence synthesis. *Review of Educational Research, 57,* 293–336.

Smith, S.C. (1987). The collaborative school takes shape. *Educational Leadership, 45*(3), 4–6.

Stainback, W., & Stainback, S. (1984). A rationale for the merger of special and regular education. *Exceptional Children, 51,* 102–111.

Thousand, J., Fox, T., Reid, R., Godek, J., Williams, W. & Fox, W. (1986). *The homecoming model: Educating students who present intensive educational challenges within regular education environments.* (Monograph No. 7-1) Burlington, VT: University of Vermont, Center for Developmental Disabilities.

Thousand, J., & Villa, R. (1989). Enhancing success in heterogeneous schools. In S. Stainback, W. Stainback, & M. Forest (Eds.), *Educating all students in the mainstream of regular education* (pp. 89–103). Baltimore: Paul H. Brookes Publishing Co.

Tindal, G., Shinn, M., Walz, L., & Germann, G. (1987). Mainstream consultation in secondary settings: The Pine County model. *The Journal of Special Education, 21*(3), 95–106.

Trumbowitz, S. (1986). Stages in the development of school-college collaboration. *Educational Leadership, 43*(5), 18–21.

Villa, R. (1989). Model public school inservice programs—do they exist? *Teacher Education and Special Education, 12,* 173–176.

Villa, R., & Thousand, J. (1988). Enhancing school success in heterogeneous classrooms and schools: The power of partnership. *Teacher Education and Special Education, 11,* 144–154.

Wang, M.C., Reynolds, M.C., & Walberg, H.J. (1988). Integrating children of the second system. *Phi Delta Kappan, 69,* 248–251.

Will, M.C. (1986). Educating children with learning problems: A shared responsibility. *Exceptional Children, 52,* 411–415.

Donna H. Dutton
Dale L. Dutton

11

Technology to Support Diverse Needs in Regular Classes

For students who need support in order to be successful in a regular classroom, technology might be just the equalizer that is needed. Computer technology in particular, as a tool under the control of the student, can provide the necessary bridge that forms the link with regular classroom activities.

All students seem to enjoy using computers in the classroom. Some students can be empowered to function on a par with the others if a computer is available as a tool. There are innumerable devices that could be mentioned as potential aids. This chapter explores a few available tools of which every educator should be aware.

First, it may be useful to define some basic terms. *Hardware* is the physical machinery and the devices attached to the machinery (for example, the computer, monitor, and printer). *Software* is the content of the programs used with the computer, usually stored on disks. Disks store program *applications* (for example, a word processor) and *data* generated by the user (for example, text in the form of stories or letters). Common *floppy disks* are circular sheets coated with magnetic material and housed in 5.25 inch square envelopes or 3.5 inch plastic casings. The computer is *booted* (started up for use) by putting a disk in a disk drive and turning on the computer; the software is *loaded* from the disk into the computer's memory and is then ready to use.

Educators who are novices in the world of technology need not feel overwhelmed. Just as no one is expected to understand music composition or electronics in order to operate a phonograph, no one is expected to have sophisticated technological expertise in order to use a computer as a tool. Where needed, training and technical assistance should be provided by school districts.

In this chapter, the following topics will be discussed: computer hardware that can enable students with diverse needs to participate in educational activities, computer software that can be helpful to students with various capabilities, and student uses for a variety of additional technologies. See the appendix at the end of this chapter for a listing of resources for learning more about these topics and for making purchases.

COMPUTER HARDWARE

Switch Access to a Computer

Most students rely on pencils to complete school work. However, a student with a physical disability may not be able to hold a pencil and thus be unable to write, even though multitudes of ideas are waiting to be expressed. The ability to provide written communication may be hampered, not by an inability to form coherent sentences, but by the inability to hold and utilize a pencil. For such a student, the computer can be a prosthesis.

Most people interact with a computer by typing on a keyboard. However, for some students, using a standard computer keyboard is impossible because of limited hand use. In this case, an alternative computer access device can be provided.

Scanning with Switches   If a student has ideas to be communicated, all that is really needed is the ability to activate a switch. This might mean pressing a small round plate with a fist, pushing against a flexible rod with a forearm, tilting a head, raising an eyebrow, pressing with a foot, leaning with an elbow, sipping as with a straw, or even gazing in a certain direction. If one muscle of the body can be consciously controlled, the student can write using a computer.

One commonly used device that makes this possible is the Adaptive Firmware Card (AFC) (Don Johnston Developmental Equipment, Inc.). It is placed inside a computer in the Apple II family. Any switch designed for this purpose can be plugged into the small AFC interface box and used to control the computer. Accompanying software will place a scanning array (an alphabet or a line of numbers or punctuation signs) at the bottom of the screen. A cursor (blinking light) highlights each letter as it moves from one character to the next. When it lands on the desired letter, the student simply hits the switch and that letter is selected and sent to the computer, just as if a student had typed that letter on the keyboard.

For example, if a student wishes to type the word "history," he or she would use the AFC software to place a scanning array at the bottom of the screen and then would load a favorite word processing program. The cursor would scan the alphabet at the bottom of the screen. When it highlighted the letter "h," the student would hit the switch. The cursor would start scanning again, and the student would hit the switch when the cursor came to the letter "i," and so on, until all the letters of the word "history" were selected. The word "history" would appear on the screen in the same way as if someone had typed the word on the regular keyboard. Variations on this concept include having the student move the cursor manually by repeatedly hitting the switch (step scanning) or communicating with the computer using Morse code.

With access to the writing process, a student with even severe physical disabilities can participate in class writing activities, just like the other students. This student may not ever learn to write with a pencil, but with a computer as a prosthesis, writing is a definite possibility.

There are devices other than the AFC that make scanning with switches possible. These include the PC A.I.D. (DADA) that will serve the same function as the AFC for an IBM or compatible computer, and the Aid + Me (ComputAbility Corporation) that will work with several different machines, including the Apple IIGS, the Macintosh, and the IBM.

The student who will be using scanning with a computer should be afforded the opportunity to try a variety of switches and mountings to discover what combination works best. Support personnel should be available to provide this service and to provide assistance with the appropriate positioning of the equipment for the student.

The classroom teacher does not need to know about the technical details of this equipment, but he or she needs to be aware that it is available to students. Trained personnel should be available to set up needed equipment and to train the student and staff on its use, as well as parents if similar equipment is available at home. Other students in the class would no doubt be excited to become experts on such fascinating equipment. After an initial training period, the daily use of switches and scanning should be simple and routine. The result will be that all students will be able to write, including the student who has no hand use.

Morse Code Scanning is clearly the slowest method that can be used for writing with a computer, and so it is perhaps the adaptation of last resort. A faster method is to use Morse code with an AFC and switches that include an encoding process. Long and short presses of one switch, according to standard Morse code, or use of two alternative switches, allows the input of letters, numbers, symbols, and so on. However, it is always preferable, if possible, for a student to use some method of direct selection of letters or numbers.

Adapted Keyboards, Expanded Keyboards, and Keyboard Emulation

Using the Standard Keyboard with Adaptations Sometimes a student with a physical disability is able to write using a standard computer keyboard that has a few minor modifications. The Apple IIGS computer, for example, allows the keyboard to be modified so that a student, who can touch a key but has trouble releasing it in a timely fashion, can avoid accidentally typing long strings of repeated letters because he or she has difficulty "letting go." This is done by carrying out a simple control panel maneuver right on the screen—open the "Options" menu, move the "Repeat Delay" option to the highest possible setting, and move the "Repeat Speed" option to the lowest possible setting.

Sometimes computer software requires the pressing of two keys simultaneously, a difficult feat for some students. A simple hard plastic keyguard with latches can remedy this problem on Apple II computers. On the Macintosh, a system resource called "Sticky Keys" converts such simultaneous keystroke commands into simple sequential steps. On IBM and compatible computers, a software resource called *Filch* (Kinetic Designs, Inc.) is one remedy. On Apple II computers, the AFC can provide additional keyboard adaptations and can "slow down" software that moves along too quickly for some.

Keyboard Emulation Various keyboard emulators are available for the Macintosh computer that allow a student to point with a mouse to letters on a picture of a keyboard right on the screen. The Headmaster (Prentke Romich Company) is a device that allows such pointing via head motions, using a headset transmitting an ultrasound signal rather than a hand-held mouse. The Free Wheel (Pointer Systems, Inc.) and the Lipstick (McIntyre Computer Systems Division) are other pointing devices that utilize on-screen keyboard emulation.

Expanded and Alternative Keyboards Expanded keyboards can be equalizers for some students and can provide an intriguing mode of access for everyone in the class. A frequent choice is the Unicorn Expanded Keyboard (Unicorn Engineering, Inc.) that looks like a 14 inch by 21 inch rectangular piece of hard plastic with a paper overlay. An enlarged picture of a keyboard or pictures of selected keys that are necessary for a certain piece of software can be placed on an overlay. When the student presses the "key" on the Unicorn overlay, the computer thinks that the standard keyboard has been accessed. For the student who needs a "target" larger than the keys on the standard keyboard this is a desirable adaptive device.

What about the student who is not able to understand letters or the words they form? This student could have overlays made with pictures, icons, or photographs that can be selected by touching them. Again, the computer thinks that the standard keyboard has been utilized. A clever educator can design overlays that will accommodate any student and provide full access to any software program, including word processing. No computer programming experience is necessary.

The Unicorn Expanded Keyboard is used in conjunction with the AFC and an Apple II computer, the PC Serial Aid (DADA) and an IBM or compatible computer, or the Aid + Me. Other special keyboards are available as well. There is even a Mini Keyboard (TASH, Inc.), which is much smaller than the standard keyboard, for people with a small range of motion.

Other Devices for Alternative Access

Some students can benefit from devices that offer unique kinds of alternative access to a computer. Some of these devices employ a selection method more direct than the standard keyboard and some are simply more fun. The devices listed here all require specially designed software and cannot be used to access general software.

Muppet Learning Keys   The Muppet Learning Keys (Sunburst Communications) is a colorful board that plugs into the back of an Apple II computer. On the board are an alphabet (in alphabetical order), numbers from zero to nine, a paint box of colors, and various other "buttons" to be pushed, like "stop," "go," and "zap." The student can use various pieces of early childhood software specially designed for use with this device. Younger students are highly motivated by "exploring" with the Muppet Learning Keys, and the accompanying software seems to be especially motivating for them.

Power Pad   The Power Pad (Dunamis, Inc.) is a square board with a 12 inch by 12 inch membrane surface on which overlays can be placed; and on the overlays are letters, numbers, drawings, or photographs. Students access the computer with software specifically designed for this device by touching the surface of the board. Several pieces of software have been programmed for this board, especially for younger children, and an easy-to-use authoring system is available, which enables educators to design their own computerized lessons without knowing computer programing. When used in conjunction with a voice synthesizer, which provides computerized speech output for selected text, simple communication boards can be constructed.

Touch Window The Touch Window (Edmark Corporation) is an input device that is a favorite of children and educators. It fits on the front of the computer monitor and is fastened with velcro. The picture on the screen shows through the Touch Window, allowing the student to "touch" and select his choices from the screen. Again, special software is needed, and an authoring system is available for constructing custom lessons. This device is especially helpful for students for whom the notion of keyboard communication with a computer is too abstract.

All of the devices mentioned in this section are alluring and captivating to *all* students in a regular classroom. Students could utilize them in pairs and in small groups. What is an access or communication device for one student may be a source of enjoyment for another.

Speech Output

Computerized speech synthesis is perhaps the most educationally helpful technological concept to be considered. The concept of computerized speech means that when letters, words, or sentences are typed into a computer, a device inside the computer produces sounds that attempt to simulate the sounds of a person who is speaking.

Speech Hardware The quality of the speech that a computer can produce varies, as might be expected, with the price of the device. There are voice synthesizers for about $4,000.00 (DECtalk from Digital Equipment Corporation) that will sound very much like human speech, and there are those in the $100.00 range (Echo from Street Electronics Corporation) that produce a robotic sounding synthesized voice as well as a more natural sounding digitized voice. In each case, it will take patience for students and educators to become accustomed to the simulated speech. Children seem to adapt to it much more easily than adults.

When computerized speech is digitized, an actual human voice has been translated into data that can be stored on a disk in words or phrases. This speech is usually of superior quality, but the computer user may only use those particular words or phrases that have been digitized. When computerized speech is synthesized, rules have been coded into the software that allow the computer to "translate" anything the person types into speech output. This is called text-to-speech.

Most speech output devices involve inserting a circuit board card into a computer and plugging an accompanying speaker into the card. They are generally easy to install. The software that is used by the student must be written to recognize the voice synthesizer, or, as is the case with IBM computers, screen-reading software must be used in addition to the software application so that the computer will be enabled to "talk."

Rationale   Why would an educator want to use such a device in the classroom? Some students who are not able to see a printed page because of vision problems could "hear" the same page of text, computerized and voiced by the synthesizer. The device would enable a student who is blind to manipulate text independently and to participate in written work of the class. Some students have severe visual perception problems that lead to difficulty in decoding. Computerized speech synthesis would enable these students to participate as well. Other students simply are stronger in the auditory mode than in the visual mode and would be helped by the reinforcement of synthesized speech. Students who are not able to speak because of deafness or lack of motor control might also be able to use the computer as one component of a communication system.

Common Uses   How could voice synthesis be used in a classroom context? The most common usage is in conjunction with the writing process. Some (or all) students may be using a word processor when they complete written assignments. Some (or all) of these students might use a word processor that is capable of speech output using a voice synthesizer. There are several such software products on the market, such as: *Keytalk* (a beginning literacy activity, PEAL Software), *My Words* (Hartley Courseware), *Language Experience Recorder* (Teacher Support Software), *Kid Talk* and *Smooth Talker* (First Byte, Electronic Arts), and *Talking Textwriter* (Scholastic, Inc.). Products specifically designed to meet the needs of students who are blind include *Pro Words* (Access Unlimited—SPEECH Enterprises), *Dr. Peet's Talk Writer* (Hartley Courseware), *outspoken* (Berkeley Systems), and *BEX* (Raised Dot Computing).

The addition of speech to text on the screen can enhance the writing process for students who cannot see, and also for those who have difficulty decoding or processing information. Dr. Laura F. Meyers (1987) researched the application of this process for students with mental retardation and observed students who are not considered educable acquire reading and writing skills.

All students in the regular classroom will be intrigued by voice synthesis. Again, what is a prosthesis for some students can provide motivation for others. A voice synthesizer can be prevented from disturbing classmates by using earphones.

Text Size Modification

What about those students who have difficulty with regular classwork because they have vision impairments that require the use of large print? These students can use the same materials as everyone else with the help of technology.

Closed Circuit Television Closed circuit televisions (Telesensory Systems, Inc. and VTEK) can be used to magnify text. The student places a book or work sheet under a camera, and the image is transmitted instantly to an enlarging monitor, giving the student control over the size of the print being viewed. Written work can also be done under such a device. With most of these products, the student has control of the size of the images being viewed.

Display Processor Display processors are manufactured by the same companies that make closed circuit televisions. These supplementary monitors are plugged into the computer and offer the student control over the size of the text on the screen. Although the text may be very small on the computer monitor, it can be enlarged many times on a display processor.

Large Print Software For those who do not need extreme magnification, there is software available that has a large font and appears magnified on the screen as well as on the printout. Four word processors for the Apple II series that include a large (20-column) font are: *Magic Slate* (Sunburst Communications), *Bank Street Writer III* (Scholastic, Inc.), *Mastertype's Writer* (Mindscape, Inc.), and *Muppet Slate* (Sunburst Communications). *Vista* (hardware and software, Telesensory Systems, Inc.) provides print enlargement on IBM and compatible computers. On the Macintosh computer, multiple-size fonts can be easily accessed by all word processors. In addition, there is a utility called *Close View* that comes with the computer and allows considerable screen enlargement. With a combination of a closed circuit television and either large print software or a display processor for a computer, the student with low vision could use all the same materials as everyone else.

Braille Students who are blind will also benefit from the technology that provides braille output from the computer. For example, a computer can be fitted with a braille printer that will print out computer files in braille. The Ohtsuki Printer (American Thermoform Corporation) is capable of printing simultaneously in braille and regular text so that everyone can read the printout. Also available are devices for people who are deaf and blind who are empowered to read by "feeling" a tactile display of "refreshable" braille, formed by vibrating pins that change under the fingertips as the text goes by (Telesensory Systems, Inc. and VTEK).

Voice Recognition

Voice recognition for computers is in its infancy but remains one of the most exciting technological developments of the 1980s. The voice recognition concept operates by translating a student's ideas directly into text for the computer. The student speaks into a "microphone" linked to the computer. The resulting text can be placed into files and saved on disks or printed out. This innovative concept, when developed fully, may well supplant the use of both pencils and keyboards in society. It is easy to envision a classroom of the future where students speak all of their ideas into a computer, or a business of the future where executives or workers instruct computers to carry out their wishes by talking to them. Many feel that this is not a far-fetched vision.

This technology, admittedly in its early stages, can assist some students now. Several devices are available that are not prohibitively expensive. The Introvoice for the IBM or Apple II series computers (Voice Connection) is one example, and the Voice Navigator (Articulate Systems) for the Macintosh is another. In each case, the person "teaches" the computer to recognize his or her voice by speaking and respeaking a series of words and phrases into a microphone. Once this process is complete, the computer can receive voice commands as well as a limited number of words that can be accepted in word processing. Unfortunately, the size of the memory of most computers prohibits the use of extensive vocabularies so users must spell additional words for the computer with their voices. Since many letters sound so much alike, they are usually spoken using a military-type alphabet (Able, Baker, Charlie for ABC).

A great deal of research and development is being done in the area of voice recognition. Clearly, there will be much more sophisticated devices available in the future. For students who are not able to use a keyboard and who find existing adapted access devices too slow or cumbersome, voice recognition is a promising alternative.

COMPUTER SOFTWARE

The selection of software for a classroom computer is a critical task for any teacher. So much software is available on the market that it is a difficult task to find and sift through the possibilities. However, there are certain categories of software that are especially useful in any classroom and that are helpful when there are students in the room who need technological assistance.

"Tool" Software

Word Processing There are many word processing programs available for classroom use. A word processor allows the user to type in text, then edit it by inserting or deleting characters, by searching for and replacing words, by moving blocks of text from one part of the page to another, by centering text, by underlining or creating bold face, by saving any desired changes for storage on a disk, and by printing the final product.

The fact that word processors provide an editing function is helpful in itself. Many students become bogged down in the writing process when they make errors. They erase and rewrite, often making the page messy. Sometimes they need to recopy their work but make new errors during the recopying process; sometimes penmanship is poor or illegible. Problems with the physical act of writing can cloud all the issues involved with putting ideas on paper. Word processing is a wonderful tool for all, because organizing, writing, and revising are handled in a simple, systematic way. Students do not focus on errors, but instead on creating and editing.

Benefits of word processing for meeting the diverse needs of students in an inclusive classroom are numerous. There are many "extras" that can be used in conjunction with word processing to aid those students who need additional help. Word processing software is available with large print options for young students and those with vision or visual perception problems. Some software includes a spell checker, which offers correctly spelled options on screen when words are identified as misspelled, or a thesaurus, which offers synonyms on screen as alternatives to trite words. Outlining programs that help the student in the writing process are available as separate programs or as an integrated part of some word processors. A prompted writing feature can allow the educator to add instructions to the student in the midst of the document.

Voice output, previously discussed, is perhaps one of the most powerful enhancements a word processor can have. Many students can benefit from having both the visual feedback of text on the screen and the auditory feedback of "spoken" text. Visual learners and auditory learners will find reading and writing at the computer to be easier with the addition of voice output. Of course, word processing can be combined with adaptive input devices, such as scanning with switches, Morse code with switches, or expanded keyboard, to provide access to the writing process for students with physical disabilities.

Data Bases Data base software can be another tool for all students in the class. The students can work in cooperative groups or as one large group to collect, organize, and compare data relevant to their curriculum (for example, data about U.S. colonies, presidents, or animals) or personally relevant data (favorite ice cream flavor, television show, or rock star). Sometimes, students can share this information to discover how much they have in common.

Spreadsheets   Spreadsheet software can be used to simulate real world financial situations. Students can learn to balance checkbooks, keep a budget, or even run a small business. Students who have difficulty mastering such concepts can rely on the computer for assistance.

Graphics and Publishing   Graphics software is fun for everybody in the class and can be highly motivating. All students can work together to create greeting cards, banners, signs, and pictures for everyone to enjoy. Performing such functions on the computer facilitates the participation of even those with severe physical or cognitive impairments.

Simulations

Simulations are programs that portray a real-life or fantasy situation on the screen, usually with colorful graphics. Students can sharpen their problem-solving skills by working through a story, solving a mystery, or dealing with a problem. This type of software does not directly instruct students in academic skills, but it does integrate many aspects of learning into one experience. Such software lends itself well to work in groups, where students with varying needs can pool their efforts and draw upon one another's strengths. Simulations have proven to be especially effective with students who have difficulty paying attention and staying on task.

Authorable Software

Drill and practice is perhaps the least innovative use for a computer in the classroom. Computers are capable of much more productive interaction with students than simply providing electronic work sheets. However, there are always those students who can benefit from simply having extra practice. For these students, drill and practice software can be helpful.

In the early years of microcomputers, math and spelling drills were available, but often the activities were designed by the programmer, and the words or problems were not especially relevant to the students at hand. Now, there are numerous authoring programs available that allow the educator or student to enter data specific to individual needs. Consequently, a student can use a spelling program that drills his or her spelling words, a vocabulary program that presents him or her with new words and definitions, or a math program that offers him or her extra help in specified areas. Authoring procedures for most of these programs are simple and designed for the novice to use.

Projection Plate and Software

One new type of technology that has become available is the projection plate. Anne Meyer and Bart Pisha (1989) have developed some interesting strategies for its use. When placed on a simple overhead projector and plugged into a computer, the plate projects the picture on the computer monitor to a movie screen. This means that all students in the classroom can view the computer screen and interact with the software at the same time. All students, as a group, can see a word processing document, a data base, or a simulation unfold before their eyes. Students can develop stories and computer graphics or take part in a problem-solving activity and learn to work in a cooperative manner at the same time.

For example, the class could work together on a story or a script for a class play. Every student could make a contribution, some small and some large, in an environment of shared responsibility. Some students would benefit markedly by simply hearing their classmates approach problems and contribute ideas. All students would be able to take pride in the accomplishments of the group.

STUDENT USES FOR A VARIETY OF TECHNOLOGIES

There are many technological innovations coming on the scene all the time, in addition to those directly related to computer access. A few primary examples are discussed here.

Environmental Control

All students feel a sense of well-being when they have physical control within the environments in which they live, study, and play. Some students have physical disabilities that make environmental control difficult. Removing such barriers can make it possible for all students, including those who use wheelchairs or who have limited hand use, to be successful and independent in the classroom.

Technology can provide power mobility to students who use wheelchairs, so that those students can control their own movements around the classroom and around the campus. Some students can operate their chairs with a hand control similar to a computer joystick; others use their chins with a switch. In any case, the use of power mobility can enable a student to participate in groups moving about the classroom, to join playground activities, to go to the cafeteria with the group, to go to the restroom, to move around in the community, and so on, with a great deal of independence.

The corollary to the availability of power mobility is carefully planned access to everything on the school grounds for students who use wheelchairs. This includes ramps in lieu of steps, doors of appropriate width, bathroom facilities at appropriate heights and with room for access, absence of obstructive bumps, and routes planned with care. Mobility training can be provided by school districts for those students who are learning to navigate their campuses.

Other aids to environmental control can easily be set up in the classroom for the purpose of enabling students to become more independent. Switches can be provided for turning lights, tape recorders, computers, and other devices on and off, and for adjusting volume, changing channels, and so forth. Control over these devices can be handled via individual switches or from a computer, which can serve as a general control unit.

Alternative and Augmentative Communication

Probably the most significant factor in classroom participation for any student is communication. The ability to communicate one's thoughts and feelings orally and in writing is central to all aspects of the learning, socialization, and relationship building process as it takes place in virtually all classrooms and school settings, and may well be a significant factor in establishing and maintaining appropriate behavior. Students for whom there are barriers to writing with a pencil can be helped by access to word processing on a computer. Students for whom speaking is difficult or impossible can participate in oral communication with the help of technology.

Communication boards that require students to point to letters, words, icons, or pictures have been used to augment communication for many years. Now, it is possible to provide electronic "speech" for a student, using a computerized device, thus making interaction and even conversation within the realm of possibility for many students. This can be accomplished in a number of ways.

Communicating via Computer   A computer equipped with a voice synthesizer can allow someone to type text and produce "speech" that can be heard by everyone. Therefore, students who are able to form sentences in their minds can type their ideas and have them heard by others.

Some students require support for either the cognitive task of constructing sentences or the physical task of typing words. In these situations, an Apple computer, equipped with an AFC and a Unicorn Expanded Keyboard, can be helpful. Using the *Talking Word Board* software that comes with the AFC, the educator can construct an array of sentences or phrases, each represented on an overlay by text, drawing, icon, or photograph that the student would touch in order to activate synthesized speech. Similar choices could be presented on the Power Pad as well.

Portable Devices   Of course, a portable augmentative communication system is much more desirable than one that is attached to a table-top computer, although such a system would be helpful in providing reinforcement and training.

There are several portable devices available in a wide range of prices. The simplest are the Wolf (ADAMLAB), the Sonoma Voice (Sonoma Developmental Center), the Alltalk (Adaptive Communication Systems, Inc.), and the Introtalker (Prentke Romich Company). These devices are all boxes that the student can carry or place on a wheelchair tray, and they are all preprogrammed with words or phrases that are spoken by either a voice synthesizer or a digitizer when certain areas of the keyboard are pressed. The system can be individualized for the user. There can be as few as one or two available words or many, with several words assigned to "levels" at each touching position, that can be represented by printed text, pictures, or photographs. The advantage of these systems is their ease of use, so that students with cognitive impairments can make use of them. The disadvantage is that students cannot use them to make unique responses, ones that were not preprogrammed, in spontaneous conversation.

More sophisticated augmentative communication systems are also available with built-in text-to-speech. With these devices, the student can type in words and phrases on the spot, using either letters or icon-based codes, and participate in complex conversations. Examples include the Touch Talker with Minspeak (Prentke Romich Company), the RealVoice with Epson HX-20 (Adaptive Communication Systems, Inc.), the Talking Notebook (Zygo Industries, Inc.), and the Vois (Phonic Ear, Inc.). The Light Talker (Prentke Romich Company), the ScanPAC (Adaptive Communication Systems, Inc.), the Scan Wolf (ADAMLAB), and the ScanWriter (Zygo Industries, Inc.) are special systems that allow use via scanning and switches for people who cannot use their hands. Some of these devices may also be used for computer access.

In this day and age, it should not be necessary to exclude anyone from full classroom participation because of a lack of ability to communicate, since such a variety of solutions is available through the use of technology. Furthermore, it is not the task of the classroom teacher to find an appropriate communication system for a student, to provide training, or to do troubleshooting. Rather, school districts should have on staff someone who is qualified to take this role. In other situations, agencies in the community are used to help identify and purchase the appropriate system and to train the student in its use. The classroom teacher only needs to be willing to learn how best to communicate with the students, and how to facilitate communication among students when one is using an augmentative device.

CONCLUSION

Essential to the process of involving all students in the activities of the classroom, with the help of technology, is a belief that all students can succeed. High expectations will go a long way in boosting morale and bringing educators and students together to work for common goals.

At the same time, teachers need to feel comfortable with the technology they are being called upon to use. School districts should provide proper training for all staff. All educators need to have time and assistance to become comfortable with the equipment they are asked to use. Not only do they need to be able to use the computers and the software, but they need to know appropriate strategies for maximizing the effects of the technology in the classroom.

Support personnel should be involved in many ways. Examples are the assistance needed from an occupational therapist in positioning a student and his or her equipment, or the assistance needed from a speech therapist in providing strategies for the use of an augmentative communication device.

Attention should be given to the implementation of computer assistance to students who change classes during the day. Portable laptop computers are now available that can be carried from class to class. However, when adaptive equipment is involved, the task of working out the logistics can become complex.

A support system must be readily available for all staff and students. Troubleshooters who can solve technical problems must be able to respond quickly. No one should feel abandoned in the process or the technology will soon be discarded.

Access to technology at home should be considered part of the total process. Although school districts may not be able to provide adapted computer systems for students at home, it is surely an issue worthy of discussion. Perhaps the school could provide a system to a family on loan. Perhaps district staff could assist parents to locate appropriate funding sources for adapted equipment for home. If the family has equipment at home, then a system should be worked out for transporting disks back and forth. When decisions are made regarding the purchase of equipment for a particular student in the classroom, attention should be given to any potentially compatible equipment that may be available at home or in the community.

In this chapter only current technology has been considered. There are some exciting new trends that will further facilitate the successful participation of all students. For example, voice recognition will soon become much more sophisticated and will become a more practical alternative for many students to access a computer. Scanners and optical character reading are coming into the marketplace. Entire pages of text are "photographed" or scanned into the computer, and special software "reads" the characters on the page and transforms them into regular text on the computer screen, which can then be "voiced" by a synthesizer or edited for other uses. This technology will be a tremendous help to people who, for one reason or another, are unable to read.

Telecommunications will allow students in one classroom to send messages to those in another far away, for students to send information from home to school and back and for everyone to access huge on-line data bases of exciting information, using a computer and a telephone. Actually, the technology for all of these applications already exists. Soon these innovations will be adopted by more and more people and will come into common use at lower prices.

Finally, it is important to remember that technology is not a "cure" for a disability, rather it is a tool for everyone in society. Focus should not be placed on how the equipment itself will work, but efforts should be placed toward developing strategies, utilizing effective teaching practices, and working with the strengths of all students in the class. Technology can help remove barriers, but it is people, working together, who learn and succeed.

REFERENCES

Meyer, A., & Pisha, B. (1989). The collaborative Macintosh. *The Macintosh Lab Monitor, 8*, 3–6.

Meyers, L. (1987, February/March). Bypassing the prerequisites: The computer as a language scaffold. *Closing the Gap, 5*, 1.

SUGGESTED READINGS

Apple computer resources in special education and rehabilitation. (1987). Allen, TX: DLM, Inc.

Behrmann, M. (1984). *Handbook of microcomputers in special education.* San Diego: College Hill Press.

Bowe, F. (1984). *Personal computers & special needs.* Berkeley, CA: Sybex.

Brandenburg, S.H., & Vanderheiden, G.C. (Eds.). (1987). *Rehab/education technology resource book series: Communication, control, and computer access for disabled and elderly individuals* (3 volumes: Communication aids, Switches and environmental controls, and Software and Hardware) Boston: College Hill Press.

CTG's 1989 resource directory: A guide to the selection of microcomputer technology for special education and rehabilitation. (1989, February/March). *Closing the Gap.* 37–179.

Gergen, M. (Ed.). (1986). *Computer technology for the handicapped, applications '85: Proceedings of Closing the Gap's 1985 National Conference.* Hutchinson, MN: Crow River Press.

Gergen, M. (Ed.). (1987). *Microcomputer technology for special education and rehabilitation: Proceedings of Closing the Gap's 1986 Conference.* Hutchinson, MN: Crow River Press.

Gergen, M., & Hagen, D. (Eds.). (1985). *Computer technology for the handicapped: Proceedings from the 1984 Closing the Gap Conference.* Henderson, MN: Closing the Gap.

Goldenberg, E., Russell, S., & Carter, C., (1984). *Computers, education and special needs.* Reading MA: Addison-Wesley.

Hagen, D. (1984). *Microcomputer resource book for special education.* Reston, VA: Reston Publishing Company, Inc.

Male, M. (1988). *Special magic: Computers and classroom strategies for exceptional students.* Palo Alto, CA: Mayfield Publishing Company.

Male, M., Johnson, R., Johnson, D., & Anderson, M. (1986). *Cooperative learning and computers.* Santa Cruz, CA: Mary Male.

Meyers, L. (1988). Using computers to teach children with Down syndrome spoken and written language. In L. Nadel (Ed.), *The neurobiology of Down syndrome.* Boston: MIT Press.

Meyers, L. (1990). *The language machine.* San Diego: College Hill Press.

Pressman, H. (Ed.). (1988). *Making an exceptional difference: Enhancing the impact of microcomputer technology on children with disabilities.* Boston: The Exceptional Parent.

Proceedings of the conference "Computer Technology and Persons with Disabilities," California State University at Northridge, October 17–19, 1985. (1986). Office of Disabled Student Services, CSUN.

Proceedings of the conference "Computer Technology and Persons with Disabilities," California State University at Northridge, October 16–18, 1986. (1987). Office of Disabled Student Services, CSUN.

Proceedings of the conference "Computer Technology and Persons with Disabilities," California State University at Northridge, October 15–17, 1987. (1988). Office of Disabled Student Services, CSUN.

Wright, C., & Nomura, M. (1985). *From toys to computers.* San Jose, CA: Christine Wright.

Appendix

Resources for Learning about and Purchasing Computer Hardware and Software

Any of the following organizations can provide up-to-date and detailed information about hardware, software, and other adaptations that are available on the market today:

National Special Education Alliance (NSEA), 2095 Rose St., 1st Floor, Berkeley, CA 94709, (415) 540–5676. Community-based technology resource centers, located throughout the country, provide places where professionals, parents, and people with disabilities can explore and evaluate computer equipment and software that might be helpful to them.

IBM National Support Center for Persons with Disabilities, P. O. Box 2150, Atlanta, GA 30055, 1-800-IBM-2133 (voice and TDD). This center provides information over the phone regarding IBM and compatible products.

Closing the Gap, P.O. Box 68, Henderson, MN, 56044. This organization provides a periodical and resource guide and holds an outstanding annual fall conference.

ABLEDATA, 8455 Colesville Rd., Silver Spring, MD 20910, (301) 588-9284. This organization makes a huge data base of technology information available to search by telephone.

MANUFACTURERS AND DISTRIBUTORS
OF ADAPTIVE HARDWARE MENTIONED IN THIS CHAPTER

Access Unlimited—SPEECH Enterprises
9039 Katy Freeway, Suite 414
Houston, TX 77024

ADAMLAB
33500 Van Born Rd.
Wayne, MI 48184

Adaptive Communication Systems, Inc.
P.O. Box 12440
Pittsburgh, PA 15231

American Thermoform Corporation
2311 Travers Ave.
City of Commerce, CA 90040

Articulate Systems
2380 Ellsworth St., Suite A
Berkeley, CA 94704

ComputAbility Corporation
40000 Grand River, Suite 109
Novi, MI 40850

DADA
1076 Butherst 87, Suite 202
Toronto, ON M5R 3G9 Canada

Digital Equipment Corporation
146 Main St.
Maynard, MA 01754-2571

Don Johnston Developmental Equipment, Inc.
P.O. Box 639
1000 N. Rand Rd., Bldg. 115
Wauconda, IL 60084

Dunamis, Inc.
3620 Highway 317
Suwanee, GA 30174

Edmark Corporation
14350 N.E. 21st St.
Bellevue, WA 98009

McIntyre Computer Systems Division
22809 Shagbark
Birmingham, MI 48010

Phonic Ear, Inc.
250 Camino Alto
Mill Valley, CA 94941

Pointer Systems, Inc.
One Mill St.
Burlington, VT 05401

Prentke Romich Company
1022 Heyl Road
Wooster, OH 44691

Raised Dot Computing
408 S. Baldwin St.
Madison, WI 53703

Sonoma Developmental Center
15000 Arnold Dr.
P. O. Box 1493
Eldridge, CA 95431

Street Electronics Corporation
6420 Via Real
Carpinteria, CA 93013

Sunburst Communications
39 Washington Ave.
Pleasantville, NY 10570

TASH, Inc.
(Technical Aids and Systems for the Handicapped)
70 Gibson Dr., Unit 12
Markham, ON L3R 4C2, Canada

Telesensory Systems, Inc./VTEK
455 N. Bernardo Ave.
Mountain View, CA 94039

Unicorn Engineering, Inc.
5221 Central Ave.
Richmond, CA 94804

Voice Connection
17835 Skypark Cr., Suite C
Irvine, CA 92714

Zygo Industries, Inc.
P.O. Box 1008
Portland, OR 97207

PUBLISHERS AND DISTRIBUTORS
OF SOFTWARE MENTIONED IN THIS CHAPTER

Access Unlimited—SPEECH Enterprises
9039 Katy Freeway, Suite 414
Houston, TX 77024

Berkeley Systems
1708 Shattuck Ave.
Berkeley, CA 94709

Don Johnston Developmental Equipment, Inc.
P.O. Box 639
1000 N. Rand Rd., Bldg. 115
Wauconda, IL 60084

First Byte, Electronic Arts
P. O. Box 7530
San Mateo, CA 94403

Hartley Courseware
P. O. Box 431
Dimondale, MI 48821

Kinetic Designs, Inc.
14231 Anatevka Lane, S.E.
Olalla, WA 98359

Mindscape, Inc.
3444 Dundee Road
Northbrook, IL 60062

PEAL Software
P. O. Box 8188
Calabasas, CA 91372

Scholastic, Inc.
730 Broadway
Dept. JS
New York, NY 10003

Sunburst Communications
39 Washington Ave.
Pleasantville, NY 10570

Teacher Support Software
P. O. Box 7130
Gainesville, FL 32605

Marsha Forest
Jack Pearpoint

12

Supports for Addressing Severe Maladaptive Behaviors

Students who exhibit severe aggressive behaviors constitute a formidable challenge to educators in terms of inclusion and support of all students in the mainstream of school and community life. In regard to students who exhibit such behaviors, there are two competing themes in the educational literature: "kick 'em out or keep 'em in."

On the "kick 'em out" side, for example, a $6.9 million institution was planned for children who are so "severely behaviorally disordered" that they *need* rooms with video surveillance and all sorts of "special" facilities. When asked who actually would be served by this institution, no clear answer was given.

However, on the "keep 'em in" side, with the recognition and utilization of innovative support options, inclusion is not only possible but highly desirable. In addition, by using millions of dollars to support educational reform, rather than building institutions, these authors believe that more worthwhile alternatives to the "kick 'em out" model exist.

The movement toward inclusive education is a process—a journey to create an educational system where excellence and equity walk hand in hand and where the highest values of the nation are respected, honored, and achieved. The purpose of this chapter is to help make inclusive education a viable option for students who have or could potentially exhibit severe aggressive behaviors. Presented in the chapter are emerging possible solutions that have been successfully used in keeping or returning such students to the educational and community main-stream.

THE PROBLEM

In a perfect world, all children would grow up in a nurturing environment in strong families (that could vary in design), and thus feel secure, loved, and confident about their future. They would have hope, dignity, and self-esteem. They would have friends and would interact with and for people because it was right—not out of greed or selfishness. They would have the desire to learn, to accept challenges, and to push themselves to their own limits, whatever they might be.

However, the future is not so rosy for an enormous number of children. Many students are experiencing little other than frustration and failure within the educational and social system; others have already fallen through the cracks. Still others have learned to be "incorrigible." Increases in teenage suicide are a barometer of how many youth view the future—they do not see one. They are imploding with despair at a time when they should be vibrant about their lives.

In a society rampant with cynicism and defeatism, it is hard to face reality optimistically. But that is exactly what must be done—people must immerse themselves in life and be with other people. It is hard, but it is healthier than the latest food/clothing or technology fad. Furthermore, it is economically sound. There are massive numbers of students having school problems who are screaming at educators with their behaviors. They are telling educators that school is irrelevant, boring, dull, not meeting their needs, and driving them crazy. These students drop out, form gangs, and get in trouble, and yet, society *continues to blame the victims rather than looking deeply at itself and the school system for creative answers and alternatives.*

STUDENTS AS SOLUTIONS

The following two case studies illustrate how students can serve as valuable and effective resources in helping classmates who exhibit challenging aggressive behavior.

Jane's Story

Jane, a 12-year old student, started doing strange things at school. The principal, teacher, and resource person agreed to call in the "behavior" specialists to design a "compliance training" program.

For a short while Jane stopped being a nuisance and life went on until she suddenly attacked a schoolmate on the school yard, knocked the girl to the ground touching her breasts and genital area. She had to be physically pulled away. The "attack" frightened the other child involved but did not seriously injure her.

The principal immediately phoned both sets of parents and to his surprise, the mother of the student who was "attacked" did not become hysterical; she realized her daughter was not hurt. Jane's entire family was called in for a serious talk with the principal.

Enlist Student Help   The following sequence is the process that was used to involve Jane's classmates in helping Jane be more accepted and welcomed by her school peers and concurrently eliminating her undesirable aggressive behaviors.

Rule #1   First the teacher, guidance counselor, or someone else on staff, should go to the students, being completely honest with them, and explain the situation. For example, "I just heard about what happened in the yard between Jane and Melissa. I think it's important that we talk about this frankly and confidentially." In this case, when the students were asked what confidentiality meant, they understood. A pin could have dropped in the room.

Rule #2   Teachers know how to teach, but many have forgotten how to talk with children or young adults as people. Children hate it when important issues are watered down or the truth skirted. Therefore, be direct. Talk to students as if they were friends. Do not lecture; rather, make the discussion a conversation.

Rule #3   Ask questions and opinions, such as, "What do you think? What do you think is happening to Jane? What's your view of the incident? Tell us your opinion."

When these questions were asked of Jane's classmates a torrent of pent up thought gushed forth and the adults later said that they were amazed at the seriousness, thoughtfulness, sincerity, and depth of the children's answers. The students basically said they felt Jane was totally isolated at school, had no friends, and was miserable and unhappy. Jane's parents, they added, treated her like a baby and would not let her go out of the house. They felt she was a real pest at school, bothering everyone, and was getting more and more out of hand. The following is an actual list of what the students in Jane's eighth grade class said about her: "lonely, depressed, empty, like an outcast, bored, horrible, upset, like in jail, like committing suicide, and dead."

Rule #4   Ask students to help and value their opinions. They should be made part of a team with the teachers to solve real problems. There are enough real-life issues and problems to deal with instead of making up games or role playing. Jane's problem was real, and the children were eager to get involved and were captured by the reality of helping a real person solve a genuinely serious problem.

Rule #5   The next step is to stop talking about the person with the problem and turn the conversation around to each students' own life. When the conversation about Jane became heated, everyone was asked to forget Jane for a moment, and think of their own lives. This was done by having each student construct their own illustration of their circles of friends. Each student was given a sheet of paper and asked to draw four concentric circles around a small one in the center of the page with each new circle progressively larger than the smaller ones. The four circles should be large enough to cover the entire page. Then the circles were explained:

A. In circle #1, the smallest and closest to the center, put the names of people who are the closest to you in your own life—the people you love most. (When everyone was finished they were asked these questions: "Why did you put those people in circle one? What do you do with the people in circle one? How do you feel about the people in circle one? How do those people feel about you?")

B. Circle #2 is exactly the same except the people included are not quite as close as those in circle #1. Follow the same procedure.

C. Circle #3 includes groups of people in your life—sports groups, teams, Boy/Girl Scouts, church groups, and so on.

D. Circle #4 are people who are paid to be in your life—teachers, doctors, hairdressers, and so on. (Throughout the procedures students were requested to share and discuss their insights).

E. The students were then asked to switch gears for a moment and think about how they would feel if they had just a few or no people in their circles. (A circle illustration of a person whose life included few friends was shown to the students).

F. How would you feel if your life looked like this?

G. How do you think you'd *act* if your life looked like this drawing? The list of actual student responses included: "silly, I'd lie, act mean, do bad things, act stupid, I'd commit suicide, I'd be scared to death, I'd think I had to go to an institution, I'd annoy people, and I'd hurt people."

When this exercise was used with children and adults in the past, without exception, they connect the "behaviors" to a person's attempt to send messages. In this case, everyone realized that Jane was behaving a certain way because she was sending a message. It was now their job to figure out the message, respond positively, and thus change the destructive behavior.

The circle process cannot be done by lecturing. People have to experientially relate Jane's suffering to their own lives and see that a person's behavior has something to do with the environment he or she is in. The person cannot be "cured" without looking at that person's whole life.

The eighth grade students immediately saw that Jane was acting in almost the same ways that they had described in their lists. What particularly scared them was the part about suicide. The final question involves *action*.

H.   "What can *we* do to get Jane back on track?" Again, a flood of response followed: "tell her right away that we're her friends, tell her we like her, invite her to our parties, go shopping with her, phone her, visit her at home, and make sure she's not alone."

An interesting event happened during this discussion. The principal of the school got so excited about the process that he went to his office and canceled recess that morning so the discussion could continue and he could participate. In short, the students did what they said they would do, and Jane's behavior has changed remarkably.

Rule #6   It is important to have a strong adult from the environment present to facilitate and assist the circle to grow and stay together. The individual with the problem behavior must also be present at all (or most) meetings. The group should name itself, but not use the name of the person.

The teacher took on the task of nurturing what had already been started. A group of 17 students from the class decided to name themselves the S.W.A.T. Team (Students Who Are Together).

Follow-Up   A follow-up of the situation was done 2 months later to find out, in the students' own words, what was happening. The following is a summary of the discussion:

> Our S.W.A.T team has a weekly meeting with Mrs. Gill (the resource teacher). Jane comes to every meeting. At the first meeting we told Jane we wanted to help and be her friends. We told her that no matter what she did, we'd be there for her. We apologized for not being around enough before. Sarah invited her to a party and Sue went to visit her at home. Danny, Rose, and Linda call her a lot. Jane's happy now because she's got the S.W.A.T. team and because she has friends. We're all making new friends, too. Jane's whole attitude has changed and she hasn't hit or attacked anyone since we talked to her.

Educators' Response   The teachers reported that they are amazed at the change in Jane and that she is: "more included in everything the other kids do, knows everyone in the class now, is generally happier, is much friendlier, and has not been in the principal's office in 2 months."

Students' Response   The S.W.A.T team was asked to write a few notes about their experience with Jane. This is what they had to say:

"A Poem About Jane"
Jane came three years ago
No one did she really know
We tried to teach her wrong from right
Tried to make her days sunny and bright
Still she walked around so sad
And we knew that we had
To make her feel like one of us
And over her we'd all fuss
Now Jane has many good friends
And I hope "our" friendship never ends.

(Tammi Washnuk)

Jane has changed since her first meeting with the S.W.A.T. team. These past couple of weeks she's really opened up. She now feels she belongs, and she knows *we are* her friends. She hasn't been acting up or annoying us like she used to. Instead she's been very friendly. She used to ignore us, now she's cheery and always talks to us.

She was just recently invited to her first party with boys. She really enjoyed it. I think Jane has really changed. She used to be so quiet and always kept to herself. Now she is more outgoing and talkative. Like any teenager, Jane needs friends and a social life.

(Melanie McDermott)

Before S.W.A.T. I found Jane moody, babyish, she swore, she spat, and once in awhile she would pee in her pants. When S.W.A.T. started helping, Jane was overjoyed. Jane would always say she didn't care about anyone or about school. About four days after saying how she didn't care about school she got suspended because she touched a kid in the private spot.

Because of S.W.A.T. she is really changing now. I called her at home and she talked to me for 10 minutes on the phone. Jane is trying to act like us! She's becoming *like* us!

(Krystyne Banakiewiczw)

When Jane first came to this school I could tell she was nervous so I became her friend. As time went on, Jane started following me everywhere I went and she wouldn't even let me talk to my friends in private.

Finally a group in my class formed the S.W.A.T. team. Jane began to change. She stopped swearing and doesn't follow me everywhere I go. She's more open to everyone. I think the S.W.A.T. team really has improved Jane's behavior and attitude toward other people.

(Nicole Salmon)

Jeff's Story

Jeff is another student at Regina Mundi school with major behavior problems. The teacher was concerned that Jeff would be in serious trouble in high school if his behavior problems continued.

After hearing about the success with Jane, Jeff's teacher wanted to ask the class members to assist Jeff with his problems. But, everyone was concerned that the seventh graders were not as good a group as the eighth graders and wondered if they would respond in a similar fashion. (Jeff's story, while described more concisely here, operated on the same rules described in Jane's story.)

If anything, the seventh graders surpassed their schoolmates in the eighth grade and surprised everyone by their sensitivity toward Jeff. The following is the student oriented intervention sequence that occurred for Jeff:

A. "What are some words to describe Jeff?" The class said: "he fights all the time, pushes, acts rough, picks on the little kids, hides, swears a lot, doesn't talk, bothers the girls, is lonely, makes rude noises when he eats, and takes things and doesn't give them back."

B. "Can you think of anything good about Jeff?" The class responded with: "he says 'hello' to some people, finishes his work, offers to help some people, listens, participates well in gym, and tries hard." (It is interesting to compare the seventh grade responses with the eighth grade group.)

C. "How would you feel if you had no one or few people in your life?" They said: "suicidal, depressed, lonely, sad, I wouldn't care about anything or anyone, down in the dumps, weird, nobody loves me."

D. "What would you do and how would you act if your life had no or few friends?" The class said: "quiet, aggressive, rude, mean, disruptive, lost, unable to concentrate, fail, immature, centered out, try to get attention, lying, making up stories, steal, bored, crying for help, lonely, want attention, want to be alone, and need someone to talk to."

With the help of the teachers, the class drew a picture using circles of friends of what Jeff's life actually looked like:

Circle #1: Jeff is very close to his older brother.
Circle #2: Jeff likes Mrs. Gill and another teacher.
Circle #3: He is not involved in any after-school activities.
Circle #4: Teachers, doctors

The students were shocked and surprised at the drawings of Jeff's life. He had few, if any, friends.

E. "How do you think Jeff feels about his life?" They answered: "depressed, lonely, sad, angry, upset, down in the dumps, and weird."

They all agreed Jeff needed friends who could understand his isolation and anger. Almost the entire class volunteered to get involved.

Conclusion: Student Solutions

Jane and Jeff are not real names, but they are real people. All other names are real. These stories can be replicated for any child at risk of being left out or kicked out at any age. All children, whether in Toronto,

Los Angeles, or a small rural town in Iowa, respond to honesty, openness, and truth.

Students, and especially teenagers, know the pressures of everyday life. They relate to suicide, death, war, and disease. They do not want to run away from these problems; rather they want and need to face them head on. Teachers can help them face life, not run from it.

It is the adults who are frightened to confront the pain of growing up and growing older. New labels are being created to mask ignorance and fear. Diseases are born: learning disabilities, behavior disorders, attention deficit disorders, and minimal brain damage. Living, however, is not a disease to be "cured" by the medical profession.

What these authors suggest costs little and is based on common sense and human kindness: *talk to children and to each other, listen to the joy, sorrow, and pain of neighbors, do not pretend to live in a Pollyanna world.*

Jane and Jeff could have ended up in jail, group homes, or on the street. Instead they are going to parties, going to the mall, and heading for a future.

This approach is practical but not magical. It is not an answer, but a process, a journey. For more stories of success like Jane's and Jeff's there needs to be:

Time
Time to listen
Time to dream
Time to hear
Time to cry and laugh
Time to work
Time to act
Time to listen again and again and again

COMMUNITY MEMBERS AS SOLUTIONS

The following is one case study of how a community member who experienced exclusion for his undesirable behavior used his experiences to assist youth considered to have severe behavior problems to learn to function and succeed in the educational and community mainstream. There are a number of such cases that can be cited, but only one is included here to illustrate that community members, including individuals many people consider to be a problem, can provide solutions if given the opportunity and support.

Charlie's Story

Some years ago, Frontier College in Toronto began a small program, originally to respond to expectations about the "literacy" needs of prisoners in Canadian jails. A great deal was learned by listening. First, it was necessary to learn how to listen, not just to the words, but to the meaning. After listening, it was discovered that "reading and writing" were not uppermost in prisoners' minds. They wanted to get out of jail and obtain a job. It was decided that these people needed help to get a job when they were released, thus a program needed to be adapted to assist them.

Most inmates do not have enormous "job skills." Standardized tests do not say much about what people can or will do, and credibility is lost by resorting to them. Therefore, a simple "test" was devised. Over coffee, inmates were asked: "What do you like? What do you want to do?"

All kinds of guesses were made about what people wanted and needed; usually they were wrong. However, by listening, and because jobs were sought that people said they wanted, the small program worked remarkably well. Then along came Charlie.

Charlie Tann had been in prison for 27 years. He was "released" to participate in the program largely because he was dying of cirrhosis. He had been given three months to live, and it was going to be more convenient to have him die "on the outside." Charlie was asked, "What would you like to do?" He replied, "I'd like to work with kids."

Charlie made his case. He argued that he had completely wasted his life, had been addicted to every drug, messed up in every conceivable way, and that was exactly what he had to offer. He argued that other adults could not really communicate with kids who were already on the skids but that he could. He could tell them that he was just like them and if they did not get smarter, they would end up just like him—dying—after having spent most of his life in jail. Charlie argued that he could do something others could not, and that he deserved the chance. He said he wanted to do something decent in his life, and he did not have long to do it.

Charlie was convincing and sold his idea to the programmers. Then the nightmare began. No responsible school official would allow a life-long criminal like Charlie near children. Therefore, the programmers retreated to the prison system. There was a "lockup" where young offenders were kept—after everyone had given up. These prison officials reluctantly agreed to let Charlie talk to these young offenders. These offenders had frustrated the officials best efforts again and again. Fundamentally, it was a waiting game—waiting for death by suicide, overdose, or murder. Since those were the choices, no one had anything to lose. Charlie was allowed access to these kids.

Charlie's "technique" was extraordinary. He went into the lockup, picked the toughest kid, and appointed himself his or her friend for life. He would simply walk in, sit down, and say, "Angie, I'm your friend."

That was all there was to his technique. He would tell them, "I am self-appointed. I have decided that I am your friend. There is nothing you can do about it. There is nothing you can do to offend me, because I have done worse. And I will find you—and I will be your friend. You are stuck with me."

This message of unconditional love coming from a hardened life-long criminal was staggering to kids. They did not know how to deal with it. Each, in their own way, tested Charlie. They ran, did drugs, stole his money and clothes. Charlie always found them and offered more. Mostly, he gave the only real thing he had to give—himself—a commodity that was in short supply.

Not all of Charlie's kids survived, but two, Angie and Kelly, made it. This author found out about Angie by accident. At a HELP staff meeting (HELP is a Frontier College program that employs approximately 37 ex-offenders to find jobs for ex-offenders) a young woman came up and asked, "Remember me?" She said, "I'm Angie . . . Charlie's Angie!" She was on the HELP staff. Since then, she has become a loving mother and a part-time graphic artist.

However, at that moment the world closed in. Charlie had died—4 years after all the doctors said he could not live another day. Charlie drove himself beyond bodily limits because he had to live to save more kids. And he did. Angie was the first of Charlie's kids. She was one of the toughest women offenders in Canadian prison history and now she is Angie.

There are hundreds just like Angie. Charlie even married one of his "stray kids." Her name was Kelly. She graduated from the university at the top of her class. One professor said he had never had a student like Kelly.

The problem Charlie, a rejected community member, became part of the solution. With Charlie's help and help from others like him, a number of "incorrigible" teens were able to turn from undesirable behaviors to more acceptable positive behaviors through acceptance, friendship, inclusion, and success in the mainstream of educational and community life.

However, Charlie could not have salvaged those youth if some "straight" people had not been willing to trust and work with him. This is not a traditional partnership based on a negotiated contract. However, if anything, the bonds are more powerful and the implications more dramatic.

Conclusion: Community Members

It is easy to think that Charlie was wonderful, but what does Charlie have to do with oil spills in Valdez, the school crisis, and so forth. The point is that there are Charlies everywhere. It is hoped that most will not have to waste 27 years in jail before someone helps them. In the family, in the classrooms, across the fence or street, at work, at school, and in a church or synagogue, there are people who need help.

As long as people are pushed out—rejected—devastation and despair will continue. People will grow more angry and more frustrated. This does not have to happen if members of society begin to accept all people in their homes, in their families, in the classrooms, in the communities, and as their friends. The accumulated anger and frustration of decades of systematic failure and refection will not disappear overnight, and there are no "microwave" solutions to long-term problems.

Charlie Tann could not possibly have helped kids. Think about it, he was an uneducated life-long criminal. But Charlie did save lives. He and others like him are among the best teachers.

CONCLUSION

Students who display severe behavior difficulties, like all children, can and should be included in the mainstream of schools and communities. The key to making it possible is relationships. It should be no great mystery that if one cannot lean over the back fence and talk to his or her neighbors as people, then similar trends cannot begin in boardrooms, international negotiations, and prison ranges. There is a common factor—people relating.

A fundamental element of relationships is that *everyone* has a role to play. Not everyone can or should be the same. Someone with a Ph.D. in theoretical physics may not be a master at human relations or be able to repair the lawn mower, while an "untrained farm hand" can talk his way through a country auction and be "Mr. Fix-it." The point is that everyone has strengths—and often the people identified as "the problem" are a key to the solution.

Together, in new and genuine partnerships, it can be done. The impossible just takes a little longer. If the people who are "labeled as problems" are invited to join, the talent, commitment, creativity, and resources will grow. It is all a matter of will.

Section III

DEVELOPING CARING AND SUPPORTIVE SCHOOLS AND COMMUNITIES

Richard A. Villa
Jacqueline S. Thousand

13

Administrative Supports to Promote Inclusive Schooling

> Leadership can be defined as the human response to the needs of a social matrix which enables it to become—to be—more fully. Quality can exist in leadership when, either in the rap of the moment or the deep mists of time, it improves the human condition. (Klopf, 1979, p. 31)

In most school systems, the educational administrator is the one who is responsible for publicly articulating the philosophy or mission of the school district and assuring that the actions of the teachers, support personnel, and students are congruent with this philosophy. Thus, the educational administrator is in a position to deliberately or incidentally shape the organizational structure of a school and the values of the school community; and these structures and values may facilitate or thwart the school's capacity to meet the needs of all students in general education environments.

The purpose of this chapter is to identify and describe strategies that the school administrator can employ to support the successful inclusion and education of all students in heterogeneous "regular" education classrooms within the local school. More specifically, strategies are included for promoting an inclusive school philosophy and a unified system of school services.

The recommendations offered to administrators in this chapter are derived from the results of research, model demonstration efforts, and surveys of Vermont general and special education administrators and teachers, as well as the authors' firsthand experiences in American and

Canadian schools that have made the commitment to educate *all* students in heterogeneous local school classrooms (Thousand et al., 1986; Thousand & Villa, 1989).

PROMOTING AN INCLUSIVE SCHOOL PHILOSOPHY

School personnel, administrators included, are driven, at least in part, by their assumptions and beliefs regarding what the goals of public education should be and their assumptions about their own and their students' capabilities to achieve these goals (Azjen & Fishbein, 1980; Donnellan, 1984). Administrators who have initiated systems change to promote the inclusion of all students in local schools stress the importance of identifying and articulating for themselves and for their staff a philosophy or vision that reflects the following assumptions: 1) all children can learn, 2) all children have the right to be educated with their peers in age-appropriate heterogeneous classrooms within their local schools, and 3) it is the responsibility of the school system to meet the diverse educational and psychological needs of all students.

However, for an administrator to clarify and share his or her inclusive vision with the school community is a necessary but not a sufficient step for the desired philosophy to be embraced by others within the school. The administrator must also take every opportunity to build understanding of the consensus regarding the vision.

Strategies for Fostering Understanding and Consensus Building

There is no single strategy for fostering understanding and consensus building that is more powerful than another. Instead, strategies are unique to the demographics, history, and the current beliefs of the membership of the school community.

In-Service and Development Activities   One strategy for building consensus is to expose people to information that provides theoretical, ethical, or data-based support for the philosophy of inclusion. For example, workshops can be arranged or guest speakers brought in to focus upon the current "best educational practices" (e.g., cooperative group learning, social integration, home-school partnership, community-based instruction) that are most readily achieved when students are educated in heterogeneous local schools. The administrator can periodically disseminate to faculty articles that point out the lack of efficacy of "pull out" and segregated special and compensatory education service delivery models (e.g., Reynolds, Wang, & Walberg, 1987; Wang, Reynolds, & Walberg, 1988) and include time for discussions of readings at small group or total faculty meetings. Arrangements can be made for groups of teachers to visit schools that have successfully integrated all of their students in general education settings and speak with parents, students, and school staff about the "how to's" and the benefits of heterogeneous grouping.

It has been pointed out that the way in which teachers understand and choose to interact with students is dependent, at least in part, upon the conceptual framework and terms they use to think and talk about students (Smith, 1988). Staff committed to educating all students in the mainstream need to acquire a common conceptual framework, language, and set of technical skills in order to communicate and implement practices that research and theory suggest will enable them to better respond to a diverse student body. If personnel of a heterogeneous school have not received this training in the past, it becomes the job of the administrator to facilitate the formulation and ratification of a comprehensive in-service training agenda. This agenda may need to extend across several years to ensure that instructional personnel have the opportunity to progress from acquisition to mastery.

It is important to avoid "one shot" learning experiences in planning the in-service agenda. Every effort should be made to follow the principles of effective instruction, with the administrator arranging for clinical supervision and peer coaching in the application of acquired knowledge and skills in the school and community settings in which they are to be used (Cummings, 1985; Joyce & Showers, 1980, 1988).

It should be noted that supervising administrators also need to become knowledgeable in the same areas as their staff if they are to promote teachers' effective and continued implementation of the understanding and skills they acquire. This may mean that administrators participate along with their instructional staff as learners during all or some of the in-service training agenda. Additionally, they need to receive training, coaching, and feedback related to their role as observer and supervisor of instructional personnel in the school (Cummings, 1985; Joyce & Showers, 1980, 1988).

Involvement in Mission Clarification   Another powerful strategy for gaining support for an inclusive school philosophy is to involve representatives of concerned school and community members in developing the school or school district's philosophy and goals for supporting the inclusion of all students in regular education. People who are given the opportunity to engage in participatory decision-making processes are more likely to develop "ownership" for their decisions and promote their agreed-upon outcomes through their words and actions than if decisions were imposed upon them (Thousand et al., 1986).

Clearly, there are risks involved in turning over such an important function to a group of people who, based upon their diverse personal and professional perspectives, will differ in the degree to which they are in support of heterogeneous schooling. This risk, however, can be minimized by ensuring that the committee include at least some participants who understand the concept of and advocate for the inclusion of all students in general school activities; also, prior to and during their involvement on the mission statement committee, all group members should receive ample opportunities to become familiar with the theoretical, ethical, and data-based support for the philosophy of inclusion.

Incentives   Schools that have been most successful in achieving a challenging mission (e.g., providing heterogeneous educational opportunities to all students) are also schools in which attention has been given to the development of a sense of *esprit de corps*—a common spirit, an inspiring enthusiasm, devotion, and strong regard for the honor of the group and the common goal (Webster's New World Dictionary, 1988). An important role of the administrator, then, is to promote this common spirit by dedicating resources and time to rewarding and publicly recognizing staff and students whose behaviors exemplify or actively promote the mission of full inclusion.

In structuring rewards and incentives, administrators are advised to keep several things in mind. First, be sure to regard *groups* as well as individuals in order to highlight the importance of and promote pride in collaborative team efforts. Second, try to spend more time with teachers, staff, and students than with other administrators; an administrator cannot provide encouragement, support, or identify excellent performance unless a great deal of time is spent "in the trenches." Third, ask staff and students what it is *they* value as a reward or incentive; what is rewarding to one person may be of little significance to another. Finally, remember that there is no "job" within the school that cannot promote the mission of full inclusion. The cafeteria worker, bus driver, custodian, secretary, community volunteer, or an individual student can do a great deal to promote inclusion or to hasten its demise. All members of the school community, therefore, must be considered candidates for recognition. Some examples of incentives, rewards, and methods of recognition that have been successfully used by administrators are as follows:

1.   Send a short note of praise (e.g., "The peer tutors in your classroom are providing effective instruction—their correction procedures are phenomenal!", "You handled that conflict in the meeting very well!").

2.   When visitors come to the school, take them to a classroom and explain in the presence of the teacher and the students why this class is being highlighted (e.g., "I wanted you to see how well the members of this class work together in cooperative learning groups.").

3. If a visitor sends a "thank you" letter, post it in the teachers' room, place a copy of the letter in the personnel file of teachers or other staff who were mentioned, and/or forward it to the superintendent or the school board chairperson so it may be shared with the community during a school board meeting.

4. Arrange for individuals and teams to make presentations regarding their innovative actions and services at faculty, school board, parent-teacher organization, or community group meetings (e.g., the employment specialist describes the functions of her job; two teachers, two students, and their parents share the benefits of team teaching).

5. Establish a monthly "pat on the back" program that provides a reward (e.g., gift certificate to a restaurant, $50.00 cash bonus, an additional day of professional leave) for an individual's exceptional actions in support of students, colleagues, or the general school community.

6. Establish annual "teacher-of-the-year," "parent-of-the-year," or "peer buddy-of-the-year" awards and widely publicize the names of the recipients and the reasons for their selection.

7. Recognize the leadership capabilities of staff, students, and community members by inviting them to participate in hiring and planning committees.

8. Give those teachers who are effective in educating a diverse student population the opportunity to serve in a mentor role with student teachers, teachers who are new to the school system, and community volunteers.

9. Create opportunities and provide release time for teachers and students to make presentations regarding their exemplary educational practices at statewide, regional, or national professional conferences.

10. Create opportunities for staff to collaborate outside of their usual work day (e.g., overnight retreats, courses taught within the school district, summer institutes, professional support groups).

A Final Word about
Promoting an Inclusive School Philosophy

While the clarification and promotion of an inclusive school philosophy in a school or school system is an important consideration that an administrator should address, it is important to recognize that not *all* instructional and support staff, parents, community members, students, or members of the administrative team need to agree and believe that the local school is a place where all of the community's children belong in order for an administrator to take actions to enhance the school's capacity to provide quality educational services for a heterogeneous group of students (Skrtic, 1987). Furthermore, although a final philosophy or mission statement can help guide change in an educational system, a school need not have a formal statement for its administrative leadership to alter the organizational structures within the school that serve as barriers to the inclusion of all students.

PROMOTING A UNIFIED SYSTEM OF SCHOOL SERVICES

Once a philosophy of inclusion has been articulated and strategies for building consensus have been initiated, the next major administrative challenge is to organize the school or school system to promote the operationalization of a unified, comprehensive system of general education services that meets the educational needs of all students.

Barriers to the Unified System

A number of characteristics of the organizational structure of the traditional American school stand in the way of heterogeneous schooling. First, most schools continue to rely upon a "lock step" curriculum approach (Stainback, Stainback, Courtnage, & Jaben, 1985); that is, what students are taught is determined not by their assessed individual needs but the grade level to which they are assigned. Students are placed in a grade according to their age and expected to master a predetermined curriculum by the end of the school year. If they fail, they are retained or referred for special services and pulled out of the classroom for part or all of the day, as "curriculum casualties" (Gickling & Thompson, 1985). This practice makes the goal of heterogeneous grouping of all students difficult, if not impossible.

Second, many schools continue to stratify their students into high, medium, and low groups through heavy reliance upon ability groupings, tracking systems, and pull-out special service models (Slavin, 1987). Third, there is a formal separation of general and special education services. Special education is a free standing *second system* (Wang et al., 1988) within the school, with its own administrators, its own department, its own teacher in-service training events, its own faculty meetings, and its own policies and procedures for student discipline, parent involvement, and access to educational services.

Finally, few school administrators encourage, expect, or structure rewards for instructional personnel to plan together, teach together, exchange professional expertise, or provide professional support to one another. Furthermore, little, if any, time is structured into the work day for collaboration to occur.

Strategies For
Promoting a Unified Service System

This section is devoted to an examination of specific strategies that administrators who are interested in educating all students together in a single unified system can use to eliminate such organizational barriers.

Consolidate Existing Curriculum   Because special education has evolved into a free standing second educational system and because students who are ejected from the mainstream into the second system rarely return, a myth has evolved regarding the *magic* of the special education curriculum (Wang et al., 1988). The myth is that what is taught in the second system is so specialized, so difficult to teach, and so different from the mainstream curriculum that it is essential to maintain this "repair shop" for an ever increasing number of students. Of course, this myth is just that—an imaginary, unverifiable notion.

Those who have worked in both the first and the second system know that, for the most part, the curriculum, and the effective instructional techniques of special education are fundamentally the same as that of general education. The majority of students eligible for special education services simply are at a different place in the curriculum sequence than their same-age peers.

For some special education students, notably students with severe disabilities, the curriculum, at first glance, appears to be quite different. The focus is upon social, work, recreation, and life skills; and the instructional setting oftentimes is not the classroom but the actual community site in which a skill is to be used. A look at general education curriculum, however, reveals that it, too, always addressed social skills (e.g., speaking and listening competencies, public speaking classes, debate clubs, co-curricular clubs and activities), life skills (e.g., home economics, technology education, consumer mathematics), recreation needs (e.g., physical education, music, competitive sports programs), and vocational instruction. Furthermore, the community has always been a place that general education has employed as an instructional setting (e.g., the behind-the-wheel instructional component of driver education, field trips to sample community experiences and potential future job choices, vocational placements in local work sites, advanced coursework at local colleges).

Administrators who wish to serve all students in a single integrated system need to first recognize the sameness of general and special education curriculum, lead others to that discovery, and work with them to create generic services that merge content, instructional staff, and instructional settings. Administrators need to examine with faculty the content of all courses and facilitate the elimination of duplicate content (e.g., a 10th-grade consumer mathematics class that covers much of the same functional content as a basic skills class offered in the resource room) and distribute instructional responsibility for common content across personnel who formerly worked exclusively with either special or general education students.

The administrator also can encourage guidance, vocational, and employment personnel within the school to examine each community training site with an eye to its use with a broader range of students. For example, the IBM or Apple computer plant in town not only may be an appropriate site for a student with severe disabilities to receive vocational instruction on an assembly line task, but an excellent place for a student with advanced computer programming skills to learn and practice new skills and social behaviors expected in a work place.

Finally, the administrator must formally alter the traditional job roles and responsibilities of special education staff members to enable skilled specialized personnel to join with and become general educators in teaching the expanded curriculum in integrated regular education and community settings and, through this union, eliminate the second system status of special education students and service providers.

Redefine Staff Roles   Job titles and the formal or informal role definitions that accompany them determine the ways in which persons behave within a school (Brookover et al., 1982). Since administrators traditionally have been responsible with input from teachers for defining the job functions of teachers, they are in an excellent position to redefine the competencies they expect teachers to demonstrate and the ways in which they expect teachers to interact with students and with one another.

For example, the title, resource room teacher, may carry with it a set of expectations: 1) this teacher works in a separate room, 2) students must leave the regular classroom to get this person's services, and 3) only those students identified as special education eligible can or will be allowed to benefit from this person's expertise. All of this, of course, leads to segregation. The resource room teacher however, may have a great deal of training and expertise in assessing students' strengths and needs, analyzing tasks and concepts, designing and implementing classroom and behavior management programs, and other areas that, if shared with classroom teachers, would help them to maximize their responsiveness to a more diverse student population within integrated regular education classes.

Suppose the special education administrator were to redefine the resource room teacher's job title and responsibilities to that of a support person who no longer worked in a separate room, but instead provided support to any number of educators in the school through modeling, consultation, team teaching, collaborative problem solving, and in-service training. Furthermore, suppose that the roles of *all* instructional personnel within the school were redefined so that classroom teachers, special and compensatory education personnel, teacher assistants, and related services personnel (e.g., speech and language pathologists, guidance counselors, school nurses, physical therapists) also were expected to collaboratively plan, deliver, and evaluate the effectiveness of instruction for all students, regardless of labels that may have been assigned to them in the past. Such a change in the professional relationships of school personnel would likely increase the adult-to-student ratio in any given classroom and result in an exchange of technical and collaborative skills, thus increasing the number of students whose needs could be met in heterogeneous regular education classrooms.

Now the question is: What can administrators do to successfully redefine roles so that the isolation of school personnel is reduced and the multiple separate educational systems that coexist in schools (e.g., general education, special education, compensatory education, vocational education, bilingual education, gifted and talented education) may be eliminated? The administrator must recognize that few schools are capable of tolerating a massive or total upheaval of the status quo. Recognizing this, the process that has been used successfully to redefine job roles is to initially develop an experimental model site within a school or system. This process has four steps.

Select the Target Group　　It is important for the administrator to determine those people in the school who are looking for or are willing to risk making a change in their job functions and enlist them to become part of an "experimental" target group. The administrator needs this first "experimental" effort to be a success, so it may serve as a model. "More is learned from a single success than from the multiple failures. A single success proves it can be done—whatever is, is possible" (Klopf, 1979, p. 40).

The composition of this first experimental group and all subsequent target groups must be heterogeneous, including regular education classroom teachers as well as personnel of specialized departments and programs. If specialized personnel are to "come out of the closet" and join the mainstream, they need regular education partners in whose classrooms they will be welcomed.

Provide Training　　Once this target group has been identified, the administrator must ensure that members receive the training, coaching, and supervisory feedback they need to be successful in their new roles. Personnel will need to acquire and demonstrate competence in at least the following areas: collaborative teaming and peer coaching; team teaching; consultation; and models for delivering effective instruction to a heterogeneous group of learners such as outcomes-based instruction, cooperative group learning, and social skills instruction (Villa & Thousand, 1988; Villa, Thousand, & Fox, 1988).

Members of this and subsequent target groups may already have skills in some of these competency areas, and the administrator should support them to provide direct instruction, modeling, and coaching to their colleagues in their respective areas of expertise. Additionally, the administrator will need to arrange for a more formal staff development program for the target group or the larger school community in order to facilitate skill development and provide the entire school with an awareness of "what the future holds." (This would need to be coordinated with and/or be a part of the in-service and development procedures for building understanding and consensus discussed earlier in this chapter.)

It is important to remember that the need for this type of in-service training never ends; training is an excellent vehicle for *inducting* the next target groups or newly hired personnel into their roles as collaborative team members. Also, the administrator will need to create expectations and multiple opportunities for members of the target group to practice and receive feedback regarding the collaborative planning and instructional skills they employ to support all students in general education classrooms.

Establish a Timeline for Change   The stage now is set for the successes of this experimental effort to be disseminated to the school community and for timelines to be established. This includes: 1) returning all students to their local schools, 2) eliminating specialized classes and pull-out services, 3) changing all job descriptions so that collaboration and accommodations for individual students are minimum expectations for all instructional personnel, and 4) providing continued in-service training for the entire school staff of the rationale for a unified school system and the specific collaborative and effective instructional competencies that have already been acquired by the initial experimental group.

Exactly how these timelines are determined and who is involved in establishing them will depend upon any number of variables, including the amount of administrative, teacher union, community, school board, and state department of education support that exists for an inclusive school model. At this stage of the change process, the role of the administrator becomes that of visionary, politician, and public relations expert with the objective of enlisting an increasing number of advocates to join in an "adhocracy" (Skrtic, 1987) that uses its collective knowledge and problem-solving capabilities to identify strategies for overcoming the organizational and attitudinal barriers to redefining professional roles and establishing a unified educational system.

Each staff person will most likely have definite beliefs regarding what appeared to work well and what yet needs to be fine-tuned or changed with regard to their new job functions, and their input should be obtained. The administrator can gather this information in a variety of ways—through written surveys or personal interviews, small group meetings, or full faculty meetings.

When responses have been summarized, they can help form the basis for the development of an action plan that proposes how job functions and resources can be realigned to better support students and staff. The action plan should not be formulated by the administrator alone. Instead, it is recommended that a core planning group be recruited to collaboratively generate the plan. Members of this team would be responsible for obtaining additional needed information, creating a plan, and soliciting feedback regarding proposed changes from their respective constituency groups (e.g., teachers at the same grade level, the other paraprofessionals).

It is critical that before any plan is proposed by this group, all members are acquainted with all the dimensions to which the plan must be responsive, such as financial, human, physical, time, legal, political, philosophical, and best educational practices.

Arrange for Continued Modification   Continued staff input is important when a plan is ready for a public hearing. Those whose job roles will be affected by the proposed changes must be given a final opportunity to modify the plan. The responsibility of the administrator at this point is to solicit a commitment from staff to experiment with their new job functions. If staff are reluctant, the administrator may need to move to an autocratic leadership style and mandate the changes in job functions. The highly participatory nature of the decision-making process makes it less likely that such a measure will be needed than if the decision-making process had excluded teacher input.

Administrators need to be cognizant that job definitions must remain fluid, that this process of redefining job responsibilities is a continual one. New knowledge in the areas of teaching technology, organizational management, human relations, and collaborative teaming continues to be generated at an accelerated pace and will suggest new ways for school staff to work with students and one another. At least annually, all school staff, from paraprofessionals and secretaries to administrators, need to have an opportunity to identify what is working well, what is not working well, and what they see as needed changes in their job roles.

Personnel Hiring Practices   Because administrators have the power to hire personnel, they have the opportunity to actively recruit new personnel who hold or are willing to adopt an inclusive philosophy and who have technical and interpersonal skills that will complement the skills of current employees. When recruiting new personnel, administrators need to consider the gaps in the current staff's technical skills and hire individuals who will strengthen the staff's ability to respond to a more diverse group of students. By bringing new personnel into the system (e.g., employment specialists, integration or support facilitators), the administrator sets the occasion for incumbent staff to modify their daily schedule and job functions to enable a new employee to deliver services to students and for staff to transfer some of their skills to other teachers in the system. In this way, new personnel who are hired to promote integrated education for all students are also likely to promote shifts in job roles.

   Promote Professional Peer Power   The more diverse a school's student population, the more skilled its teachers must be as a collective instructional body. Local schools have within them a natural and oftentimes untapped pool of "experts." Each teacher's unique skills and interests may be of value to another teacher or a broader range of students than those for whom he or she is directly responsible. A key to successfully meeting the educational needs of all students is promoting collaborative relationships and professional growth among the school staff so that expertise may be shared.

   Mentor and Coaching Opportunities   The school administrator can structure multiple mentoring and coaching opportunities to promote an understanding of the school philosophy or mission, the exchange of skills, and peer support among instructional staff. For example, each newly hired teacher may be assigned a "peer buddy"—a veteran teacher who can articulate the inclusive philosophy of the school; orient the new person to school policies, discipline procedures, and the material and human resources within the building; and demonstrate effective instructional, classroom management and collaborative teaming strategies that are responsive to a diverse student population.

   Professional Teaming   The administrator can also play a primary role in determining how personnel with specialized expertise—those people formerly labeled special educators, compensatory education reading teachers, speech and language pathologists—are paired with classroom teachers to deliver in-class student support services, serve as the teacher's advocate for additional support resources and/or serve as team teachers. The administrator's responsibility here is to maintain a global perspective to weigh and balance the collective needs of teachers and students across the entire system for which he or she is responsible when making or approving assignments of specialized personnel to support classroom teachers. Among the questions administrators may ask themselves and others in order to make the most appropriate matches are the following:

1. Who are the classroom teacher's most challenging students and which specialists have the skills that most directly address those students' needs?
2. Of all of the specialized personnel, with whom does the classroom teacher already have a trusting relationship?
3. Which of the classroom teachers are "ready" for a change such as multiage student grouping or team teaching? Pair these teachers with specialists who have an "energetic and assertive" style and the organizational skills to structure and introduce the innovation into the classroom as rapidly as possible.
4. Which of the classroom teachers are reluctant to initiate instructional innovations such as peer tutoring or cooperative group learning? Pair these teachers with specialists with whom they have a trusting relationship and who will be highly supportive, reinforcing, and incremental in their introduction of the innovation.
5. Which of the classroom teachers are actively resistant to change? Encourage the specialized personnel who work with these teachers to involve the administrator directly in team meetings to resolve conflict and set timelines for change and to reference administrative directives in order to promote the desired change rather than making the recommended changes themselves. This puts the specialist in the role of teacher advocate rather than adversary and builds trust and credibility with the resistant teacher.

Just as it is recommended that job responsibilities be reassessed at least annually, the composition of teams assigned to support a teacher must also remain fluid. When students move on to the next grade, teachers and administrators must decide whether specialists move on with their students, whether they remain with the teachers to whom they currently are assigned and with whom they have developed a close working relationship, or whether they will be assigned to a new set of students and classroom teachers.

Providing teachers with such opportunities to meld their complementary skills through the organization of collaborative planning and teaching teams has proven to be a powerful strategy for broadening the range of responses instructional and support personnel can make to any individual student (Johnson & Johnson, 1987; Thousand et al., 1986). It provides support to teachers through the natural exchange of knowledge and skills that occurs during collaboration, and in this way is a vehicle for ongoing professional growth for all parties involved in the team effort.

Situation Structuring   An administrator may structure a variety of other situations that go beyond the traditional job functions of a teacher in order to foster professional growth. These methods include:

1. Job "shadowing," where one professional follows another through the work day or work week, is a method for acquainting a staff member with specific job roles (e.g., paraprofessional training and supervision, community-based instruction) and classroom organizational and instructional practices that they may not yet employ (e.g., multiage grouping for reading or math, the use of peer tutors, cooperative learning group lessons).
2. Asking teachers to observe one another and then confer with one another is also a method for exposing teachers to new practices. This experience fosters professional growth by giving teachers practice in leadership roles (e.g., mentor, expert, clinical supervisor) that recognizes their competence in making professional judgments and in providing positive support and constructive criticism to another professional.
3. Administrators can use staff meetings for disseminating and structuring discussions of current literature regarding integrated education. These regularly scheduled discussions build support for and improve employees' skills in operationalizing the school's inclusive philosophy.

Develop Schedules to Promote Collaboration   As the above discussion points out, a common denominator of schools striving to successfully educate all students in a single unified system is the presence of collaborative relationships among school staff through which expertise may be shared. The school administrator can play a vital role in structuring collaborative opportunities. However, one problem that the administrator must address when attempting to create these opportunities is how to modify the school's organizational structure to enable staff to meet and work as teams.

To build a coordinated and responsive master schedule, the administrator must first ask professional staff to identify the various peer collaboration arrangements in which they currently are involved or which they would like to structure. There are a multitude of possible collaborative combinations. For example, there are classroom-based teams comprised of the classroom teacher, one or more specialists, and possibly a paraprofessional or two; these teams need to meet at least weekly to develop and modify lesson plans. There are teachers who team teach, and they may meet from one to five times per week. There are also supervisory (e.g., professional-paraprofessional and professional-peer tutor) combinations. The school may have one or more *student support teams* comprised of a cross-section of the school's instructional personnel that meet regularly to develop interventions for students experiencing difficulties, plan for the smooth transition of a student from one grade to the next or from secondary to post-secondary options, or develop and monitor the individualized education plan (IEP) of students in need.

The task of the administrator at this juncture is to develop a master school schedule that meshes the planning and meeting needs of the collaborative teams with schoolwide functions (e.g., faculty meetings, parent-teacher conferences, in-service training events, curriculum development committee meetings) and special events (e.g., "I Love to Read Week"). The Winooski School District is an example of one Vermont school district that has taken a number of steps to create a coordinated master schedule. Building-based faculty meetings occur on the second Wednesday of each month, the curriculum and in-service steering committee meets on the fourth Wednesday, and the district administrative team meets on the first and third Wednesdays. Periods at the beginning and the end of each Tuesday and Thursday are reserved for student support team meetings to develop interventions for individual students, determine students needing specialized services, and develop student IEPs. On Mondays, a time block from 2:45 to 3:30 is reserved for departmental and curriculum committee subgroup meetings. Teams of teachers may also request to use time during in-service training days to meet for a variety of purposes, including transition planning for individual students, the development of curriculum and instructional programs, the training of paraprofessionals, and parent meetings.

Teachers who share students or who team teach are given common preparation periods, and efforts are made so that "specials" (e.g., music, art, physical education) and special events such as assemblies do not conflict with regularly scheduled collaborative planning and teaching times. In this district, it was determined that junior high school students would benefit if all of their content area teachers had a common daily planning period that supplemented their individual planning times. This was considered a priority and was arranged for in the master schedule. These teachers now have a structured agenda for their common planning period that addresses a host of curricular issues and includes meetings with students, families, or specialized student support staff.

Specialized personnel (e.g., teachers certified in special education, speech and language pathology, employment specialists, reading specialists) also have a weekly 2-hour time block set aside during the school day to coordinate and complete required paperwork (e.g., student IEPs, comprehensive evaluations) for students who are eligible for services from several specialists, to determine specialized support personnel and paraprofessionals that will work with each of the classroom teachers, to assist one another to develop or modify behavioral or academic interventions for individual students, to develop or deliver in-service training content for paraprofessionals, and so on. Arrangements also have been made for a substitute to be hired once or twice a month, as needed, to relieve classroom teachers so they may participate in meetings concerning challenging students in their class.

It is unrealistic for an administrator to set an expectation that teachers will collaborate unless efforts also are made to create opportunities, incentives, and rewards for such collaboration. The Winooski example is simply one *example* of how a school's administration has manipulated the master schedule, made available resources such as substitute teacher time, and expanded the use of in-service training time to enable a diverse instructional staff to come together and collaboratively respond to the educational needs of a diverse student body.

CONCLUSION

The enactment of PL 94-142, the law that was intended to eliminate segregation and exclusion of children with disabilities from educational opportunities open to their peers, was passed in 1975. Yet, barriers to full inclusion still remain in many schools. Among these barriers are: 1) the lack of a schoolwide inclusive vision, 2) a curriculum that is still too narrow to meet the increasingly diverse needs of students, 3) the continued separation of general and special education faculty and services, 4) the lack of expectations for collaboration among faculty members, 5) a failure to appreciate the need for rewarding those who actively promote the mission of full inclusion, and 6) the absence of common knowledge, language, and skills among school personnel to enable them to communicate effectively about their own and student needs and to accommodate for student diversity.

This chapter presents administrators with a broad range of strategies, each of which is intended to address one or more of the above barriers to the full inclusion of all students in the mainstream of education. By implementing strategies such as those recommended in this chapter, administrators simply are doing their job—exercising the power and the rights of their leadership position to promote and reward particular values and actions, alter organizational structures, and bring new knowledge and skills to instructional staff for the good of children.

> Use of authority within a framework of a commendable and humane value system is better than laissez faire approaches to leadership which may

permit inadequate learning environments for children to exist. (Klopf, 1979, p. 35)

REFERENCES

Azjen, I., & Fishbein, M. (1980). *Understanding attitudes and predicting social behavior.* Englewood Cliffs, NJ: Prentice-Hall.

Brookover, W., Beamer, L., Efthim, H., Hathaway, D., Lezzotte, L., Miller, S., Passalacqua, J., & Tornatzky, L. (1982). *Creating effective schools: An inservice program for enhancing school learning climate and achievement.* Holmes Beach, FL: Learning Publications.

Cummings, C. (1985). *Peering in on peers.* Edmonds, WA: Snohomish Publishing Company.

Donnellan, A.M. (1984). The criterion of least dangerous assumption. *Behavior Disorders, 7,* 141–150.

Gickling, E.E., & Thompson, V.P. (1985). A personal view of curriculum-based assessment. *Exceptional Children, 52,* 205–218.

Johnson, D., & Johnson, R. (1987). Research shows the benefit of adult cooperation. *Educational Leadership, 45*(3), 27–30.

Joyce, B., & Showers, B. (1980). Improving inservice training: The messages of research. *Educational Leadership, 37*(5), 379–385.

Joyce, B., & Showers, B. (1988). *Student achievement through staff development.* New York: Longmen Publishing Co.

Klopf, G.J. (1979). *The principal and staff development in the school – with a special focus on the role of the principal in mainstreaming.* New York: Bank Street College of Education.

Reynolds, M.C., Wang, M.C., & Walberg, H.J. (1987). The necessary restructuring of special and regular education. *Exceptional Children, 53,* 391–398.

Skrtic, T. (1987). An organizational analysis of special education reform. *Counterpoint, 8*(2), 15–19.

Slavin, R.E. (1987). Ability grouping and student achievement in elementary school: A best-evidence synthesis. *Review of Educational Research, 57,* 293–336.

Smith, C. (1988, March). *What's in a Word? On our acquisition of the concept language learning disability.* Paper presented at the First Vermont Symposium on Learning Disabilities, Rutland, VT.

Stainback, W., Stainback, S., Courtnage, L., & Jaben, T. (1985). Facilitating mainstreaming by modifying the mainstream. *Exceptional Children, 52,* 144–152.

Thousand, J., Fox, T., Reid, R., Godek, J., Williams, W., & Fox, W.(1986). *The homecoming model: Educating students who present intensive educational challenges within regular education environments* (Monograph No. 7-1). Burlington, VT: University of Vermont, Center for Developmental Disabilities.

Thousand, J., & Villa, R. (1989). Enhancing success in heterogeneous schools. In S. Stainback, W. Stainback, & M. Forest (Eds.) *Educating all students in the mainstream of regular education* (pp. 89–103). Baltimore: Paul H. Brookes Publishing Co.

Villa, R., & Thousand, J. (1988). Enhancing success in heterogeneous classrooms and schools: The powers of partnership. *Teacher Education and Special Education, 11,* 144–154.

Villa, R., Thousand, J., & Fox, W. (1988). *The Winooski model: A comprehensive model for providing a quality education for all learners with and without handicaps within an integrated public school setting.* (Available from Richard Villa, Winooski School District, Winooski, VT)

Wang, M.C., Reynolds, M.C., & Walberg, H.J. (1988, November). Integrating children of the second system, *Phi Delta Kappan,* 248–251.

Webster's New World Dictionary (3rd college ed.). (1988). New York: Simon and Schuster.

Barbara E. Buswell
C. Beth Schaffner

14

Families Supporting Inclusive Schooling

Many families of children with disabilities have a vision of what they want for their children's lives, and they are working to actualize that vision. The vision begins by having all children learn side-by-side in an integrated classroom to ensure that they all have the skills and experiences necessary to live together in the community. Families can support and encourage inclusive schooling in a number of ways:

• The parents of a high school student who has been labeled as severely and multiply disabled spent a good portion of their personal funds to send their daughter's special education teacher to Canada to attend a seminar on full inclusion and to visit model schools where children are fully integrated.

• At the end of the school year, a family requested copies of the textbooks their child will be using in his regular classes next year so that they can begin to generate ideas for adapting the curriculum to meet their child's unique needs with input from some of the child's friends from his class.

• The mother and father of an elementary student who has significant physical challenges alternately take off work to go on field trips with their child's class to provide support so that their child can participate.

• A mother meets regularly with her child's science teacher to brainstorm ways to adapt the sixth-grade science curriculum and develop activities that she can help her child with at home so that his needs can be better met in the regular class.

These families have a very strong commitment to integrated, inclusive schooling for their children. This is evidenced in the extraordinary efforts they have put forth in helping to support school personnel to make regular education a place that meets the diverse needs of all students. They have utilized much of their personal time, energy, and even their financial resources because they want their children to be valued, participating members of their schools and to learn with their same-age peers.

Their dreams for their children's futures are not unlike what any parent wants for his or her child: a good life, happiness, friends, support, a job to feel good about, a nice place to live, active membership in the community. They understand that the only way their children can realize these dreams in the future is if they are fully included in their school and neighborhood communities now.

MOTIVATING FAMILY SUPPORT

In the past, families of children with challenging needs have not been able to dream of these kinds of futures for their children. Special education services have traditionally segregated children and have focused on remediating deficits; thus, parents have had little hope for their children having successful lives in the community.

However, when families learn about the possibilities of inclusive schooling—that all children can be valued, participating members of their schools, can develop friendships with other children, and can be active members of their communities—then they begin to reclaim lost dreams and to develop a clearer, positive vision for the future.

It is this clear vision that enables families to work toward supporting inclusive, integrated education for their children. One parent shared her feelings in the following way after hearing a presentation on integration:

> Today, a whole new world opened up for myself and my son. I learned of a new world for children—a kaleidoscope world. I've learned that my child can learn along with other non-handicapped children. There are so many new ways to help my child grow to be a complete human being filled with the joys and sorrows of life before only offered to the [so-called] average child. . . . So, I'm looking forward to my child's future. (Schaffner & Buswell, 1988, p. 95)

Segregated, special education has often conditioned families to focus only on what their children cannot do—those skills that are perceived as needing remediation. When family members are given the opportunity to think about their children in terms of their capabilities and their gifts, a new world of possibilities opens up to them.

Once a family's vision for a child becomes clear and alive, there is a tremendous urgency to actualize it. Parents feel that they cannot wait for systems to slowly evolve and change service delivery modes because every day of waiting is a day of lost opportunities for their child. This sense of urgency can empower families to become actively involved in the goal of inclusive schooling for their child.

WHY FAMILY SUPPORT?

Why are families a necessary component for bringing about the inclusion of students with challenging needs in schools? Full inclusion is a new concept to many. Educators report that they have become so accustomed to a system that uses a segregated "fix-it" model for educational services that this new full inclusion model seems totally foreign, too challenging to implement, and beyond their realm of expertise. Therefore, parents who have the vision of full inclusion for their children must often become the pioneers and help guide the educational system through the necessary changes to make inclusive schooling possible.

It is important to note that not all parents, or other family members (grandparents, siblings, cousins, etc.), can be expected to be as empowered to work toward integration as those described above. Some may not have experienced exposure to the possibilities inclusive schooling can open up for their children and, therefore, do not have a clearly defined vision for their child. Others may just not have the expertise or the sheer energy required for such an effort. Still others, because they do not have children who have been segregated or excluded from the educational mainstream, may simply not be aware of the school and classroom needs inherent in operating inclusive educational settings in which all students are accepted, supported, and belong as equal members. It is evident, however, that families who have that goal of full inclusion for their children can be a tremendous resource to schools.

THE ROLE OF FAMILIES

Vision

A family's primary role in supporting inclusive, integrated schooling is to share their vision of what is possible for the child. Since parents have the big picture of the child's life, their goals, hopes, and dreams reflect a global perspective. They are concerned with the kind of life the child will live when he or she becomes an adult. They recognize the kind of skills that the child will need to be successful.

Attitudes

In addition to vision, families exhibit three attitudes they can share with school personnel that support inclusion of children in the family and the mainstream of school life. Biklen (1985) described two of these as *unconditional acceptance* and *unconditional commitment*. Families accept children as they are and then commit themselves to support them successfully. A third attitude is that families *focus upon the capabilities or strengths* of the child rather than the challenges.

Advocacy

A related role that family members serve in the inclusive schooling movement is contributing their energy and commitment. Since families are the primary advocates for their child and have the big picture of the child's life and future, they have ongoing commitment and energy to persevere in advocating for their child. Since parents live with their children year after year, they have had practice coping with challenges and obstacles and, as a consequence, have developed skills and strength to keep going even in the face of challenges. Their drive to proactively problem solve on the child's behalf maintains momentum even when difficulties arise and the process appears more challenging. Families' ongoing involvement, sharing commitment, and energy can keep the inclusive school process moving.

The vision, attitudes, and advocacy provided by parents and other family members can bring a focus to inclusive schooling that can help guide educational programming for each student that is positive, supportive, caring, and purposeful. Parents and family members working with teachers, support people, and students can use their best thinking, knowledge, and problem-solving skills to support any child to learn successfully with his or her peers. When families work with the school in program planning, there is a greater likelihood of all students meeting their individual goals, making friends, and participating actively in their school and community.

FAMILY SUPPORT STRATEGIES

Presented in this section are some strategies that families can use to positively affect the necessary changes needed to make full inclusion of all children a reality in schools. While a number of strategies are presented, it is not expected that any parent or family would be involved in *all* of them. Based on the interests, time available, and individual talents inherent in any family, one or more of these or other strategies might be used. Also, parents should expect full inclusion of all their children with any necessary adaptions and supports in the mainstream of the school, whether the family becomes involved or not.

Offer Current Resources

Families who have worked to educate themselves on state-of-the-art practices and successful integration models can offer the resources that they have encountered to schools. Videos, articles, and books that describe individual children in model integrated programs are quickly emerging. Parents report that sharing these resources and discussing them with administrators, teachers, and support people can be helpful in conveying their vision for what is possible and what they want for their child. A parent who shared materials for inclusive schooling with his child's educational team stated:

> The integration materials [we shared with the school] were invaluable in educating the administration and staff as to the many benefits that will accrue not only to our son, but to the other non-labeled children, the teachers, and to the school as a whole. As a result, our child's IEP reflects a consensus of strong support for his integration into the regular classroom. (B. A. Drummond, personal communication, May 22, 1989)

Often, family members encounter individuals experienced with inclusive/integrated education at conferences, in support group meetings, or through newsletters from advocacy groups. Families can connect these resource people with their school. A strategy that some families have arranged is to contact advocacy groups, professional organizations, and their state department of education to inquire about prominent integration leaders who are scheduled to appear in their state. Parents then contact the presenter and arrange for him or her to spend some time visiting at their child's school, meeting with the school staff, conferring on particular issues the school is facing, brainstorming ideas, or speaking to a group in the community to build vision. A third grade classroom teacher stated: "Sharing the expertise of integration leaders was reinforcing, refreshing, and educational. It allowed me to gain a different perspective and to be reaffirmed in my efforts" (K. H. Maher, personal communication, May 1, 1989).

Another strategy parents have used successfully is to invite school personnel to visit model programs in the community, state, or even elsewhere in the country to observe together the kind of supports that might be successful in integrating their child in the local school. A mother traveled with her child's principal and teacher to an elementary school that is fully integrating all students in regular classes. The team agreed that this opportunity to observe and explore new possibilities for supporting children enabled them to successfully and proactively design new strategies to facilitate the child's full inclusion in his neighborhood fourth-grade class.

Integrate in the Total Community

Some children have few friends in their neighborhood and are quite isolated. When parents are in touch with the school, they can facilitate after-school activities for their child with children in the class. Teachers can notice particular friendships that are emerging; parents and other family members can then encourage these relationships in their neighborhoods. Parents can assist their children by inviting peers to their home to participate in family outings, birthday parties, and other activities. Friendships made at home or in the community can carry over into the school. A friend or friends can help a child feel more welcomed and secure at school.

Families can access typical community resources that schoolmates of the child use day-to-day. For instance, scouting is an activity in which all children can participate and enjoy outside of school. Community recreation and parks programs offer activities after school, on weekends, and during summer vacations. Accessing other community resources such as church or synagogue youth groups, YMCA recreation programs, museum after-school enrichment classes, or youth bowling leagues are steps families can take.

One family whose son had previously attended only segregated summer camps for children with disabilities enrolled their child in the regular YMCA camp. Their initial apprehensions gave way to positive feelings at the end of the week when they saw the tremendous benefit of their child's presence at camp both to him and to the other campers. A key in deciding which avenues to pursue is observing other children in the neighborhood who are the same age and scheduling one's own child in the same activities.

Since supports a child may require (e.g., transportation, interpreter for sign language) are not automatically provided in community activities as they are during the school day, parents often need to arrange for supports on their own. Sometimes parents hire a teenager to support the child in community and family activities. Other times, supports can be provided by the organization itself if parents assist with preparation and modeling prior to the activity. For example, the staff at a park and recreation day camp discovered that they were able to assist a child who uses a wheelchair to participate in rugged camp activities after parents spent some time instructing them about their child's support needs.

Family members can also volunteer as advisers, sponsors, or helpers for activities. A tip that is quite successful is signing the child up for activities with a friend who knows the child well. The friend can then share with, model supports, and advocate for his or her buddy. The more that children are able to interface and interact outside the school, the more easily they can relate in school.

Offer Problem-Solving Strategies

Whenever people are pioneering and attempting new ways of doing something, challenges can arise. When challenges emerge at school, parents are key resources in offering suggestions for successful resolution. Usually families have confronted and learned ways to address or redirect similar situations at home. Accepting this fact as a matter of course assists in handling stumbling blocks.

Some challenges that teachers find especially difficult to deal with center around behavior. Teachers can panic if troublesome behaviors emerge that they do not know how to handle. Parents can offer input and reassure teachers in these situations. If teachers understand ways parents handle particular behaviors at home, then it may be helpful to them when they are developing successful strategies for resolving challenges that arise at school. Parents can identify key situations or factors that precipitate certain behaviors so that activities can be structured in ways in which the child can be successful.

For example, a 9-year-old boy got into trouble at the end of each day as the children lined up to wait for the school buses. Various discipline techniques did not work. After conferring with the child's mother, the teacher learned that standing in line is difficult for this child and his behavior is most challenging in this situation. Together the teacher and mother came up with the following solution: each day when the class got their backpacks and lined up at the door, two friends would spend time at a table near the door doing an activity with the child until his bus came. The problem behaviors stopped as soon as this process was in place.

Lobby for Policies and Resources to Improve Educational Options

The way children are integrated has much more to do with the policies and practices of the particular school district in which they live than their individual, unique needs (Blackman, 1989). In addition, resources are frequently allocated to segregated special education programs or classrooms rather than to support individual students who are integrated. Thus, oftentimes when students are in regular classrooms in their neighborhood, few resources are available.

In situations like this, families and educators feel that systems change in both policy and practice is necessary to increase opportunities and resources for students in integrated settings. When situations require policy change, parents can often have more impact than can individuals working within the system. Parents can lobby for policies, resources, or supports that the school needs to effectively educate the child in regular classes. Parents can speak to administrators, school board members, other parents, and leaders on various advisory committees of the school district about needs that exist. Also, parents can ensure that supports the child needs (including adaptive equipment, particular resource people, or materials) are listed on the individualized education program (IEP).

Participate in General School Activities

Parents committed to inclusive schooling are most successful in actualizing the process when they themselves are fully integrated in the activities of their child's school. There are many avenues for participation. Joining the PTA or other parent groups working for the good of the entire school as well as one's own child increases a parent's credibility and ability to effect change significantly. Serving as a room parent, adviser for an after-school club, member of the activities committee for the prom or graduation, library volunteer, or a sponsor for the student council can be helpful. Serving on the school's administrative committees (such as the accountability, fund raising, or playground committee) is also useful. Attending school or class activities such as sporting events, musical performances, special assemblies, art shows, or drama productions demonstrates commitment and support to the school as well.

Parents also can participate by assisting on field trips. Having an extra adult to work with a group during the outing can personalize and streamline the trip. In addition, the parent can model unobtrusive ways to support children in need of assistance, build a relationship with the teacher, observe interactions among children, and learn which children relate most easily with his or her child.

If it is a common practice for other adults to be involved in the classroom, parents, grandparents or other family members of elementary age students can assist by working with small learning groups, sharing some particular expertise with the whole class, or assisting the teacher with clerical tasks so that he or she is free to spend more time with the children. This involvement demonstrates support to the teacher and school and also enables the parent to see firsthand the day-to-day activities.

This approach does not mean that the adult family members come in to serve as paraprofessionals to work only with a particular child. They may work individually with a particular child briefly but also should be seen as a resource to the classroom, teacher, and school as a whole. Neither the child nor the child's family members should be isolated as "special" or different.

Help with Adapting Curriculum

The more familiar parents are with day-to-day classroom activities, the easier it is for them to provide input and assistance with appropriate learning goals and curriculum adaptations for their child. When teachers share curriculum goals and learning activities for particular subjects, parents can often suggest ways the child can be involved that meet his or her own learning goals. For example, when a first-grade class was working on math using Cuisenaire rods, a parent suggested that this would be the perfect time for her child to work on color identification and sorting, which were goals on the child's IEP. Sharing this input enabled all the students to use the same materials at the same time to address their particular needs.

The father of a middle-school student integrated in a science class procured an actual blueprint of a new city park and designed adapted activities for his son when the class assignment was to design a park habitat that was ecologically sound for people and animals. Especially when typical activities appear to be "inaccessible" or inappropriate for a child, parents can collaborate with teachers to determine ways to involve the child in a meaningful way and still meet the learning goals for all the students.

All parents, of course, will not have the time, energy and resources to do these types of activities. But, for those who can, it may help not only their child, but others as well.

Help Create a Support Network

Frequently, support and advocacy groups exist for families who have children with needs similar to their child's. In these settings, parents have access to current thinking and innovative models for supporting children. These groups also serve as a forum for solidifying families' values, problem solving, and empowerment. Support groups can serve the same function for teachers and offer many practical strategies. In Canada, an Integration Action Group composed of both parents and educators has developed to meet the needs of parents, teachers, and others who are committed to inclusive schooling. Parents can invite teachers to attend support groups or organize a new forum to include educators and others who are committed to working towards full school inclusion.

Use the IEP Effectively to Facilitate Integration

Parents can use the IEP process to support their child's integration. Since parents are required by law to be participants in the process, this is a logical place for their input in structuring successful integration. First, parents can ensure that the child's strengths are stated directly so that the educational program and supports can be designed to capitalize on the strengths. Also, parents can see that the child's primary needs for integration, such as building friendships, having positive role models, feeling part of the classroom and school, and participating fully in all activities, are addressed on the IEP. These needs can then serve as guidelines for developing educational goals as well as implementation of the daily classroom activities.

Parents also can ensure that the services designated on the IEP are child-oriented rather than program-oriented. This can help to focus specific supports around a particular child. Parents can request that team processes such as MAPS (see Vandercook & York, Chapter 7, this volume) become a part of the program planning for their child to help strengthen the IEP and focus on the child's capabilities.

CONCLUSION

Though the responsibility for educating all children in the mainstream rests with the school system, in this pioneering period of including all students in all classrooms, family members, and particularly parents, can play a key role in expediting the process and paving the way for future successes. As stated earlier, not all parents or other family members will have the desire, expertise, or energy to be as actively involved as described here. However, all parents and other family members should be involved to whatever degree possible. When parents and other family members are involved, their vision, expertise, commitment, and energy can serve the diverse needs of *all* students, not just the student(s) with a disability. It should be noted that when family members, particularly siblings, support one another socially and educationally, they should be recognized and encouraged. While all children should be encouraged to support and care for one another, care must be exercised that a child is not inadvertently given too much responsibility for a brother or sister.

The process through which total inclusion of students with challenging needs in neighborhood schools will happen is a dynamic one. As the movement evolves, the need for intense family participation in the process will change. As the value of full inclusion becomes more a part of the basic belief system of educators and as they become more committed and better able to strategize to meet all students' needs, families will no longer have to spend so much of their personal energy to see that their children are included and supported. More natural inclusion and support systems will evolve.

What are the effects of involving family members as key team participants? First, differences in perspective will be a constant factor in the planning process. Though unsettling for everyone at times, this diversity of opinion can offer significantly more options and opportunities for children. The chances of genuinely meeting an individual child's needs are significantly increased.

In addition, the education of children will be more holistic and genuine when the family is involved. The school day and curriculum will build on the rest of the child's life, and the child's home life can complement school activities.

The final element present in involving families actively to support inclusive schools and communities is that all those involved (teachers, administrators, parents, and the child) will learn a great deal in this creative process that opens new possibilities for all students. The end result of families and educators collaborating for full inclusion in the schools is children who lead richer, less fragmented lives in their school and communities.

In the pioneering period, family members can bring a great deal to the inclusive schooling movement. The role of the families should not be underestimated. As Biklen stated:

> If we ask ourselves, is there any place within our society in which people with disabilities are fully integrated, the answer is yes. If we look at families that include a child with a disability, we can see total acceptance and full participation. In families, we can see a vision of what we must achieve in schools, workplaces, recreation and leisure—in all of community life. (D. P. Biklen, personal communication, May 17, 1988)

REFERENCES

Biklen, D. (1985). *Achieving the complete school.* New York: Teachers College Press.

Blackman, H.P. (1989). Special education placement: Is it what you know or where you live? *Exceptional Children, 55* (5), 459–462.

Schaffner, B., & Buswell, B. (1988). *Discover the possibilities: A curriculum for teaching parents about integration.* Colorado Springs: PEAK Parent Center, Inc.

Mary A. Falvey
Jennifer J. Coots
Kathryn D. Bishop

15

Developing
a Caring
Community to Support
Volunteer Programs

When members of a community care about themselves, each other, and the world around them, those values spread naturally to and throughout the schools in that community. The local school has often been seen as a community itself, but should also be viewed as a member of a larger community. "Community is not only a place to be, it is a feeling of belonging among other human beings" (Taylor, Biklen, & Knoll, 1987, p. xvii). A community is not only a geographic location, but also a network of interactions between people (Nesbit & Hagner, 1988).

Schools are viewed as both communal entities and elements of the surrounding community. The ability of a local school to foster an internal sense of community is closely related to the potential of its graduates to promote and develop the community in the larger society. A school whose mission reflects a narrow restrictive vision of academic skills only leads to narrow restrictive options for its' graduates and often results in myopic restricted individuals. However, a school whose mission is to seek state-of-the-art advances in curricula, instructional technologies, peer support, community involvement, and employment preparation is attempting to provide effective quality education for all students. If schools are committed to teaching students the values of accepting individual differences and providing all people in the society with equal access and opportunities, then the schools must model such inclusionary values by being open and accessible to all students.

Many members of the community feel that the schools have deteriorated and are not motivating for students. For example, businesses have become concerned about the ways in which schools are preparing students for the work world as evidenced by an article in the *Wall Street Journal Reports*, "Retooling The Schools," (Graham, 1989). This article cited statistics concerning the deplorable conditions schools are in; for example, there is a 60% dropout rate in some cities in this country. The report concluded that the low level of skills of job applicants is evidence that the schools are not "making it."

> Last year 44% of the job applicants at the Newark, New Jersey Office of Prudential Insurance Company couldn't read at the 9th grade level. "They are 17 years old and virtually unemployable for life," says Robert Winters, Prudential's chief executive. Other employers can report similar experiences. (Graham, 1989, p. R3)

Businesses are also realizing the need to provide assistance in improving educational services. In Philadelphia, for example, volunteers from the city's largest companies joined with university representatives to form the "committee to support Philadelphia schools." They have developed a 5-year plan to decrease the dropout rate, improve students employability skills, and increase college attendance, raising $5 million to fund their efforts. The business community is sponsoring training for school administrators and workshops in specific subject areas for teachers. Businesses have "adopted" specific schools or pooled funds for districts (Lopez, 1989). In addition to employment skills, concerns have been raised about the opportunities students have to learn to assist one another.

> Today it is possible for American teenagers to finish high school yet never be asked to participate responsibly in life in or out of the school, never be encouraged to spend time with older people who may be lonely, to help a child who has not learned to read, to pick up the litter on the street, or even to do something meaningful at the school itself. (Boyer, 1983, p. 209)

Such efforts demonstrate that there is support within the community to help make schools successful educational environments for all students. Other community groups have formed tutoring programs, support groups, partnerships with business and industry, and so forth in an effort to develop opportunities for students to learn how to interact and assist one another (Frady & Dunphy, 1985).

Developing a community with members who are actively participating in everyday events and who care about and assist one another is essential to the development of a caring community. To this end, schools must strive to become an integral part of the community. There are several strategies that schools can use to accomplish this "community sense." First, teachers, students, and families must be allowed and encouraged to participate in "running" the school. Second, members of the community must be encouraged to become actively involved. Third, the curriculum offered in the schools should reflect the diverse cultural values and practices of its members. Fourth, students should study issues reflecting problems and challenges of the community and make recommendations for solving such problems (e.g., homelessness, gang violence). Community leaders should listen to and seriously consider these recommendations from the students. Fifth, the education and the profession of teaching must be valued by the members of the community, and schools must work with the community to foster such valued attitudes. Sixth, schools should be open and accessible to the community in a safe manner. Finally, schools should be available to all students within that community in order to teach values of inclusion.

In facilitating schools to include all students within that community, at least two major actions must occur. First, the resources previously used to segregate students in "special" schools and classrooms must be reassigned to the regular classroom; second, creative strategies should be used to provide enough support for students to successfully and fully participate in their neighborhood schools. A major strategy for providing such support is the establishment of active and effective volunteer programs.

Much of the school reform movement calls for the ". . . introduction of parents and volunteers into the school setting" (Macchiarola, 1989, p. xvii). In order to strengthen schools to provide high quality educational opportunities for all students, members of the community must be recruited to become involved in the teaching process of children. Business leaders, community organizations, college students, and other groups, including senior citizens and retired citizens, should be sought after and welcomed into the schools in the process of providing high quality educational programs.

The success of a volunteer program is determined from two perspectives. One perspective is the positive impact that the time and effort from the volunteers has on the school and the students. The second is the positive impact that volunteering has on the volunteer. In developing and maintaining successful volunteer programs, the second perspective is often overlooked.

Bishop and Falvey (1989) discussed the difference between volunteerism that is patronizing and volunteerism that is meaningful. Meaningful volunteerism makes a difference and leads to change. An individual volunteer who is respected as a vital piece of a process that creates positive change will be more invested in the program. The expectation of a successful volunteer program should yield an expectation of volunteers as valued, vital people supporting schools. One way to ensure this is to facilitate the volunteer's participation in meaningful activities as opposed to trivial tasks that "no one else wants to do." Valuing volunteers in society directly contributes to the development of a caring community.

STRATEGIES FOR DEVELOPING VOLUNTEER PROGRAMS

The key to running a successful volunteer effort is organization. Someone must take responsibility for assisting teachers and other school staff to identify areas in which they may require assistance. Organizing the volunteer program might be undertaken by the PTA.

Some teachers may want a volunteer to assist students directly, teaching them skills such as reading or math, interacting and playing with friends on the playground, or buying lunch in the high school snack bar. Volunteers can be effective at providing individual and small group instruction where schools are unable to due to budget constraints.

Volunteers can be used to provide information to students in appreciating human differences. They would receive comprehensive training and go from school to school presenting lessons to students exemplifying how to treat others with respect and how to appreciate each individual's unique contributions to society.

Some teachers may require assistance with indirect service, such as preparing pictures to update an augmentative communication device, cutting out objects for an art project, or reading and critiquing students' essays from an English class. A formal in-service meeting for teachers and other staff, such as speech therapists, explaining the volunteer program and potential program enhancement through volunteers, may help these teachers and staff members to begin thinking of possible roles for volunteers. A questionnaire might be used by teachers to help them identify the ways in which they could use the assistance of a volunteer with their students. The volunteer coordinator then could match the needs of teachers with the skills and interests of the volunteers.

Recruitment

If an active and effective volunteer program in the school has not been established, then volunteers must be actively recruited. It is important that the purpose of volunteering be made clear to prospective volunteers. For example, in this book the focus is on efforts to assist all students in succeeding in the regular education class and in the local community so that they can grow to be contributing members of society. Volunteers may assist in individual or small group instruction, in preparing materials, or with supervision on field trips. Volunteers should be "matched" with the job they would like to do and can do well.

The orientation mentioned above could be given to prospective volunteers in a formal presentation by an effective school spokesperson to service clubs and other groups. A carefully written document presenting and "selling" the volunteer program can also be sent to groups. The following are examples of groups that may have members willing and able to assist with volunteering:

Rotary, Kiwanis, and so forth
Chamber of commerce
Junior League
College students (classes, sororities, fraternities, and so forth)
Retired teachers
Let Older Volunteers Educate (L.O.V.E.)
Retired Seniors Volunteer Progam (R.S.V.P.)
Volunteers in Action
Future teacher groups
High school students
Parent organizations

Advertising in newspapers or over radio and television can assist in locating persons interested in volunteering. Such advertising programs may support the effort to recruit volunteers if it effectively communicates or "sells" the purpose and need for volunteers. Since schools are generally nonprofit, these ads can be public service announcements and therefore be aired at no charge. Television and radio stations are required to air public service announcements and so may welcome this opportunity.

As mentioned earlier in this chapter, businesses have become interested in assisting the educational system to meet the needs of all students. Some businesses have adopted schools or have given employees extra breaks or time off to assist in volunteering. An effective spokesperson can contact businesses in the community to present the need for volunteers and to inform these businesses of the long-range benefits for them in assisting in the education of students.

Once volunteers have been recruited, a face-to-face meeting with a volunteer coordinator can clarify the purpose of the volunteer effort and assist with identifying the appropriate job match for the volunteer. It is important that these meetings be informative and a good use of the volunteer's time as they are truly "giving" their time to this effort.

Training

Once volunteers have been recruited, they must be efficiently and effectively trained. Once a position has been selected for the volunteer, the person most knowledgeable of the job should train the volunteer. Again, the training should be organized efficiently so that the volunteers' time is well spent.

Training could be conducted through demonstration where someone models the job the volunteer will perform or provides coaching. Coaching is where the volunteer is given instruction, attempts to perform the job, and then receives feedback from the trainer. For example, for several days the teacher could demonstrate for the volunteer effective strategies to guide a group of students to play "four-square," providing a student who has physical challenges with an adaptation. The volunteer could observe the teacher implementing the targeted strategies on the playground and then attempt to model those strategies, receiving feedback about what worked well, what did not, and why. Videotaped training can also be used effectively. Physical management (positioning and handling) techniques for specific students with physical challenges could be videotaped and studied by the volunteer before being trained to work directly with the student.

Communication is the key to effective training. The volunteer and trainer must understand and listen to each other. Goals, objectives, and strategies must be made explicitly clear to the volunteer without wasting his or her time. Ongoing communication and feedback is also important.

Maintaining Volunteers

Volunteers may tire of their job at some point, as most people do; therefore, feedback and positive reinforcement for a job well done are critical to long-term efforts. Communication with the supervising teacher or staff member keeps the volunteer informed and updated. Recognition and thanks from others through letters and luncheons may assist the volunteer in realizing that his or her efforts are noticed and appreciated. If the job becomes tedious or the volunteer does not feel effective, new strategies for the job may be required (e.g., working with different students) or a new job altogether may be necessary. Keeping volunteers feeling content and effective is critical.

Monitoring Volunteers

The supervising staff members must monitor the volunteer on an ongoing basis to make sure the job as described is being implemented. Volunteers must be monitored to ensure the appropriateness of their interactions with students, to ensure their ability to teach a skill according to students' needs, and so forth. When problems are noticed, additional assistance from the staff member may be required. Monitoring and assistance can be provided in a manner that makes the volunteer feel competent though they may still be in need of help. Again, in order to maintain volunteers, they must be kept informed, involved, and reinforced along the way. The school staff are responsible for volunteers' efforts.

Liability

Most school districts have existing policies and procedures that cover liability issues concerning volunteers. For example, most volunteers are covered by Workers Compensation for accidents on the job if they have registered with the school district and sign in and out each day they volunteer. If accidents occur on the job, volunteers can be treated as any other employee. It should be stressed to volunteers that they must fill out the appropriate forms and follow the procedures in order to receive the necessary coverage.

VOLUNTEER PROGRAM EXAMPLES

Volunteer programs have been organized to successfully meet all students' educational needs. Frady and Dunphy (1985) stated in _To Save Our School, To Save Our Children:_

> There is little doubt that the schools must open their doors to the communities, if the communities are to open their ears and pocketbooks to the schools. This open-door policy can be fostered in several ways: first, by making the activities of the school known and participated in by a wider segment of the general public; second, by acting on what the public conceives to be crucial to school success; and finally, by initiating programs which serve community needs. (p. 178)

The following hypothetical examples based upon real experiences demonstrate how an "open-door" policy involving volunteers might benefit a specific school and the greater community:

> A large corporation adopted an elementary school. The company raised money and helped purchase computers and adaptive equipment to be used in the computer lab by students with and without visual and developmental disabilities. They released two employees for 2 hours per week to participate in one or several of the following activities: teaching computer literacy and new computer games; teaching small groups of students a unit on "The 1950s: What were they really like?"; teaching an art or drama class; preparing classroom materials; teaching a small group of students how to use the public library.

> Students from a local high school went weekly to a local elementary school to tutor individual students. Some assisted students integrated into age-appropriate classroom activities, some provided extra assistance to students who required more information or a different way of getting information than was provided by the teacher, and others provided additional assistance to students who had completed their work and needed more advanced work.

The local chamber of commerce provided T-shirts as awards to "citizens of the week" that were given to students who assisted each other and went out of their way to be helpful.

Senior citizens participating in an R.S.V.P. group provided assistance to students in the library conducting research, locating materials they can read, taping materials for students who cannot read, reading to students, or teaching students how to use the audio visual equipment in the library.

Numerous other opportunities exist within communities to expand the resources of the school by including volunteers and volunteer programs. School personnel can access and use such resources in facilitating the integration of students previously excluded from regular education, including students with disability labels.

CONCLUSION

This chapter focuses on two components of facilitating quality education for all students. The first component is the perception of school as a microcosm of the larger community/society. If the goal of education is to teach children to function effectively and contribute positively to society as adults, then that society in all of it's diversity must be reflected and experienced in the school setting.

The second component suggests that schools that access volunteers from the community will facilitate bridging the school with the "real" world. Utilizing and valuing volunteers develops closer school-community ties. A successful volunteer program can also provide additional support to enhance a school's efforts to meet the individual needs of an increasingly diverse student population. Successful volunteer programs involve planning and organization of the recruitment, training, monitoring, and maintaining of individuals who volunteer in active and meaningful ways.

If educational efforts are to be taken seriously, then all students must receive and experience effective education together. Effective education will allow students to learn with and from each other, their teachers, and the members of their community. Access to and involvement with volunteers as individuals or organizations will only serve to broaden the experiences that are meaningful to the developemnt of all students. Such efforts will not only enhance the value of the community to schools but will emphasize the value of schools to the community as well.

REFERENCES

Bishop, K.B., & Falvey, M.A. (1989). Employment skills. In M.A. Falvey (Ed.), *Community-based curriculum: Instructional strategies for students with severe handicaps* (2nd ed., pp. 165–287). Baltimore: Paul H. Brookes Publishing Co.

Boyer, E.L. (1983). _High school: A report on American secondary education._ New York: Harper & Row.

Frady, M., & Dunphy, J.S. (1985). _To save our schools, to save our children._ Far Hills, NJ: New Horizons Press.

Graham, E. (1989, March 31). Retooling the schools. _The Wall Street Journal Reports,_ pp. R1–3.

Lopez, J. (1989, March 31). System failure. _The Wall Street Journal,_ pp. R12–13.

Macchiarola, F.J. (1989). Foreword. In D.K. Lipsky & A. Gartner (Eds.), _Beyond separate education: Quality education for all_ (pp. xi–xix). Baltimore: Paul H. Brookes Publishing Co.

Nesbit, J., & Hagner, D. (1988). Natural supports in the workplace: A re-examination of supported employment. _Journal for The Association for Persons with Severe Handicaps, 13_(4), 260–267.

Taylor, S., Biklen, D., & Knoll, J. (1987). _Community integration for people with severe disabilities._ New York: Teachers College Press.

Initial Steps for Developing a Caring School

This book discusses the theoretical arguments as well as practical approaches for transforming schools so that they meet the needs of all students within a single, inclusive system. The authors of each chapter have presented pieces of this vision. They have identified specific ways in which teachers can implement classroom instructional strategies that enhance the learning of all students and have proposed schoolwide models that address the role changes that will be necessary for all school staff to work together on full integration.

This book is also about change, changing policies of separate education to full inclusion. It is about getting from where we are now to where we want to be, about moving teachers, schools, and students in new directions. There are three important elements of the change process that can be identified here. First, change is a long-term process. No teacher or administrator can wave his or her magic wand and instantly transform a school into one which meets the needs of all children. Precisely because change is a process rather than a specific outcome, it takes time. It takes endless meetings and lots of discussion. Nothing worth accomplishing ever happened overnight.

Second, change is not easy; if it were, schools would have been transformed long ago. Many people are involved in the change process, and people with long histories of seeing things one way, doing things one way, are not always easily persuaded to implement a change. Bureaucracies, funding patterns, and existing school structures often seem to stand in the way of what is hoped to be accomplished.

Third, real change is inclusive and comprehensive. Creating schools that truly meet the needs of a range of students within heterogeneous structures will involve changes in many areas. It requires all of us to rethink how the classrooms are organized, the instruction that is provided, the roles school staff play within a building, the ways in which parents are involved, and so on. The list can seem endless. Each desired change seems linked to a dozen others; changing one piece of the puzzle often seems to necessitate rearranging the entire picture.

As we educators and community members think about changing schools, we are often left paralyzed by two feelings. Precisely because change is a long-term process, difficult and comprehensive, it is easy to feel overwhelmed by all that needs to be done. Sometimes it is hard to know where to begin; we are often immobilized because we *do* see the larger picture! How can educators and community members change school structures when categorical funding systems exist? How can the ways that teachers interact within schools be changed when they are trained to hold such discrete positions and titles? How can change take place when classrooms have too many students and insufficient and inadequate materials?

In addition to feeling overwhelmed by all that needs to be done, the other feeling that is often overpowering is one of isolation and loneliness. How can one person be expected to change so much? What will happen to that person in the process? People often become frustrated and throw up their hands muttering, "Do they expect me to do all *that* by myself?"

However, hope can come from several directions. First, we must remember that *everything* does not change at once. Not everything is known about the best ways to totally transform schools, but we, as educators, *do* know a lot already. There are many changes that can be made that will move schools closer towards integration and full inclusion, even with the acknowledgment that there is more to be done. And, perhaps more importantly, little changes can mean a lot. Every small act has meaning and significance. Ayers (1989) wrote that the "secret of teaching is in the detail of everyday practice." Similarly, the "secret" of educational change can lie in individual acts of transformation—new ways of thinking, new ways of talking, new ways of doing things. Without negating the fact that change is comprehensive and inclusive, we can begin to think about specific changes that can be made within our own settings that will help the school move toward the ultimate vision. Furthermore, no one should feel or act alone; there are numerous allies in the change process, including other teachers, parents, school staff, administrators, the students themselves, and volunteers. Change need not be a lonely or isolating process. It can become the occasion for people who formerly viewed themselves as quite different to share their visions, their goals, and to work with one another on creating a new reality in their educational systems.

This chapter, then, is devoted to 10 steps, 10 directions, that can be undertaken immediately by educators who are committed to working towards more inclusive, integrated schools. Each of these must be undertaken with the acknolwedgment and understanding that there is more to do and that each step alone is not sufficient. These represent places to begin, not places to end. The desire is not to trivialize the complexity and magnitude of the change process, but rather to empower individual educators and groups of educators to begin the process. And, as each step is taken, new steps will become apparent, other steps will follow, connections will become obvious. As Gandhi is quoted as saying: "Whatever you do may seem insignificant, but it is most important that you do it."

TAKE THE LABELS OFF
THE DOORS, TAKE THE LABELS OFF THE STUDENTS

One step of the change process is to take the labels off the students. No classroom has to be labeled the special class, "Educably Mentally Retarded," the "Learning Disability" room, or the class for students with severe handicaps. Classrooms can bear the names of the teachers: Ms. Hernandes' or Mr. Weintraub's room. A principal in Madison, Wisconsin, Don Stoddard, decided that yearbook pictures did not need to identify any students as "special needs" students, but should, instead, identify all students by last name (Anderson, William; Bermani, Luigi) and by activity (glee club, hall patrol). Announcements over the public-address system, school newsletters, awards assemblies can all identify students by name and accomplishment without labels. All students in the schools can be referred to by name, as individuals. There is little or no reason to divide classrooms or students into those who are special or regular. They all can be discussed and referred to as just classrooms and students.

TAKE THE LABELS OFF THE TEACHERS

A second step is to take the labels off the teachers. Encourage all teachers to see themselves as responsible for all the students in the school. Stop referring to teachers as "the gifted teacher," the "learning disability teacher," or, "the teacher of the severely disabled." Teachers should be thought about in terms of their expertise areas (individualization of instruction, community-referenced instruction) and decisions about which students they interact with based on who might benefit from their knowledge or expertise. Be creative in designing activities and structures that permit teachers to interact with a broader range of students, including coaching and after-school responsibilities, teacher exchanges, and cooperative projects between classes. If the specialist in hearing or visual differences, for example, is also the drama teacher, then students', teachers' and parents' perceptions all shift. A first grade teacher might really enjoy the opportunity to work with sixth graders on a special project and vice versa.

ESTABLISH A SCHOOL PHILOSOPHY OF CARING

A third step toward more inclusive schools is to develop a school philosophy relative to inclusion and the school's response to student diversity. Stress the importance of affective and social concerns throughout the school. Think about how every decision will be felt and interpreted by the students. Do not give students a mixed message by telling them that social relations are important and then only teaching and evaluating academics. Set social outcome goals for students, implement social learning programs as central to the school's objectives, and give students and parents feedback on the extent to which students meet the goals of listening, caring, and cooperating. Remove any and all barriers to friendships between students, teachers, and staff. Allow time for relationships to be built—schedule special times for students to have "lunch with the secretary," or for teachers to plan parties and treats for one another and for students. Encourage one another to be fully human at all times; when wonderful things happen to anyone in the school community (promotions, prizes, births, etc.), let the whole school celebrate. When sad things happen (illness, death, injuries, stolen bicycles, and other disappointments) allow these to be shared and grieved or lamented as well.

CONSIDER THE WHOLE STAFF

A fourth step toward building a community that is inclusive is to think about *all* the people who work in the school, including cafeteria workers, secretaries, teacher's aides, custodians, and so forth, in planning and activities. When Jerry Johnson, a principal in Madison, Wisconsin, wanted to integrate the hearing impaired students into the life of the school, he offered in-service training on signing for *all* school staff as well as for students. George Conrad, a principal in Bennet, Nebraska, asked the school secretary, Ruby King, to share with him all the ways in which she makes the students in the school feel special and valued. He has empowered her to think of herself as a vital member of the school community, and she responded with all the things she does to validate students when they come to the office with injuries and how she talks about students with parents and other staff members. Both the principal and the secretary are conscious of the fact that parents' and visitors' first contact with the school is generally through the central office and that the values communicated by the secretarial staff are extremely significant.

BUILD THE SCHOOL AS A COMMUNITY

Another step is to build the school as a community. All students should attend assemblies and other similar school functions together. Encourage school sing-alongs, celebrate all student, teacher, and staff birthdays. Community is built when a student in special education, the school secretary, a fifth grade athlete, and the third grade teacher all find that they share the same birthday. Encourage school spirit, publish a school-wide newsletter that lists everyone's accomplishments, design cooperative bulletin boards that cross grade-levels and areas. Involve everyone in the Red Cross food project, the school beautification project, the school carnival. Develop a school logo, a school motto, sell school T-shirts, hold special dress-up (dress-down) days at school.

Mix students in as many ways as possible. Have theme tables at lunch; anybody interested in talking about something special (baseball, dinosaurs, problems with big sisters) can identify a table and any/all interested students can sit together. Encourage parents to be active participants in the school community. Encourage grandparents, aunts, uncles, and older siblings of students in the school to volunteer as aides and tutors. Provide baby-sitting at school (using high school students) so that all parents can attend school activities. Extend the early-childhood tradition of parent involvement to all grade levels. Send home questionnaires asking parents what goals they would like to set for their children. Call parents and tell them about their child's successes as well as the problems that come up. One third grade teacher has a system where she calls one parent a night; in a little over a month, she has cycled through her entire class and can begin again.

HONOR AND CELEBRATE DIVERSITY

A sixth step is to set as a goal that students will not just "tolerate" or "accept" each other's differences, but celebrate them. Find ways to draw attention to the many kinds of diversity in the school and to be respectful of differences. School bulletin boards can reflect the ethnic diversity of the school. Biklen (1978) suggested initiating a student poster campaign on themes relevant to mainstreaming, integration, and inclusion: Everyone Has Rights, A Little Respect Beats a Lot of Pity, and We All Fit In. Librarians can set up special displays of books that explain and promote positive responses to differences and help teachers build these books into their ongoing teaching and story times. Outside speakers can be brought in to address students: a community leader with disabilities, a man or a woman who holds a nontraditional job, a foreign visitor, the parent of a child whose background is dissimilar to others in the school. Rather than celebrating only Christian holidays (Halloween, Christmas, Easter), either celebrate the widest possible range of holidays (Chinese New Year, Native American holidays, Syttende Mai) or have nonholiday celebrations and themes (teddy-bear week, etc.). Encourage students and teachers to use nonexclusive, nonsexist language. Explore with students the ways in which much of what passes for humor is offensive to various groups; post a "joke of the day" that is nonsexist, nonracist and not offensive to any ethnic group. Encourage students and staff to bring in contributions for sharing.

THINK ABOUT CURRICULUM BROADLY

Another step toward the change process is to encourage the development of multilevel curriculum that allows students at all levels to participate. If the school is learning about space, then students at all grade levels and all levels of ability can undertake projects in the same theme area. Promote the sharing of materials and curriculum projects across grade and age levels. Establish a central place for teachers to put materials they feel might be of interest to other groups of students and teachers. Develop community-based education for all students. Use integration as a catalyst to the reorganization of the total curriculum; maybe *all* students would profit from learning math by making purchases at the local store—perhaps the work sheets that seem so inappropriate for some children are really inappropriate for *all* children.

Take the labels off activities. Establish a club for anyone interested in animals, regardless of age or ability level. Ask teachers to sponsor after-school activities that draw a broad range of participants, but do not group students by disability, age, or sex. Think more broadly of all the people who can teach within a school. Establish a schoolwide yellow pages: for information/help on jumping rope, see Nicole in Room 3; for information/help on Chinese cooking, see Mr. Lau in Room 7. Encourage peer teaching projects; in one school, students offered miniworkshops after school on ski waxing, cookie baking, crocheting, and basketball skills.

STRESS COOPERATION RATHER THAN COMPETITION

Teaching strategies that encourage cooperation among students, rather then competition, should be developed as another step. Have workshops on cooperative learning and encourage the use of heterogeneous grouping for learning. Restructure physical education classes and outdoor play times so that students are engaged in cooperative games, rather than in competition that draws negative attention to differences and creates winners and losers. Do not give awards or citations to students that are competitively based; post improvement scores for individuals and classes. Have groups set their own goals and then strive to meet them. Encourage students to notice and report on others' good deeds and accomplishments; plant a "Good Deed Tree" in the front hallway where students place notes telling what acts of kindness they have noticed and then read and share these on a regular basis.

Encourage students and staff to cooperate across grade levels. Assign peer tutors within classrooms and across classrooms. In Lord Roberts Community School in Winnipeg, sixth graders are assigned to work with younger children with large motor difficulties. They work individually with children on ball bouncing, hopping, and throwing. Assign students in special education classes as assistants in classes of "typical" students. Establish friendship circles for children who are isolated; encourage students to take responsibility for one another. Train students in creative conflict resolution; let groups of trained students break up fights on the playground and negotiate conflicts.

Encourage teachers to work together as well. Think beyond having all the fourth grade teachers group for reading; try some experimental team teaching. When principal George Conrad was a teacher, he combined his sixth grade with the first grade for a 3-week period of study using the newspaper to facilitate peer coaching. Students and teachers all benefited from the experience. Do not label certain classrooms as "special" and isolate them in one wing of the school. People talk most often to those who are physically closest to them. Give teachers a regular time to work together. Use in-service moneys to pay for a school-wide substitute so that teachers can visit each others' classrooms and observe.

EMPOWER EVERYONE IN THE SCHOOL

Empowering everyone in the school is another critical step. Establish task forces within the school to look at individual problems and situations and come up with solutions. Make committees as diverse as possible, including teachers, parents, administrators, and students. The inclusive way the issue is discussed will help people to see the problem differently; solutions may emerge simply from the dialogue. Take seriously the idea of a suggestion box in the hall. Encourage students to put in their ideas. Challenge the whole school with a problem: "Kids are being teased on the playground. What should we do?" Ask people for suggestions, hold meetings to discuss what is generated, and try to implement some of the suggestions. Remember that when power is shared and spread around, everyone acts more powerfully. One fourth grade teacher seats her students in "families," clusters of five desks, and the classroom rule is that any student with any kind of a problem must ask for help and solutions first from their group family before coming to the teacher for assistance. Students have become resourceful in helping one another, empathic about the difficulties of their classmates, and the teacher has been relieved of an endless stream of questions and demands on her time. Think about the poster that reads: "None of us is as smart as all of us."

THIS STEP IS UP TO YOU

There are, of course, far more things that can be done to encourage a philosophy of inclusive schooling. Many of them are apparent only to the people whose lives are most directly affected. Think, dream, plan. Engage in a little "blue-skying"—"if the sky were really always blue, what would I want my school to be like?" Share those dreams with someone, maybe they share the same dreams. Keep a sense of humor (essential in the change process) and do not give up.

CONCLUSION

These 10 steps are only one way of looking at what will surely be a long and complex process. There is a well-known Talmudic saying "You are not required to complete the task, but neither are you free to refrain from it." Now is the time to go forward to begin the process and meet the challenges, remembering that barriers are only problems waiting to be solved.

REFERENCES

Ayers, W.C. (1989). *The good preschool teacher: Six teachers reflect on their lives.* New York: Teacher's College Press.
Biklen, D. (1978). Decisions that make a difference. In D. Biklen (Ed.), *The elementary school administrator's practical guide to mainstreaming.* New York: Scholastic Book Services.

Index

AutoPro

66

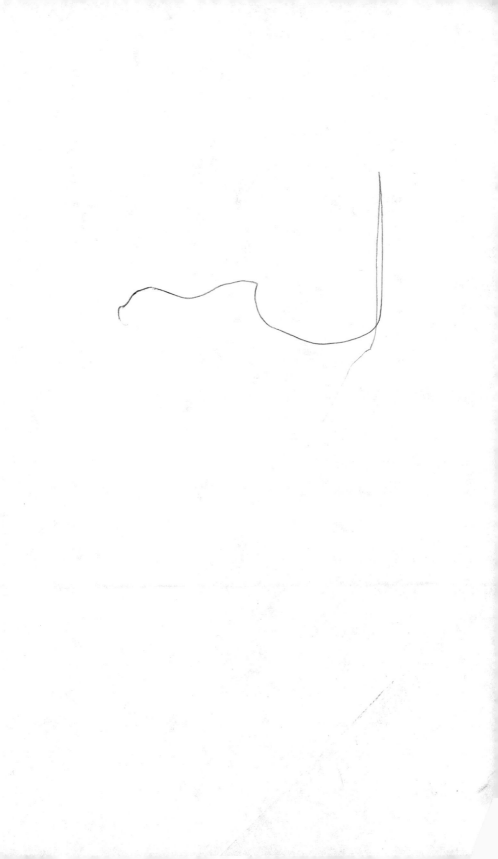